BACK IN TIME 3104 B.C. TO THE GREAT PYRAMID

EGYPTIANS BROKE THEIR BACKS TO BUILD IT
HOW THE GREAT PYRAMID WAS REALLY BUILT

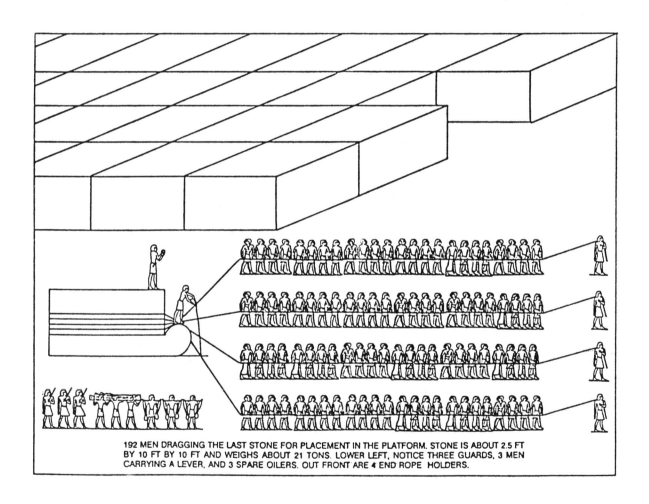

192 MEN DRAGGING THE LAST STONE FOR PLACEMENT IN THE PLATFORM. STONE IS ABOUT 2.5 FT
BY 10 FT BY 10 FT AND WEIGHS ABOUT 21 TONS. LOWER LEFT, NOTICE THREE GUARDS, 3 MEN
CARRYING A LEVER, AND 3 SPARE OILERS. OUT FRONT ARE 4 END ROPE HOLDERS.

SOCRATES G. TASEOS

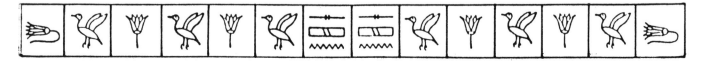

HERE'S WHAT EGYPTOLOGISTS HAD TO SAY OF
BACK IN TIME 3104 B.C. TO THE GREAT PYRAMID

● A COLLECTOR'S AND A RARE SOURCE BOOK ON "HOW" THE GREAT PYRAMID WAS REALLY BUILT. IT IS A TREASURE CHEST ON THE THREE METHODS MOST HISTORIAN BELIEVE ON "HOW" THE ANCIENT EGYPTIANS ERECTED SUCH A TIMELESS MONUMENT FOR KING KHUFU'S (CHEOPS) TOMB, THE SECOND KING OF THE FOURTH DYNASTY (3124-2840 B.C.)

● A BOOK THAT THE AUTHOR COVERS WITH EXTRAORDINARY THOROUGHNESS AND DETAIL OF THESE METHODS FOR THE FIRST TIME EVER IN ONE BOOK.

● A BOOK IN WHICH THE AUTHOR CONVINCINGLY SHOWS HOW THE CREATIVE-GENIUS-BUILDER USED THE PYRAMID ITSELF TO LIFT THE HUGE BLOCKS OF LIMESTONE THAT WENT INTO ITS CONSTRUCTION. MANY DRAWINGS CLEARLY SHOW HOW THESE BLOCKS WERE TRANSPORTED.

● A BOOK YOU WILL NEED IF YOU ARE PLANNING TO VISIT EGYPT TO SEE THE GREAT PYRAMID. TRAVEL THERE FIRST IN THE PAGES OF THIS BOOK--THEN YOUR VISIT TO EGYPT WILL BE MORE ENJOYABLE.

● A BOOK THAT GIVES A CLEAR INSIGHT OF THE SIMPLE TOOLS, LABOR AND METHODS USED FOR ERECTING EGYPT'S HUGE MONUMENTS OF STONE.

● A BOOK THAT IS NOT ONLY INNOVATIVE, INFORMATIVE BUT BREATHTAKING TO READ.

● A BOOK FILLED WITH PRICELESS MONUMENTS, SKETCHES, AND DRAWINGS WHICH MAKE IT UNIQUE AND A PLEASURE TO SEE. THEY TELL THE READERS SO MUCH ABOUT THESE ANCIENT EGYPTIAN PEOPLE.

● A BOOK THAT CONTAINS A MATHEMATICAL COMPUTER MODEL OF THE GREAT PYRAMID WHICH WAS BASED ON TWO OF THE ORIGINAL CASING STONE FOUND AT ITS BASE. IT ESTABLISHES FOR THE FIRST TIME AN ACCURATE ACCOUNTING OF THE NUMBER OF LIMESTONE BLOCKS, THEIR SIZES AND WEIGHTS THAT WERE USED FOR THE PYRAMID.

● A BOOK THAT VIVIDLY TRACES, FROM HIGH UP IN THE AFRICAN MOUNTAINS FROM ITS SOURCE IN LAKE VICTORIA, THE NILE RIVER DOWN ITS LONG COURSE OF 3,473 MILES, THROUGH SIX CATARACTS, TO THE MEDITERRANEAN SEA.

● A BOOK THAT IS A TREASURE CHEST FILLED WITH INFORMATION ON THE KINGS AND THEIR DYNASTIES OF ANCIENT EGYPT.

● A BOOK THAT CONTAINS DETAILED DESCRIPTIONS WORTH THEIR WEIGHT IN GOLD ON THE HIEROGLYPHIC LANGUAGE USED BY TEMPLE PRIESTS AND THEIR SCRIBES. MANY TRANSLATIONS OF INSCRIPTIONS IN THIS BOOK WILL DRAW THE READERS CLOSE TO THESE ANCIENT PEOPLE AND THEY WILL APPRECIATE AND UNDERSTAND HOW THESE ANCIENTS LIVED WAY BACK THERE IN THE DIME PAST.

● A BOOK THAT IS ONE OF THE MOST COMPREHENSIVE ONES AVAILABLE ON THIS SUBJECT.

● A BOOK THAT IS A REFRESHING COVERAGE ON THIS SUBJECT. A CLASSIC.

● THIS BOOK IS AVAILABLE AT SPECIAL QUANTITY DISCOUNTS FOR BULK PURCHASES FOR SALES PROMOTION, PREMIUMS OR FUND RAISING.

● FOR DETAILS WRITE TO S O C PUBLISHERS, DIV. OF S O C CORP., 7306 SHEFFINGDELL DR., CHARLOTTE, NC 28226, AND OR CALL 1-704-541-3497.

BACK IN TIME 3104 B.C.
TO THE GREAT PYRAMID

EGYPTIANS BROKE THEIR BACKS TO BUILD IT
HOW THE GREAT PYRAMID WAS REALLY BUILT

I STUDIES ON THREE METHODS FOR BUILDING THE GREAT PYRAMID. ONLY ONE OF THESE WAS ACTUALLY USED.

II OVERVIEW OF THE NILE

III KINGS OF EGYPT

IV HIEROGLYPHICS - ANCIENT EGYPTIAN FIGURE LANGUAGE

By SOCRATES G. TASEOS

B.S. Chemical Engineering, University Of NH; M. Ed. University of Massachusetts; Teacher of mathematics and computer sciences.

S O C Publishers, Div. Of S O C Corporation, Inc.
Charlotte, NC 28226

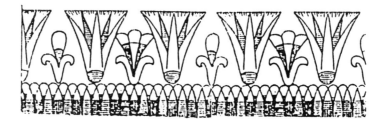

A paper cover edition of this book is published by S O C Publishers, Div. of S O C Corporation, Inc.

The List of Egyptian Hieroglyphic Figures in the Fount of Messrs. Harrison and Sons (a printer's catalogue) is used in this Book.

International Standard Book Number: 0-9626053-0-1
Library of Congress Catalog Card Number: 90-81671

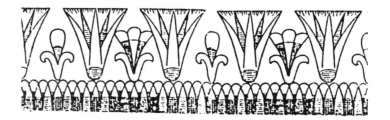

TABLE OF CONTENTS

LIST OF FIGURES, TABLES, AND DRAWINGS

PREFACE

This book is divided into four Chapters: (I), a stone by stone, and ramp by ramp studies to determine "How" king Khufu's Great Pyramid of Giza was built; (II), the Nile River was the flowing heart of the ancient Egyptian people; (III), the kings of Egypt; and (IV), the ancient Egyptian Hieroglyphic Figure Language.

This book is full of Egyptian monuments, sketches, inscriptions, Hieroglyphics and their translations. The reader will become acquainted, understand and appreciate the ancient Egyptians.

This is a rare source book, one of a kind. It answers, once and for all, "Who", "Why" and "How" The Great Pyramid was built.

Ten miles south of the modern city of Cairo, on a tract of land about 100 feet in elevation, stand the three Pyramids of Giza, (Figure No.1). The largest of these is called The Great Pyramid. It represents the culminating efforts of Imhotep, designer of the Stepped Pyramid at Sakkarah, as well as other pyramid builders. It is the largest monument of its kind ever constructed for excellence of workmanship, accuracy of planning and beauty of proportion. It remains, after thousands of years, the chief of the Seven Wonders of the Ancient World.

It is astonishing that so little is known about king Khufu, (Egyptian name) and Cheops, (Greek name). He is credited with ordering the erection of The Great Pyramid as the eternal home of his mortal body. He was the son and successor of king Seneferu, by queen Hetepheres, the daughter and heiress of king Hu. He married more than one wife and had many sons and daughters.

No known records have survived to tell how long he reigned and "How" The Great Pyramid was built. Herodotus states in his "History" that he ruled for fifty-six years. He was the second king of the Fourth Dynasty, 3124-2840 B.C., (see Lepsius in Table No. 1).

Herodotus and Egyptologists present three different methods for the construction of The Great Pyramid: (1) Herodotus - use the Pyramid Steps, Levers, Wedges, Rollers, Ropes and Thousands Of Workers to raise the large-heavy blocks of stone as the Pyramid grew in height; (2) First Group Of Egyptologists - use One Huge Ramp that increased in height and length, as the Pyramid rose, to lift the blocks of stone; and (3) Second Group Of Egyptologists - use many Add-On-Ramps attached to the sides of the Pyramid, as it rose, to elevate the blocks of stone.

LOTUS FLOWER COLUMNS SUPPORTING THE ANCIENT EGYPTIAN SKY (GODDESS NUT)

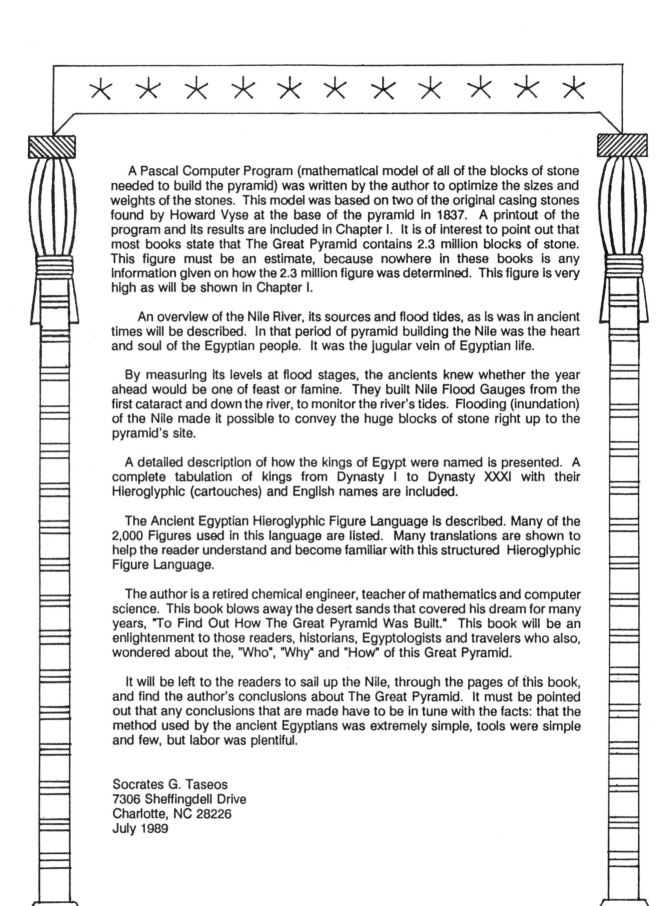

A Pascal Computer Program (mathematical model of all of the blocks of stone needed to build the pyramid) was written by the author to optimize the sizes and weights of the stones. This model was based on two of the original casing stones found by Howard Vyse at the base of the pyramid in 1837. A printout of the program and its results are included in Chapter I. It is of interest to point out that most books state that The Great Pyramid contains 2.3 million blocks of stone. This figure must be an estimate, because nowhere in these books is any information given on how the 2.3 million figure was determined. This figure is very high as will be shown in Chapter I.

An overview of the Nile River, its sources and flood tides, as is was in ancient times will be described. In that period of pyramid building the Nile was the heart and soul of the Egyptian people. It was the jugular vein of Egyptian life.

By measuring its levels at flood stages, the ancients knew whether the year ahead would be one of feast or famine. They built Nile Flood Gauges from the first cataract and down the river, to monitor the river's tides. Flooding (inundation) of the Nile made it possible to convey the huge blocks of stone right up to the pyramid's site.

A detailed description of how the kings of Egypt were named is presented. A complete tabulation of kings from Dynasty I to Dynasty XXXI with their Hieroglyphic (cartouches) and English names are included.

The Ancient Egyptian Hieroglyphic Figure Language is described. Many of the 2,000 Figures used in this language are listed. Many translations are shown to help the reader understand and become familiar with this structured Hieroglyphic Figure Language.

The author is a retired chemical engineer, teacher of mathematics and computer science. This book blows away the desert sands that covered his dream for many years, "To Find Out How The Great Pyramid Was Built." This book will be an enlightenment to those readers, historians, Egyptologists and travelers who also, wondered about the, "Who", "Why" and "How" of this Great Pyramid.

It will be left to the readers to sail up the Nile, through the pages of this book, and find the author's conclusions about The Great Pyramid. It must be pointed out that any conclusions that are made have to be in tune with the facts: that the method used by the ancient Egyptians was extremely simple, tools were simple and few, but labor was plentiful.

Socrates G. Taseos
7306 Sheffingdell Drive
Charlotte, NC 28226
July 1989

LOTUS BUD COLUMNS SUPPORTING THE ANCIENT EGYPTIAN SKY (GODDESS NUT)

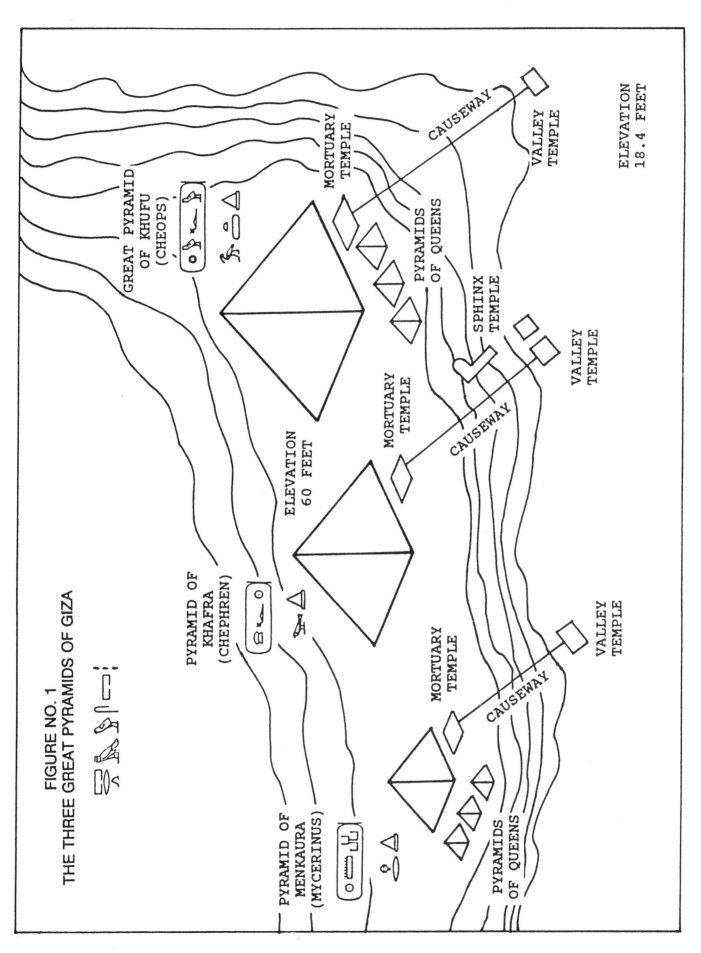

FIGURE NO. 1
THE THREE GREAT PYRAMIDS OF GIZA

PYRAMID OF MENKAURA (MYCERINUS)

PYRAMID OF KHAFRA (CHEPHREN)

GREAT PYRAMID OF KHUFU (CHEOPS)

ELEVATION 60 FEET

ELEVATION 18.4 FEET

MORTUARY TEMPLE

PYRAMIDS OF QUEENS

VALLEY TEMPLE

CAUSEWAY

SPHINX TEMPLE

VALLEY TEMPLE

MORTUARY TEMPLE

CAUSEWAY

MORTUARY TEMPLE

PYRAMIDS OF QUEENS

VALLEY TEMPLE

CAUSEWAY

3

TABLE N0. 1

DATES ASSIGNED TO THE EGYPTIAN DYNASTIES BY EGYPTOLOGISTS

Dynasty B.C.	Champol. B.C.	Boeckh. B.C.	Lepsius B.C.	Brugsch. B.C.	Unger B.C.	Mariette B.C.	Lieblein B.C.
I	5869	5702	3892	4400	5613	5004	3893
II	5615	5449	3639	4133	5360	4751	3630
III	5318	5147	3338	3966	5058	4449	3328
IV	5121	4933	3124	3733	4845	4235	3114
V	4673	4650	2840	3566	4568	3951	2862
VI	4426	4402	2744	3300	4310	3703	2830
VII	4222	4199	2592	3100	4137	3500	2612
VIII	4147	4128	2522	----	4107	3429	2506
IX	4047	4056	2674	----	3967	3358	2414
X	3947	3647	2565	----	3558	3249	2367
XI	3762	3462	2423	----	3374	3064	2321
XII	3703	3404	2380	2466	3315	2851	2268
XIII	3417	3244	2167	2235	3009	----	2108
XIV	3004	2791	2136	----	2702	2398	1925
XV	2520	2607	2101	----	2518	2214	1831
XVI	2270	2323	1842	----	2258	----	1737
XVII	2082	1806	1684	----	2007	----	1641
XVIII	1822	1655	1591	1700	1796	1703	1490
XIX	1473	1326	1443	1400	1404	1462	1231
XX	1279	1183	1269	1200	1195	1288	1022
XXI	1101	1048	1091	1100	1060	1110	950
XXII	971	934	961	966	930	980	887
XXIII	851	814	787	766	810	810	773
XXIV	762	725	729	733	721	721	728
XXV	718	719	716	700	715	715	684
XXVI	674	658	685	666	665	665	678
XXVII	524	529	525	527	525	527	527
XXVIII	404	405	425	---	424	406	404
XXIX	398	399	399	399	399	399	398
XXX	377	378	378	378	382	378	378
XXXI	339	340	340	340	346	340	340

The above list starts with the god-kings of Dynasty 1 and ends with the Persian-kings of Dynasty XXXI. Which preceeded the Macedonian-kings starting with Alexander The Great. There were approximately 297 kings from Dynasty I to XXXI. The source of knowledge for most of these kings are:

(1) The Tablet of Sakkarah containling fifty-three names of kings, found in the grave of Thunurei, who lived during the reign of Rameses II. (2) The Tablet of Karnak drawn up in the time of Thothmes III and it contained the names of sixty-one of his ancestors. (3) The Tablet of Abydos, found in the Temple of Osiris at Abydos. It lists the names of seventy-six Dynastic kings, beginning with Mena and end with Seti, father of Rameses II. The Turin Papyrus, which contains a complete list of kings, beginning with the god-kings and continuing to the end of the ruler, Hyksos (shepherd king) about 1600 B.C.

Khufu (Cheops) was the second king of Dynasty IV (3124-2840 B.C.). Which included the following six kings: Seneferu (father of Khufu), Khufu, Tchetfra, Khafra, Menkaura (Mycerinus, son of Khufu), and Shepseskaf.

Dynasty	IV and V	3124-2840 B.C.	The "Old Empire"
"	VI	2744 B.C.	" " "
"	XII	2380 B.C.	The "Middle Empire"
"	XIII	2136 B.C.	" " "
"	XVIII	1591-1443 B.C.	The "New Empire"
"	XIX	1443-1269 B.C.	" " "
"	XX	1269-1091 B.C.	" " "

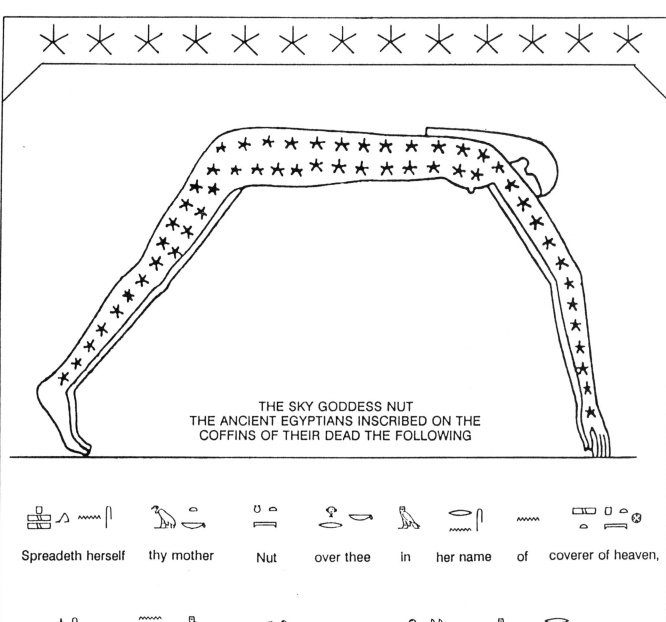

THE SKY GODDESS NUT
THE ANCIENT EGYPTIANS INSCRIBED ON THE
COFFINS OF THEIR DEAD THE FOLLOWING

| Spreadeth herself | thy mother | Nut | over thee | in | her name | of | coverer of heaven, |

| she maketh | thee to be | as | a god | without | thine enemy | in | thy name | of |

| god, | she withdraweth thee | from | thing | every | evil | in her name |

| of "Defender from every evil, great | lady; | and from Ura | whom | she hath brought forth;" |

5

ACKNOWLEDGEMENT

Thanks to H. J. Cole for his survey of The Great Pyramid which furnished at long last its accurate dimensions and Howard Vyse for finding two of the original casing stones at the base of the pyramid. These contributions made it possible to calculate the number of blocks of stone needed to build the pyramid.

To William M. Petrie and John Taylor for their informative books on The Great Pyramid.

To Peter Tompkins for his exhaustive research at the Library of Congress, which resulted in 335 references on Egypt.

Warmest thanks to E. A. Wallis Budge who spent most of his professional life at the British Museum. He wrote thousands of notes and translations, on small pieces of paper, about the flood of ancient Egyptian artifacts that flowed into the museum. These notes ripened into some of the sweetest, informative books on ancient Egypt: its people, kings, queens, monuments, gods, religion, history and culture.

Again to E. A. Wallis Budge, this great leading Egyptologist of the 19th. and 20th. centuries, for his excellent dictionaries on the ancient Egyptian Hieroglyphic Figure Language. It is through these books that it was possible to learn how to read some Hieroglyphics. Thus the author was able to cook up this book giving it a delicious ancient Egyptian flavor and color.

To General Napoleon Bonaparte, his savants and soldiers for clearing off the desert sands and reporting piles of information about The Great Pyramid. Also, for finding that gem, The Rosetta Stone, which eventually led to the decipherment of Hieroglyphics.

Thanks to the following decipherers of Hieroglyphics for their efforts and dedication in establishing a formal, structural way of interpretation: Jean Francois Champollion (father of the decipherment), Dr. Thomas Young, J. Zoega, DuThell, A. I. Silvestre de Sacy, J. D. Akerbald, Athanasius Kircher, E. A. Wallis Budge and many others on a very long list.

Special thanks also belong to the ancient Scribes for their sketches and inscriptions on so many timeless monuments, as well as to Herodotus for his "History" which gave a few clues about The Great Pyramid Pyramid.

Socrates G. Taseos
7306 Sheffingdell Drive
Charlotte, NC 28226
July 1989

Palm Leaf Columns Supporting The Ancient Egyptian Sky (goddess Nut)

INTRODUCTION

Historical Information On The Great Pyramid

Information on "How" The Great Pyramid was built can't be found. The only major historian of ancient Egypt Manetho (323-283 B.C.), a priest, wrote a history of Egypt for Ptolemy II but it was lost.

Strabo, a geographer, took a trip up the Nile in 24 B.C. He wrote forty-seven books of history, which were lost. In the appendix, which survives, he describes an entrance on the north face of the pyramid made of a hinged stone which is indistinguishable from the surrounding masonry when it lay flush with the casing stones. Strabo reports that this small opening gave way to a narrow passage, about 4 by 4 feet. It descends 375 feet into a damp, vermin-infested pit dug into the bedrock 150 feet below the base of the pyramid.

The great library of Alexandria, Egypt, accidentally damaged by Julius Caesar was restored by Mark Anthony. It was intentionally destroyed by a Christian mob on orders of the Christian emperor Theodosius in 389 A.D. Anything that may have existed in it on The Great Pyramid was lost.

Diodorus Sicules, the Greek historian, who lived soon after the time of Christ, described The Great Pyramid's 22 acres of polished casing stone as being complete and without the least decay.

The Roman Pliny tells of natives capering up the polished sides to the delight of Roman tourists.

Herodotus (484-425 B.C.), a Greek traveller and historian was born a Persian subject in the Greek provinces of Asia Minor. These were part of the vast dominant empire of Persia. Xerxes, the weak minded-ruler came to the throne of this great empire one year before the birth of Herodotus. Herodotus visited Egypt in about 459 B.C. and in his "History" of his travels, he briefly describes the three pyramids of Giza.

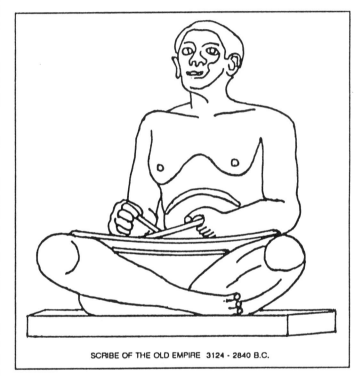

SCRIBE OF THE OLD EMPIRE 3124 - 2840 B.C.

Over the years the Arabs removed the 22 acres of the limestone casing. Then they built two bridges for dragging the stones across the Nile up to Cairo. All of the casing stones were carried away during and after the thirteenth century.

In 1356 A.D. the Sultan Hasan, one of the younger sons of Sultan Nasir, built the Grand Minareted Mosque in Cairo with stones taken from The Great Pyramid. It is close to the Citadel, and is generally considered to be the grandest in Cairo. Its construction took three years, 1358-1356 A.D. Hasan's tomb is situated on the east side of the buildings. The remaining minaret is about 280 feet high and the greatest length of the mosque is about 200 feet. The walls are 113 feet high. In the open court are two fountains which were formerly used, one by the Egyptians and one by the Turks. On the eastern side, still to be seen, are a few cannon balls which were fired at the mosque by Napoleon's army.

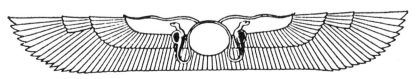

THE SUN'S DISC, WITH BRIGHTLY COLOURED WINGS, THE EMBLEM OF A VICTORIOUS KING.

Herodotus' History Book II

The exact dates of his travels in Greece, the Aegean, Asia Minor, Egypt, Cyrene, Syria and the northern coast of the Black Sea are not known. During these wanderings, he collected a boat full of information about these countries. In Book II of the Nine Books in his "History", he tells the "Who", "Why" and "How" of The Great Pyramid in the following two pages.

His Greek writings about the Nile, The Great Pyramid, king Khufu (Cheops) were translated by A. D. Godley, Hon. Fellow of Magdalen College, Oxford, England, 1920.

97. Ἐπεὰν δὲ ἐπέλθῃ ὁ Νεῖλος τὴν χώρην, αἱ πόλιες μοῦναι φαίνονται ὑπερέχουσαι, μάλιστά κῃ ἐμφερέες τῇσι ἐν τῷ Αἰγαίῳ πόντῳ νήσοισι· τὰ μὲν γὰρ ἄλλα τῆς Αἰγύπτου πέλαγος γίνεται, αἱ δὲ πόλιες μοῦναι ὑπερέχουσι. πορθμεύονται ὦν, ἐπεὰν τοῦτο γένηται, οὐκέτι κατὰ τὰ ῥέεθρα τοῦ ποταμοῦ ἀλλὰ διὰ μέσου τοῦ πεδίου. ἐς μέν γε Μέμφιν ἐκ Ναυκράτιος ἀναπλώοντι παρ' αὐτὰς τὰς πυραμίδας γίνεται ὁ πλόος· ἔστι δὲ οὐδ' οὗτος, ἀλλὰ παρὰ τὸ ὀξὺ τοῦ Δέλτα καὶ παρὰ Κερκάσωρον πόλιν· ἐς δὲ Ναύκρατιν ἀπὸ θαλάσσης καὶ Κανώβου διὰ πεδίου πλέων ἥξεις κατ' Ἀνθυλλάν τε πόλιν καὶ τὴν Ἀρχάνδρου καλευμένην.

97. When the Nile overflows the land, the towns alone are seen high and dry above the water, very like to the islands in the Aegean sea. These alone stand out, the rest of Egypt being a sheet of water. So when this happens folk are ferried not, as is their wont, in the course of the stream, but clean over the plain. From Naucratis indeed to Memphis the boat going upwards passes close by the pyramids themselves; though here the course runs not so, but by the Delta's point and the town Cercasorus; but your voyage from the sea and Canobus to Naucratis will take you over the plain near the town of Anthylla and that which is called Archandrus' town.

124. Μέχρι μὲν νυν Ῥαμψινίτου βασιλέος εἶναι ἐν Αἰγύπτῳ πᾶσαν εὐνομίην ἔλεγον καὶ εὐθηνέειν Αἴγυπτον μεγάλως, μετὰ δὲ τοῦτον βασιλεύσαντα σφέων Χέοπα ἐς πᾶσαν κακότητα ἐλάσαι. κατακληίσαντα γάρ μιν πάντα τὰ ἱρὰ πρῶτα μὲν σφέας θυσιέων τουτέων ἀπέρξαι, μετὰ δὲ ἐργάζεσθαι ἑωυτῷ κελεύειν πάντας Αἰγυπτίους. τοῖσι μὲν δὴ ἀποδεδέχθαι ἐκ τῶν λιθοτομιέων τῶν ἐν τῷ Ἀραβίῳ ὄρεϊ, ἐκ τουτέων ἕλκειν λίθους μέχρι τοῦ Νείλου· διαπεραιωθέντας δὲ τὸν ποταμὸν πλοίοισι τοὺς λίθους ἑτέροισι ἐπέταξε ἐκδέκεσθαι καὶ πρὸς τὸ Λιβυκὸν καλεύμενον ὄρος, πρὸς τοῦτο ἕλκειν. ἐργάζοντο δὲ κατὰ δέκα μυριάδας ἀνθρώπων αἰεὶ τὴν τρίμηνον ἑκάστην. χρόνον δὲ ἐγγενέσθαι τριβομένῳ τῷ λεῷ δέκα ἔτεα μὲν τῆς ὁδοῦ κατ' ἣν εἷλκον τοὺς λίθους, τὴν ἔδειμαν ἔργον ἐὸν οὐ πολλῷ τεω ἔλασσον τῆς πυραμίδος. ὡς ἐμοὶ

124. Till the time of Rhampsinitus Egypt (so the priests told me) was in all ways well governed and greatly prospered, but Cheops, who was the next king, brought the people to utter misery. For first he shut up all the temples, so that none could sacrifice there; and next, he compelled all the Egyptians to work for him, appointing to some to drag stones from the quarries in the Arabian mountains to the Nile: and the stones being carried across the river in boats, others were charged to receive and drag them to the mountains called Libyan. They worked in gangs of a hundred thousand men, each gang for three months. For ten years the people were afflicted in making the road whereon the stones were dragged, the making of which road was to my thinking a task but a little lighter than the building of the pyramid,

δοκέειν· τῆς μὲν γὰρ μῆκος εἰσὶ πέντε στάδιοι, εὖρος δὲ δέκα ὄργυιαι, ὕψος δέ, τῇ ὑψηλοτάτη ἐστὶ αὐτὴ ἑωυτῆς, ὀκτὼ ὄργυιαι, λίθου δὲ ξεστοῦ καὶ ζῴων ἐγγεγλυμμένων· ταύτης τε δὴ τὰ δέκα ἔτεα γενέσθαι καὶ τῶν ἐπὶ τοῦ λόφου ἐπ' οὗ ἑστᾶσι αἱ πυραμίδες, τῶν ὑπὸ γῆν οἰκημάτων, τὰς ἐποιέετο θήκας ἑωυτῷ ἐν νήσῳ, διώρυχα τοῦ Νείλου ἐσαγαγών. τῇ δὲ πυραμίδι αὐτῇ χρόνον γενέσθαι εἴκοσι ἔτεα ποιευμένῃ· τῆς ἐστὶ πανταχῇ μέτωπον ἕκαστον ὀκτὼ πλέθρα ἐούσης τετραγώνου καὶ ὕψος ἴσον, λίθου δὲ ξεστοῦ τε καὶ ἁρμοσμένου τὰ μάλιστα· οὐδεὶς τῶν λίθων τριήκοντα ποδῶν ἐλάσσων.

for the road is five furlongs long and ten fathoms broad, and raised at its highest to a height of eight fathoms, and it is all of stone polished and carven with figures. The ten years aforesaid went to the making of this road and of the underground chambers on the hill whereon the pyramids stand; these the king meant to be burial-places for himself, and encompassed them with water, bringing in a channel from the Nile. The pyramid itself was twenty years in the making. Its base is square, each side eight hundred feet long, and its height is the same; the whole is of stone polished and most exactly fitted; there is no block of less than thirty feet in length.

125. Ἐποιήθη δὲ ὧδε αὕτη ἡ πυραμίς· ἀναβαθμῶν τρόπον, τὰς μετεξέτεροι κρόσσας οἱ δὲ βωμίδας ὀνομάζουσι, τοιαύτην τὸ πρῶτον ἐπείτε ἐποίησαν αὐτήν, ἤειρον τοὺς ἐπιλοίπους λίθους μηχανῇσι ξύλων βραχέων πεποιημένῃσι, χαμᾶθεν μὲν ἐπὶ τὸν πρῶτον στοῖχον τῶν ἀναβαθμῶν ἀείροντες· ὅκως δὲ ἀνίοι ὁ λίθος ἐπ' αὐτόν, ἐς ἑτέρην μηχανὴν ἐτίθετο ἑστεῶσαν ἐπὶ τοῦ πρῶτου στοίχου, ἀπὸ τούτου δὲ ἐπὶ τὸν δεύτερον εἵλκετο στοῖχον ἐπ' ἄλλης μηχανῆς· ὅσοι γὰρ δὴ στοῖχοι ἦσαν τῶν ἀναβαθμῶν, τοσαῦται καὶ μηχαναὶ ἦσαν, εἴτε καὶ τὴν αὐτὴν μηχανὴν ἐοῦσαν μίαν τε καὶ εὐβάστακτον μετεφόρεον ἐπὶ στοῖχον ἕκαστον, ὅκως τὸν λίθον ἐξέλοιεν· λελέχθω γὰρ ἡμῖν ἐπ' ἀμφότερα, κατά περ λέγεται. ἐξεποιήθη δ' ὦν τὰ ἀνώτατα αὐτῆς πρῶτα, μετὰ δὲ τὰ ἐχόμενα τούτων ἐξεποίευν, τελευταῖα δὲ αὐτῆς τὰ ἐπίγαια καὶ τὰ κατωτάτω ἐξεποίησαν. σεσημανται δὲ διὰ γραμμάτων Αἰγυπτίων ἐν τῇ πυραμίδι ὅσα ἔς τε συρμαίην καὶ κρόμμυα καὶ σκόροδα ἀναισιμώθη τοῖσι ἐργαζομένοισι· καὶ ὡς ἐμὲ εὖ μεμνῆσθαι τὰ ὁ ἑρμηνεύς μοι ἐπιλεγόμενος τὰ γράμματα ἔφη, ἑξακόσια καὶ χίλια τάλαντα ἀργυρίου τετελέσθαι. εἰ δ' ἔστι οὕτω ἔχοντα ταῦτα, κόσα οἰκὸς ἄλλα δεδαπανῆσθαί ἐστι ἔς τε σίδηρον τῷ ἐργάζοντο καὶ σιτία καὶ ἐσθῆτα τοῖσι ἐργαζομένοισι, ὁκότε χρόνον μὲν οἰκοδόμεον τὰ ἔργα τὸν εἰρημένον, ἄλλον δέ, ὡς ἐγὼ δοκέω, ἐν τῷ τοὺς λίθους ἔταμνον καὶ ἦγον καὶ τὸ ὑπὸ γῆν ὄρυγμα ἐργάζοντο, οὐκ ὀλίγον χρόνον.

127. Βασιλεῦσαι δὲ τὸν Χέοπα τοῦτον Αἰγύπτιοι ἔλεγον πεντήκοντα ἔτεα, τελευτήσαντος δὲ τούτου ἐκδέξασθαι τὴν βασιληίην τὸν ἀδελφεὸν αὐτοῦ Χεφρῆνα· καὶ τοῦτον δὲ τῷ αὐτῷ τρόπῳ διαχρᾶσθαι τῷ ἑτέρῳ τά τε ἄλλα καὶ πυραμίδα ποιῆσαι, ἐς μὲν τὰ ἐκείνου μέτρα οὐκ ἀνήκουσαν·

125. This pyramid was made like a stairway with tiers, courses, or steps. When this, its first form, was completed, the workmen used levers made of short wooden logs to raise the rest of the stones; they heaved up the blocks from the ground on to the first tier of steps; when the stone had been so raised it was set on another lever that stood on the first tier, and a lever again drew it up from this tier to the next. It may be that there was a new lever on each tier of the steps, or perhaps there was but one lever, and that easily lifted, which they carried up to each tier in turn; I leave this uncertain, both ways being told me. But this is certain, that the upper part of the pyramid was the first finished off, then the next below it, and last of all the base and the lowest part. There are writings on [2] the pyramid in Egyptian characters showing how much was spent on purges and onions and garlic for the workmen; and to my sure remembrance the interpreter when he read me the writing said that sixteen hundred talents of silver had been paid. Now if that is so, how much must needs have been expended on the iron with which they worked, and the workmen's food and clothing? seeing that the time aforesaid was spent in building, and the hewing and carrying of the stone and the digging out of the underground parts was, as I suppose, a business of long duration.

127. Cheops reigned (so the Egyptians said) for fifty years; at his death he was succeeded by his brother Chephren, who bore himself in all respects like Cheops. Chephren also built a pyramid, of a less size than his brother's.

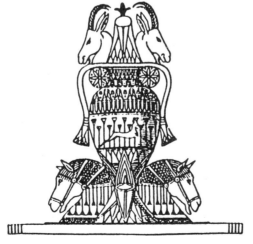

A BEAUTIFUL SMALL VASE AT GIZA
LOTUS FLOWER HANDLE WITH HEADS OF GAZELLES AND HORSES

The History Of Herodotus

The greek historian, Herodotus, in his "History Book II", writes about his trip to Egypt and gives a few clues on how The Great Pyramid was built. The FIRST HINT is how it was possible for boats carrying blocks of stone to sail close to the pyramid's site: "When the Nile overflows the land, the towns alone are seen high and dry above the water, like the islands in the Aegean sea. These alone stand out, the rest of Egypt being a sheet of water. Boats no longer keep the course of the river, but sail right across the plain. On the voyage from Naucratis to Memphis at this season, YOU PASS CLOSE TO THE PYRAMIDS THEMSELVES."

The SECOND HINT is that the causeway was used for dragging blocks of stone to the pyramid's site. "Till the time of king Rhampsinitus, Egypt was always well governed and greatly prospered, but Cheops, who followed him, ruled most miserably. He closed all the temples first, so that none could sacrifice there. Next, he compelled all of the Egyptians to work for him, appointing some to drag stones from the quarries in the Arabian mountains to the Nile. The stones being carried across the river in boats, and then dragged them to the Libyan mountain (pyramid site). They worked in gangs of a hundred thousand men, each for three months. For ten years the people were afflicted in making the ROAD WHEREON THE STONES WERE DRAGGED. For me a task but a little lighter than building the pyramid. This road is 3,051 feet in length, 60 feet in width, and 48 feet in height. Ten years went to making of this road and of the underground chambers on the hill whereon the pyramid stand. These the king meant to be the burial place for himself, and encompassed them with water, bringing in a channel from the Nile."

"The pyramid was twenty years in building. Its base is square, each side is eight hundred feet long, and its height is the same; yes the stones were polished and fitted; there is no stone less than thirty feet in length."

He gives the THIRD, FOURTH, and FIFTH HINTS: "THE PYRAMID WAS MADE LIKE A STAIRWAY WITH TIERS, COURSES, OR STEPS. When this, its first form, was completed, THE REST OF THE STONES WERE RAISED WITH LEVERS MADE OF SHORT WOODEN LOGS, they heaved up the blocks from the ground on to the first step, when the stone had been so raised, it was set on another lever that stood on the first step, and a lever again drew it up from this step to the next. It may be that there was a lever on each step, or perhaps there was but one lever which was easily lifted and carried up to each step in turn. I leave this uncertain, both ways being told me."

"THE UPPER PART OF THE PYRAMID WAS FINISHED FIRST. THEN THE MIDDLE, AND FINALLY THE PART WHICH WAS LOWEST AND NEAREST THE GROUND."

"The Egyptians say that this Cheops reigned fifty years, and when he died, his brother Chephren succeeded him."

Some Costs

"There is an inscription in Egyptian characters on the pyramid which records the quantity of radishes, onions, and garlic consumed by the workers who constructed it. I perfectly well remember that the interpreter, who read the writing to me, said that the money expended was 1,600 talents of silver. If this be the case, how much more was expended in iron tools, in bread, and in clothes for the workers, since they were occupied in building the works for the time which I mentioned, and no short time besides, as I think, in cutting and drawing the stones, and in forming the subterraneous excavations."

WEST SIDE OF QUEEN'S HATSHEPUT'S OBELISK AT KARNAK
SEE APPENDIX FOR TRANSLATION

If it is assumed that the 1,600 talents of silver was for one day's wages for 100,000 workers, and an average of 4.16 radishes, 1.66 onions and .83 of a garlic bulb were consumed by each worker each day, then the Egyptian characters for their wages and vegetables for one year are:

576,000 talents of silver

150,000,000 radishes

60,000,000 onions

30,000,000 garlic

When, By Whom, Why The Great Pyramid Was Built

Egyptologists vary considerably as to the time when The Great Pyramid was built, (see Table No. 1). However by using the Dynasty dates assigned by Lepsius, it is estimated that it was built after 3124 B.C.

They agree that Khufu built The Great Pyramid. That is, high up near the top, inside the pyramid, above the king's chamber are hieroglyphics painted on the walls of five shallow chambers that contain three different variations of Khufu's name and the number 17:

, indicating that the construction reached this point in 17 years. Similar marks, in red, but occasionally in black, were also found on stones in the first six courses of the pyramid, behind the casing blocks.

The Great Pyramid was built as Khufu's tomb. It is the largest tomb ever built for a single individual, and the most famous monument of antiquity. Never before and never since, did any king have such a sublime resting place. Although it failed to protect Khufu's body, it did succeed in preserving his name. As long as it stands on the edge of the Libyan plateau, the name of Khufu will endure. Khufu called his pyramid khut,

Death in ancient Egypt was considered the beginning of a new life in another world. This life, assuming certain precautions were taken, would last forever. Because life on earth was relatively short, the Egyptians built their houses of mud. They built their tombs of stone since life after death was eternal.

The Egyptians believed that besides a physical body everyone had a soul called a Ba, and a spiritual duplicate of themselves called a Ka. When the body died, an individual's Ba continued to exist here on earth, resting within the body at night. His or her Ka, on the other hand, traveled back and forth between the earth and the other world. Eternal life depended on both the Ba and Ka being able to identify the body. For this reason, corpses were preserved by the process of mummification.

The tomb into which a body was placed had two functions: It was designed to protect the body from the elements and from thieves who might try to steal the gold and precious objects placed in and around the coffin. It also had to serve as a house for the Ka. The more important the person, the greater his tomb. Since at death kings became gods, their tombs were the largest and most elaborate of all.

FRONT OF KING THOTHMES III'S OBELISK AT KARNAK
SEE APPENDIX FOR TRANSLATION

11

The Great Pyramid Was Khufu's Tomb

There exists no evidence to suggest that The Great Pyramid was built to serve for the purpose of astronomical uses, a standard of measurement, and or magical happenings.

Surveys And Observations On The Great Pyramid

The ancient past is silent about plans that give information on the dimensions of the pyramid and how it was built. This information has to come from present day surveys and inspections of the pyramid and its site. Then the number of limestone blocks that went into its construction can be calculated. Also, its method of construction can be determined.

No monument in Egypt has been surveyed and measured as often as the pyramid. So many people were involved in these surveys that it would take a small book to mention all of them. The more significant include: Colonel Howard Vyse and J. S. Perring (1837-8), John Taylor (1864), William M. Petrie (1893), and J. H. Cole (1925).

From their observations the average measurements are: base - north 755.43 ft.; south 756.08 ft.; east 755.88 ft.; and west 755.77 ft.. These dimensions show no two sides are identical; however, the difference between the longest and shortest side is only 7.8 inches.

Each side is oriented almost exactly with the four Cardinal Points. The following being the estimated errors: north side 2'28" south of west; south side 1'57" south of west; east side 5'30" west of north; and west side 2'30" west of north.

Four corners were almost perfect right angles: north-east 90°3'2"; north-west 89°59'58"; south-east 89°56'27", and south-west 90°0'33".

When completed, it rose to a height of 481.4 ft., the top 31 feet of which are now missing. Its four sides incline at an angle of about 51°51' with the ground. At its base, it covers an area of about 13.1 acres.

It is not known whether the pyramid was built on the accretion (layer) plan. It was built in 201 stepped tiers, which are visible because the casing stones have been removed. It rises to the height of a modern forty-story building.

The pyramid is built partly upon a solid, large, bedrock core and a platform of limestone blocks which can be seen at the northern and eastern sides. A few blocks of the fine limestone casing remain at the base of the northern side and show how accurately the stones were dressed and fitted together. Howard Vyse found two of these casing stones which measured 5 ft. by 8 ft. by 12 ft. with the pyramid's face angle of 51°51' cut on one of the 12 foot sides.

The core masonry, behind the casing stones, consists of large blocks of local limestone, quarried right on the spot, built around and over the bedrock core. The size of this core can't be determined, since it is completely covered by the pyramid.

The casing stones were of highly polished pure white limestone, which must have been a dazzling sight. Unlike marble, which tends to become eroded with time and weather, limestone becomes harder and more polished. The workmanship on the casing stones, some of which weighed up to 40 tons, is quite remarkable. The faces were so straight and so truly square that when the stones had been placed together the fine film of mortar between them was, on the average, no thicker then 1/50 of an inch over an area of several square feet. The average variation of the layout of the casing stones from a straight line was about 1/100 of an inch on a length of ten feet. To place these stone in exact contact with cement in joints would be difficult to do by present day masons. The fine texture of the cement was so strong, even after thousands of years, that the stones shattered before the cement would yield.

CURVATURE OF THE GREAT PYRAMID'S FACES

It is of interest to note that Napoleon's savants observed that the exposed blocks on each face were slightly concave. They made note of this curvature as a line along the apothem of the faces in one of their drawings. This was overlooked for almost 100 years when in April of 1893 William M. Petrie made the same observation of this curvature which is difficult to observe with the naked eye (see Figure No. 2 below).

FIGURE NO. 2
CURVATURE OF THE GREAT PYRAMID'S FACES

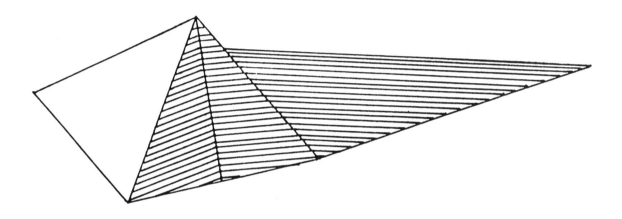

EGYPTIAN CEILING AND WALL ORNAMENTATION
CONSISTING OF CONVENTIONAL LOTUS FLOWERS

PYRAMID BUILT IN SEVEN PHASES

Some of these sections will be discussed in detail. While others will only be briefly pursued. Thus, this Chapter 1 will keep its course up the Nile to the pyramid site to study three methods for building The Great Pyramid.

I   Selection And Preparation Of The Site.
II Planning The Great Pyramid.
III Quarrying Of The Blocks Of Stone.
IV Transporting The Blocks Of Stone.
V   Shaping And Polishing The Blocks Of Stone.
VI Building The Pyramid - Three Methods.
    a) Levers, Rollers, And Wedges Made Of Short Wooden Logs.
    b) One Long Ramp.
    c) Side Ramps.
VII Description Of The Interior Chambers And Passages.

I Selection And Preparation Of The Site

The builder of this pyramid was very wise to choose this site because most of the stones, with the exception of the casing stones, some granite and basalt stones, could be cut right on the spot and in the near by quarry. This practical choice made it possible to reduce considerably the time and back-breaking labor needed to drag the stones from distant quarries across the Nile.

The many surveys done on the pyramid proved that the Egyptians located the sides of the pyramid along the four Cardinal Points with extreme accuracy. Whether they used the stars, and/or the rising and setting sun, can't be determined. One thing is certain, that whatever method they used was direct and very simple.

Once the sand, gravel and loose rocks had been removed, down to the solid bedrock of the plateau, the whole pyramid site was open-cast quarried into blocks, leaving a square core for the center of the pyramid. These blocks were then stored outside a low wall, made of mortared stone, that surrounds the core. Today there still remains the foundation of this wall on the north, south, and west sides of the pyramid, at an average distance of 66 feet from the outer edge of the base casing stone (see Figure No. 3).

This core gives the pyramid stability from the downward and horizontal forces that will develop from the superimposed loads of blocks of stones that are piled up, as the pyramid rises. Also, from the prevailing north-west winds that exert enormous pressures on the huge areas of the pyramid's faces, thus increasing these forces further.

Levelling of the entire pyramid site was accomplished by flooding the area inside the wall with water, leaving just the high spots. Then these were cut down to the level of the surface of the water. Next, some of the water was released and the high spots again were cut down to the water's surface. This process was repeated until the entire pyramid site, between the core and the four walls, was levelled down to the base of the pyramid's platform.

FRONT OF KING THOTHMES III'S OBELISK AT HELIOPOLIS
SEE APPENDIX FOR TRANSLATION

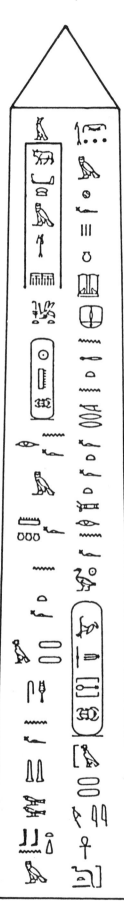

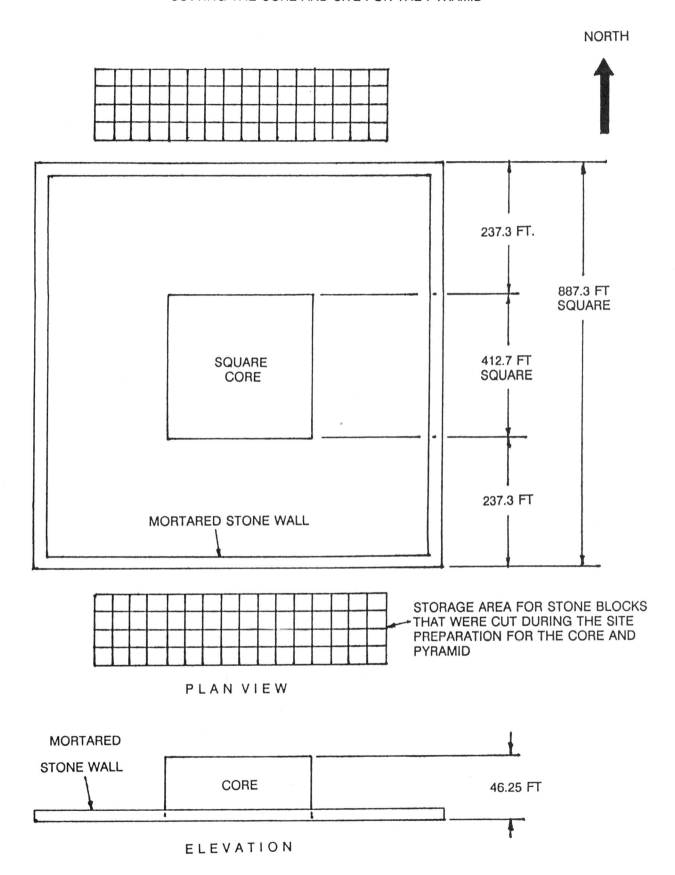

FIGURE NO. 3
CUTTING THE CORE AND SITE FOR THE PYRAMID

NORTH

237.3 FT.

887.3 FT
SQUARE

412.7 FT
SQUARE

237.3 FT

SQUARE
CORE

MORTARED STONE WALL

STORAGE AREA FOR STONE BLOCKS
THAT WERE CUT DURING THE SITE
PREPARATION FOR THE CORE AND
PYRAMID

P L A N   V I E W

MORTARED

STONE WALL

CORE

46.25 FT

E L E V A T I O N

The Pyramid's Bedrock Core

Some known facts about the pyramid can help establish rough dimensions of its bedrock core. From the pyramid's entrance at the 16th step, a passageway descends into the heart of the pyramid, at an angle of 26°30'. At a distance of 130 feet down, the passageway cuts into the bedrock. With this intersection, the Step heights in Table No. 2 and a few calculations, it can be determined approximately how far in from the base edge of the casing stone the core begins. That is, point B, where the descending passageway meets the bedrock.

Calculation Of Point B (See Figure No. 4)

P, the length of the descending passageway at the point where it meets the bedrock = 130 feet.

$X/130$ = cosine 26°30', X = 116.3 feet.

$H/130$ = sine 26°30', H = 58.0 feet.

$58.0/R$ = tangent 51°51', R = 45.6 feet.

E, from Table No. 2 = $(60+59+58+57+56+55+54+53+52+51+50+49+48+47+46+45)/12$ = 70 feet.

$S = E - H = 70.0 - 58.0$ = 12 feet.

$12/T$ = tangent 51°51', T = 9.4 feet.

$B = X + R + T = 116.3 + 45.6 + 9.4$ = 171.3 feet.

From Table No. 2, the length = width of Step No. 1, to the outside edge of the casing stones = 9063.85 inches, or 9063.85/12 = 755.3 feet. Therefore, the bedrock core left to give stability to the pyramid = (755.3 - 2 x 171.3) = 412.7 feet square.

It is impossible to determine the height of the bedrock core. However, it will be assumed to reach to the top of Step No. 10 = $(60+59+58+57+56+55+54+53+52+51)/12$ = 46.25 feet. The reasons for this assumption are: (1) A core height of 46.25 feet seems reasonable compared to the pyramid's height of 481.3 feet. And (2) The number of large heavy blocks of stone to be cut will be reduced. (See Table No. 2 for the above Step heights).

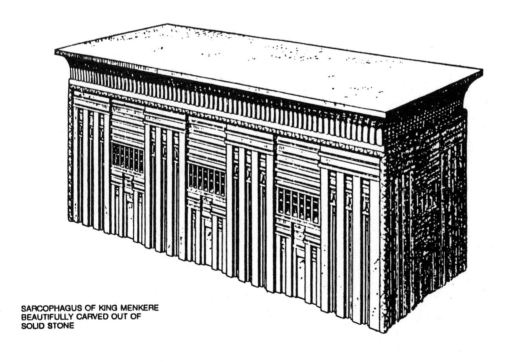

SARCOPHAGUS OF KING MENKERE
BEAUTIFULLY CARVED OUT OF
SOLID STONE

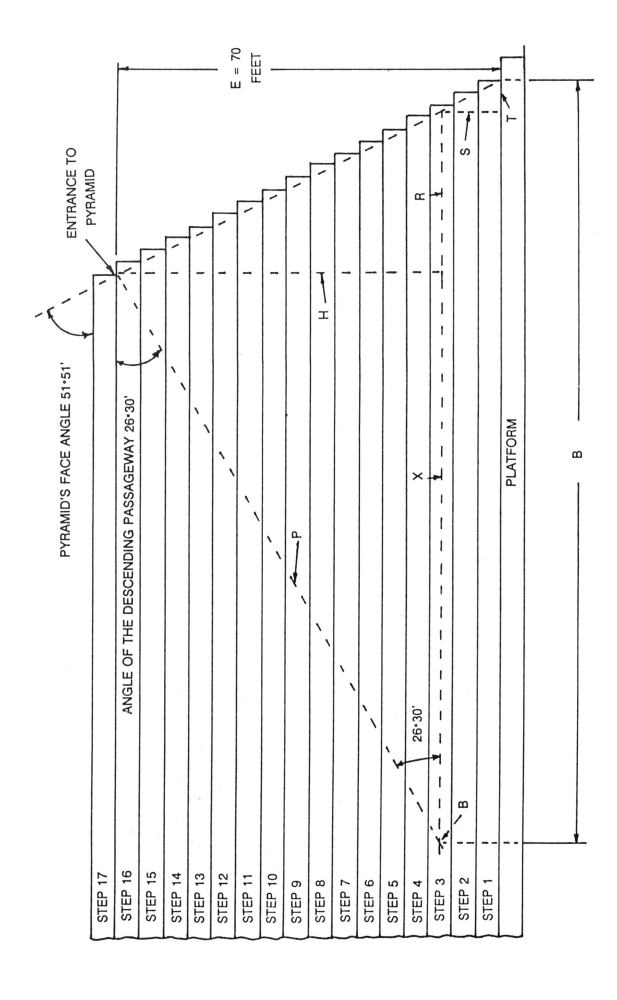

FIGURE NO. 4
B - POINT WHERE THE DESCENDING PASSAGEWAY MEETS THE BEDROCK
(DRAWING IS NOT TO SCALE)

17

II Planning The Great Pyramid

FIRST: From the surveys done on The Great Pyramid, its dimensions were calculated and a layout was made of them. SECOND: Then a computer was used to calculate every block of stone in The Great Pyramid and a layout out them was drawn. All block sizes were scaled from the two original casing stones, 5 ft. by 8 ft. by 12 ft. found by Howard Vyse at the base of the pyramid.

The Great Pyramid's Dimensions And Their Layout

One acre = 43,560 square feet, or 208.71 feet on a side. For the pyramid's base, length = width = (square root of 13.097144 acres) x 208.71 feet = 755.321 feet. Or 755.321 x 12 = 9063.85 inches. Height = (755.321 x tangent 51•51')/2 = 480.783 feet. Or 480.783 x 12 = 5769.403 inches. For the Cap stone base: length = width = (32.18x2)/tangent 51•51' = 50.55 inches. The layout of The Great Pyramid's dimensions are shown below.

FIGURE NO. 5
LAYOUT OF THE GREAT PYRAMID'S DIMENSIONS
(LAYOUT IS NOT TO SCALE)

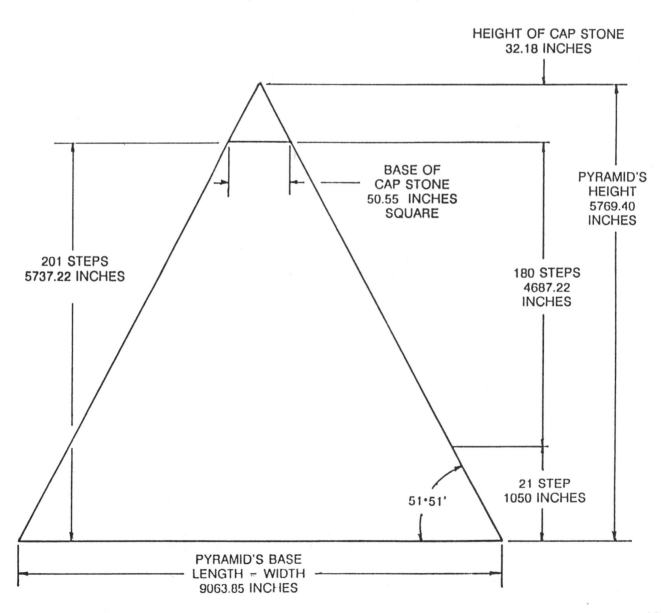

HEIGHT OF CAP STONE
32.18 INCHES

BASE OF
CAP STONE
50.55 INCHES
SQUARE

PYRAMID'S
HEIGHT
5769.40
INCHES

201 STEPS
5737.22 INCHES

180 STEPS
4687.22
INCHES

51•51'

21 STEP
1050 INCHES

PYRAMID'S BASE
LENGTH = WIDTH
9063.85 INCHES

Method For Controlling The Symmetry Of The Pyramid As It Rises

In 1798, Napoleon Bonaparte's savants found the original reference-squares just outside each of the pyramid's four corners. These were shallow, square hollows, cut into the bedrock. In April of 1865, Piazzi Smyth, the Royal engineer-surveyor, went over the surfaces of these squares, with a level, and found them to be perfectly flat.

These reference-squares were used by the ancient Egyptians to continuously check, as the pyramid rose, the edge lengths of each of its 201 steps, and their four corner stones for accuracy of placements. In this way the pyramid's symmetry was maintained. What instruments they used is not known.

They did this checking by sighting along the diagonals of the reference-squares and their extensions, across the pyramid's corners to see if the opposite corners lined up along these diagonals. Today modern skyscrapers are inspected, during their construction, in the same way. However, extremely accurate laser beams of light are used in these modern day optical instruments. It is difficult to believe that these ancient Egyptians used this same method more that 4,000 years ago see below.

FIGURE NO. 6
METHOD FOR CONTROLLING THE SYMMETRY OF
THE PYRAMID'S STEPS AND ITS PLATFORM

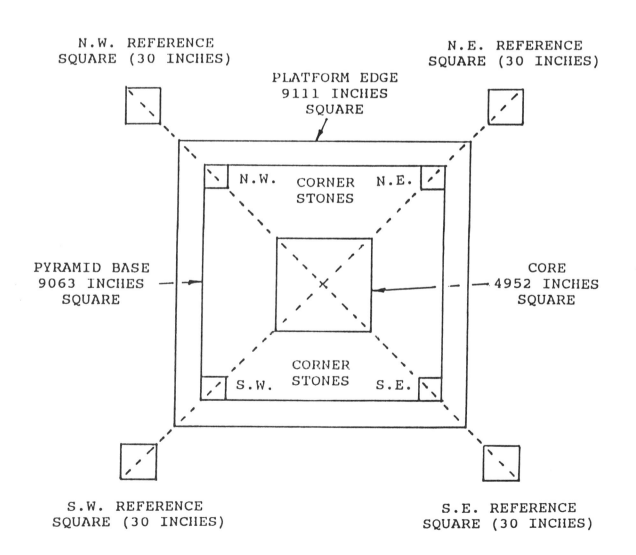

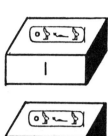

Detailed Calculations Of Every Block Of Stone In The Great Pyramid

Since the volumes of the pyramid's passageways and internal chambers are very small compared to the huge volume of the pyramid, they are ignored at this time, just as though the pyramid was built of solid stone blocks with mortared joints. With this approach, the calculations of the sizes and weights of the blocks needed for the pyramid are greatly simplified.

These calculations are based on two of the original casing stones found by Howard Vyse at the base of The Great Pyramid which were 5 ft. by 8 ft. by 12 ft. One of the 12 foot sides of each stone was bevel to 51·51' which was the angle that the pyramid faces made with the ground.

Initially, a scientific solar-powered calculator was used to determine the number of blocks, their sizes and weights. These results were used to write a Pascal Computer Program to optimize the block sizes for each of the 201 steps by letting a computer do the calculations. That is, it is important to have the largest blocks in the lower steps to give stability to the pyramid. Also, to gradually reduce the sizes of these blocks, from step to step, so that the effort by the workers to raise the blocks would likewise be reduced as the pyramid rises.

Several computer runs were made to optimize the block sizes and weights. To minimize the errors, the dimensions of the blocks were carried to the nearest one-hundredth of an inch.

As mentioned earlier, most books and encyclopedia state that there are 2.3 million blocks of stone in The Great Pyramid, with no method given as to how the figure was conceived. Table No.2 shows that 603,728 blocks were determined. When the 13,016 blocks are deducted for the volume of the bedrock core, the total blocks needed is equal to: (603,728 -13,016) = 590,712. This figure is (2,300,000 - 590,712) = 1,709,288 blocks less than the often published 2.3 million value.

BLOCK PULLING CREWS
BLOCKS OF STONE WITH KHUFU'S NAME ARE NUMBERED 1 TO 20 (IN HIEROGLYPHICS)
(ONE FOR EACH OF THE TWENTY YEARS IT TOOK TO BUILD THE GREAT PYRAMID)

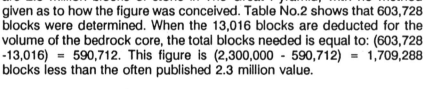

Explanation Of The Calculated Results In Table No. 2

To help understand Table No. 2 and its long columns of block calculations refer to Figures No. 5, No. 7, and the following:

Column (1): SN, Number of Steps in the pyramid, starts at 1 and ends at 201.

Column (4): ST, Step Thickness, starts at 60.00 inches for Step No. 1. This figure is reduced 1 inch for each succeeding Step until Step No. 21 is reached. In this way the total thickness of the first 21 Steps will be equal to 1,050 inches. Then the Step thickness in each of the remaining 180 Steps is fixed at 26.04 inches so that the sum of their thickness equals 4,687.22 inches.

Column (5): CCSL = CCSW, Casing Corner Stone Length = Casing Corner Stone Width, are set at 96.00 and 84.00 inches alternatively between Steps No.s 1 and 21. Then they are reduced alternatively to 72.00 and 60.00 inches between Steps No.s 22 to 126 inclusively. Finally, for Steps No.s 127 to 200, they are alternatively set at 48.00 and 40.00 inches.

Column (7): CS1SN, Number Of Casing Side Stones One Side of the pyramid is set at 61 for Steps No.s 1 to 127 inclusively. Between Steps No.s 128 to 200 this number is gradually reduced from 61 to 1.

Step No. 1 Calculations

Column (1): SN, Step No. 1.

Column (2): SL = SW, Step Length = Step Width, Starts at 9063.85 inches.

Column (3): DTSB, Distance From The Top Of The Pyramid To Step Base, Starts at 5769.70 inches.

Column (4): ST, Step Thickness, Starts At 60.00 inches.

Column (5): CCSL = CCSW, Casing Corner Stone Length = Casing Corner Stone Width, Starts at 96.00 inches.

Column (6): CCSWTE, Casing Corner Stone Weight Of Each, equals (ST x CCSL x CCSW x 165)/(12 x 12 x 12 x 2000) = 26.40 Tons.

Column (7): CS1SN, Casing Stones One Side Number of is set at 61.

Column (8): CSSL1S, Casing Side Stones Length Of One Side, equals (SL - 2 x CCSL) = 9063.85 - 2 x 96 = 8871.85 inches.

Column (9): CSSLE, Casing Side Stone Length Of Each, equals (CSSL1S/CS1SN) = (8871.85/61) = 145.44 inches.

Column (10): CSSWTE, Casing Side Stone Weight Of Each, equals (ST x CCSL x CSSLE x 165)/(12 x 12 x 12 x 2000) = 40.00 Tons.

Column (11): CS4SN, Casing Stones 4 Sides Number Of, equals (4 x CS1SN) = 4 x 61 = 244.

Column (12): COSL = COSW, Core Stone Length = Core Stone Width, equals CSSLE = 145.44 inches.

Column (13): COSWTE, Core Stone Weight Each, equals (ST x COSL x COSW x 165)/(12 x 12 x 12 x 2000) = 60.59 Tons.

Column (14): COSTN, Core Stones Total Number, equals (CS1SN x CS1SN) = 61 x 61 = 3721 stones.

Column (15): TNPS, Total Number Pyramid Stones, equals (4 Corner Stone + CS4SN + COSTN) = 4 + 244 + 3721 = 3969 stones.

Step No. 2 Calculations

Column (1): SN, Step No. 2.

Column (2): SL = SW, Step Length = Step Width, equals ((5769.40 - 60) x 2)/tangent 51°51' = 8969.64 inches.

Column (3): DTSB, equals (5769.40 - 60) = 5709.40 inches.

Column (4): ST, equals (60.00 - 1.00) = 59.00 inches.

Column (5): CCSL = CCSW, set at 84.00 inches.

Column (6): CCSWTE, equals (ST x CCSL x CCSW x 165)/(12 x 12 x 12 x 2000) = 19.88 Tons.

Column (7): CS1SN, is set at 61.

Column (8): CSSL1S, equals (8969.64 - 2 x 84) = 8801.64 inches.

Column (9): CSSLE, equals (8801.64/61) = 144.29 inches.

Column (10): CSSWTE, equals (59 x 84 x 144.29 x 165)/(12 x 12 x 12 x 2000) = 34.14 tons.

Column (11): CS4SN, equals (4 x 61) = 244 stones.

Column (12): COSL = COSW, equals CSSLE = 144.29 inches.

Column (13): COSWTE, equals (59 x 144.29 x 144.29 x 165)/(12 x 12 x 12 x 2000) = 58.64 Tons.

Column (14): COSTN, equals (61 x 61) = 3721 stones.

Column (15): TNPS, equals (4 + 244 + 3721 + 3969) = 7938 stones.

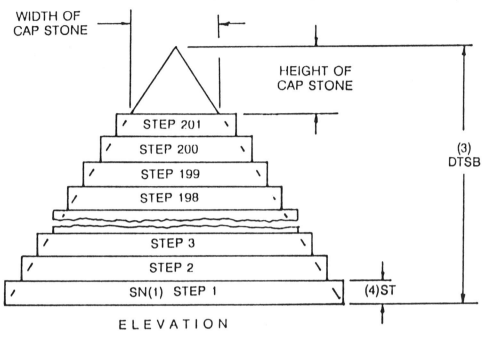

FIGURE NO. 7
LAYOUT OF THE PYRAMID'S STEPS AND STONES
(NOT TO SCALE)

WIDTH OF
CAP STONE

HEIGHT OF
CAP STONE

(3)
DTSB

STEP 201
STEP 200
STEP 199
STEP 198

STEP 3
STEP 2
SN(1) STEP 1

(4)ST

ELEVATION

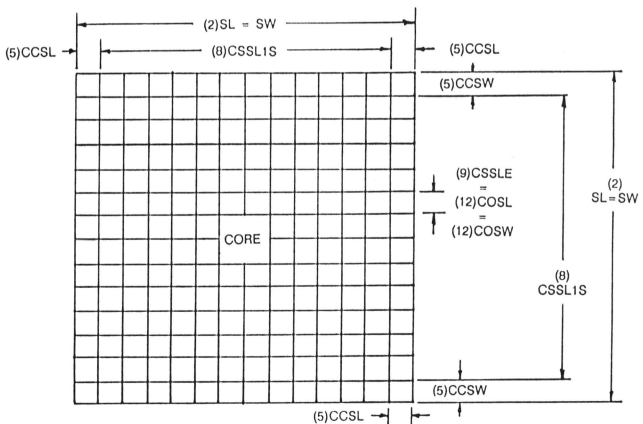

(2)SL = SW

(8)CSSL1S

(5)CCSL

(5)CCSL

(5)CCSW

(9)CSSLE
=
(12)COSL
=
(12)COSW

(2)
SL = SW

CORE

(8)
CSSL1S

(5)CCSW

(5)CCSL

PLAN VIEW-STEP NO. 1

```pascal
PROGRAM PYRAMID;
Uses Printer;
Label 100,200,300,400,500,600,700,800,900;

(Written by Socrates G. Taseos, July 11,1989. Calculation of the number)
(of limestone blocks needed to build Cheop's Great Pyramid at Giza,Egypt,)
(No provision was made for interior chambers and passageways. The Pyramid)
(is in the form of 201 steps. The casing stones are rectangular, unfinished)
(with no slant angle. The pyramid is 9063.85 inches square at the base and)
(5769.40 inches in height. The density of limestone is 165 lbs per cubic ft.)
(The pyramid's casing stones will be finished, top-to-bottom, after all)
(blocks have been placed, to an angle of 51°51' with the ground)

Var   SL,SW,DTSB,ST,CCSL,CCSW,CCSWTE,CS1SN,CSSL1S,CSSLE    :REAL;
      CSSWTE,CS4SN,COSL,COSW,COSWTE,COSTN,SUMTNPS,TNPS      :REAL;
                                               STEP    :INTEGER;



Begin
Writeln;Writeln;Writeln;
Writeln(Lst,'                                          TABLE NO. 2');
Write(Lst,'                          DETAILED CALCULATIONS OF EVERY STONE');
Writeln(Lst,' IN THE GREAT PYRAMID');
Write(Lst,'                                       (SEE FIGURE NO. 7 FOR LAYOUT');
Writeln(Lst,' OF STONES)');
Write(Lst,'(1)   (2)       (3)      (4)     (5)     (6)     (7)     (8)     (9)');
Writeln(Lst,'  (10)   (11)   (12)   (13)   (14)   (15)');
Write(Lst,'STEP STEP     DISTAN. STEP   CASING CASING CASING CASING   CASING');
Writeln(Lst,' CASING CASING CORE   CORE    CORE    TOTAL');
Write(Lst,'NO   LENGTH   TOP        THICK- CORNER CORNER STONES SIDE     SIDE');
Writeln(Lst,'    SIDE    STONES STONES STONES STONES NUMBERS');
Write(Lst,'       EQUALS  OF        NESS   STONE  STONE  1 SIDE STONES   STONE');
Writeln(Lst,'  STONE   4SIDES LENGTH WEIGHT TOTAL   OF');
Write(Lst,'        STEP   PYRAMID          LENGTH WEIGHT                 LENGTH');
Writeln(Lst,' WEIGHT NUMBER EQUALS EACH   NUMBER PYRAMID');
Write(Lst,'        WIDTH    TO STEP          EQUALS EACH    NUMBER LENGTH OF');
Writeln(Lst,'     OF     OF     WIDTH        OF      STONES');
Write(Lst,'                 BASE             WIDTH          OF      1 SIDE  EACH');
Writeln(Lst,'    EACH');
Write(Lst,'                                 CCSL                               ');
Writeln(Lst,'                  COSL');
Write(Lst,'SN    SL=SW    DTSB    ST    CCSW   CCSWTE CS1SN   CSSL1S   CSSLE');
Writeln(Lst,'  CSSWTE CS4SN  COSW   COSWTE COSTN  SUMTNPS');
Write(Lst,'      INCHES   INCHES  INCHES INCHES TONS            INCHES   INCHES');
Writeln(Lst,' TONS          INCHES TONS');
SL:=9063.85;
DTSB:=5769.40;
ST:=60.00;
CCSL:=96.00;
CS1SN:=61.00;
SUMTNPS:=000000.0;

   FOR STEP:= 1 TO 21 DO
     BEGIN
       CCSWTE:=(CCSL*CCSL*ST*165.0)/(12.0*12.0*12.0*2000.0);
       CSSL1S:=SL-2.0*CCSL;
       CSSLE:=CSSL1S/CS1SN;
       CSSWTE:=(CSSLE*CCSL*ST*165.0)/(12.0*12.0*12.0*2000.0);
       CS4SN:=4.0*CS1SN;
```

```
        COSL:=CSSLE;
        COSWTE:=(COSL*COSL*ST*165.0)/(12.0*12.0*12.0*2000.0);
        COSTN:=CS1SN*CS1SN;
        TNPS:=4+CS4SN+COSTN;
        SUMTNPS:=SUMTNPS+TNPS;
        WRITE(LST,STEP:3,SL:9:2,DTSB:8:2,ST:6:2,CCSL:7:2,CCSWTE:7:2,CS1SN:6:1);
        WRITE(LST,CSSL1S:10:2,CSSLE:7:2,CSSWTE:6:2,CS4SN:7:1,COSL:8:2);
        WRITELN(LST,COSWTE:6:2,COSTN:6:0,SUMTNPS:9:0);
        IF CCSL=96.00 THEN GOTO 100;
        IF CCSL=84.00 THEN GOTO 200;
100:    CCSL:=84.00;
        GOTO 300;
200:    CCSL:=96.00;
300:    SL:=((DTSB-ST)*2.0)/1.27305;
        DTSB:=DTSB-ST;
        ST:=ST-1.00;
     End;

CCSL:=72.00;
ST:=26.04;
     FOR STEP:= 22 TO 126 DO
      BEGIN
       CCSWTE:=(CCSL*CCSL*ST*165.0)/(12.0*12.0*12.0*2000.0);
       CSSL1S:=SL-2.0*CCSL;
       CSSLE:=CSSL1S/CS1SN;
       CSSWTE:=(CSSLE*CCSL*ST*165.0)/(12.0*12.0*12.0*2000.0);
       CS4SN:=4.0*CS1SN;
       COSL:=CSSLE;
       COSWTE:=(COSL*COSL*ST*165.0)/(12.0*12.0*12.0*2000.0);
       COSTN:=CS1SN*CS1SN;
       TNPS:=4+CS4SN+COSTN;
       SUMTNPS:=SUMTNPS+TNPS;
       WRITE(LST,STEP:3,SL:9:2,DTSB:8:2,ST:6:2,CCSL:7:2,CCSWTE:7:2,CS1SN:6:1);
       WRITE(LST,CSSL1S:10:2,CSSLE:7:2,CSSWTE:6:2,CS4SN:7:1,COSL:8:2);
       WRITELN(LST,COSWTE:6:2,COSTN:6:0,SUMTNPS:9:0);
       IF CCSL=72.00 THEN GOTO 400;
       IF CCSL=60.00 THEN GOTO 500;
400:   CCSL:=60.00;
       GOTO 600;
500:   CCSL:=72.00;
600:   SL:=((DTSB-ST)*2.0)/1.27305;
       DTSB:=DTSB-ST;
     END;

CCSL:=48.00;


     FOR STEP:=127 TO 200 DO
      BEGIN
       CCSWTE:=(CCSL*CCSL*ST*165.0)/(12.0*12.0*12.0*2000.0);
       CSSL1S:=SL-2.0*CCSL;
       CSSLE:=CSSL1S/CS1SN;
       CSSWTE:=(CSSLE*CCSL*ST*165.0)/(12.0*12.0*12.0*2000.0);
       CS4SN:=4.0*CS1SN;
       COSL:=CSSLE;
       COSWTE:=(COSL*COSL*ST*165.0)/(12.*12.0*12.0*2000.0);
       COSTN:=CS1SN*CS1SN;
       TNPS:=4+CS4SN+COSTN;
       SUMTNPS:=SUMTNPS+TNPS;
       WRITE(LST,STEP:3,SL:9:2,DTSB:8:2,ST:6:2,CCSL:7:2,CCSWTE:7:2,CS1SN:6:1);
```

```
      WRITE(LST,CSSL1S:10:2,CSSLE:7:2,CSSWTE:6:2,CS4SN:7:1,COSL:8:2);
      WRITELN(LST,COSWTE:6:2,COSTN:6:0,SUMTNPS:9:0);
      IF CCSL=48.00 THEN GOTO 700;
      IF CCSL=40.00 THEN GOTO 800;
700:  CCSL:=40.00;
      GOTO 900;
800:  CCSL:=48.00;
900:  SL:=((DTSB-ST)*2.0)/1.27305;
      DTSB:=DTSB-ST;
      CS1SN:=CS1SN-0.82;
End;
Begin
Write(Lst,'201     91.49    58.24 26.04   45.74    2.60 (ONLY 4 CORNER STONES)');
Writeln(Lst,'                                    4    603728');
Writeln(Lst,'   CAP STONE, BASE=50.58IN., HEIGHT=32.20IN, WEIGHT=3.93 TONS');
Writeln; Writeln; Writeln;
END;
WRITELN(LST,#12);
END.
```

TABLE NO. 2

DETAILED CALCULATIONS OF EVERY STONE IN THE GREAT PYRAMID

(SEE FIGURE NO. 7 FOR LAYOUT OF STONES)

(1) STEP NO	(2) STEP LENGTH EQUALS STEP WIDTH	(3) DISTAN. TOP OF PYRAMID TO STEP BASE	(4) STEP THICK-NESS	(5) CASING CORNER STONE LENGTH EQUALS WIDTH CCSL	(6) CASING CORNER STONE WEIGHT EACH	(7) CASING STONES 1 SIDE NUMBER OF	(8) CASING SIDE STONES LENGTH 1 SIDE	(9) CASING SIDE STONE LENGTH OF EACH	(10) CASING SIDE STONE WEIGHT OF EACH	(11) CASING STONES 4SIDES NUMBER OF	(12) CORE STONES LENGTH EQUALS WIDTH COSL	(13) CORE STONES WEIGHT EACH	(14) CORE STONES TOTAL NUMBER OF	(15) TOTAL NUMBERS OF PYRAMID STONES
SN	SL=SW INCHES	DTSB INCHES	ST INCHES	CCSW INCHES	CCSWTE TONS	CS1SN	CSSL1S INCHES	CSSLE INCHES	CSSWTE TONS	CS4SN	COSW INCHES	COSWTE TONS	COSTN	SUMTNPS
1	9063.85	5769.40	60.00	96.00	26.40	61.0	8871.85	145.44	40.00	244.0	145.44	60.59	3721	3969
2	8969.64	5709.40	59.00	84.00	19.88	61.0	8801.64	144.29	34.14	244.0	144.29	58.64	3721	7938
3	8876.95	5650.40	58.00	96.00	25.52	61.0	8684.95	142.38	37.85	244.0	142.38	56.13	3721	11907
4	8785.83	5592.40	57.00	84.00	19.20	61.0	8617.83	141.28	32.29	244.0	141.28	54.32	3721	15876
5	8696.28	5535.40	56.00	96.00	24.64	61.0	8504.28	139.41	35.78	244.0	139.41	51.97	3721	19845
6	8608.30	5479.40	55.00	84.00	18.53	61.0	8440.30	138.37	30.52	244.0	138.37	50.27	3721	23814
7	8521.90	5424.40	54.00	96.00	23.76	61.0	8329.90	136.56	33.80	244.0	136.56	48.08	3721	27783
8	8437.06	5370.40	53.00	84.00	17.85	61.0	8269.06	135.56	28.81	244.0	135.56	46.50	3721	31752
9	8353.80	5317.40	52.00	96.00	22.88	61.0	8161.80	133.80	31.89	244.0	133.80	44.45	3721	35721
10	8272.10	5265.40	51.00	84.00	17.18	61.0	8104.10	132.85	27.17	244.0	132.85	42.98	3721	39690
11	8191.98	5214.40	50.00	96.00	22.00	61.0	7999.98	131.15	30.05	244.0	131.15	41.06	3721	43659
12	8113.43	5164.40	49.00	84.00	16.51	61.0	7945.43	130.25	25.60	244.0	130.25	39.69	3721	47628
13	8036.45	5115.40	48.00	96.00	21.12	61.0	7844.45	128.60	28.29	244.0	128.60	37.90	3721	51597
14	7961.04	5067.40	47.00	84.00	15.83	61.0	7793.04	127.75	24.08	244.0	127.75	36.62	3721	55566
15	7887.20	5020.40	46.00	96.00	20.24	61.0	7695.20	126.15	26.60	244.0	126.15	34.95	3721	59535
16	7814.93	4974.40	45.00	84.00	15.16	61.0	7646.93	125.36	22.62	244.0	125.36	33.76	3721	63504
17	7744.24	4929.40	44.00	96.00	19.36	61.0	7552.24	123.81	24.97	244.0	123.81	32.20	3721	67473
18	7675.11	4885.40	43.00	84.00	14.49	61.0	7507.11	123.07	21.22	244.0	123.07	31.09	3721	71442
19	7607.56	4842.40	42.00	96.00	18.48	61.0	7415.56	121.57	23.40	244.0	121.57	29.63	3721	75411
20	7541.57	4800.40	41.00	84.00	13.81	61.0	7373.57	120.88	19.88	244.0	120.88	28.60	3721	79380
21	7477.16	4759.40	40.00	96.00	17.60	61.0	7285.16	119.43	21.90	244.0	119.43	27.24	3721	83349
22	7414.32	4719.40	26.04	72.00	6.44	61.0	7270.32	119.19	10.67	244.0	119.19	17.66	3721	87318
23	7373.41	4693.36	26.04	60.00	4.48	61.0	7253.41	118.91	8.87	244.0	118.91	17.58	3721	91287
24	7332.50	4667.32	26.04	72.00	6.44	61.0	7188.50	117.84	10.55	244.0	117.84	17.27	3721	95256
25	7291.59	4641.28	26.04	60.00	4.48	61.0	7171.59	117.57	8.77	244.0	117.57	17.18	3721	99225
26	7250.68	4615.24	26.04	72.00	6.44	61.0	7106.68	116.50	10.43	244.0	116.50	16.87	3721	103194
27	7209.77	4589.20	26.04	60.00	4.48	61.0	7089.77	116.23	8.67	244.0	116.23	16.79	3721	107163
28	7168.86	4563.16	26.04	72.00	6.44	61.0	7024.86	115.16	10.31	244.0	115.16	16.49	3721	111132
29	7127.95	4537.12	26.04	60.00	4.48	61.0	7007.95	114.88	8.57	244.0	114.88	16.41	3721	115101
30	7087.04	4511.08	26.04	72.00	6.44	61.0	6943.04	113.82	10.19	244.0	113.82	16.11	3721	119070
31	7046.13	4485.04	26.04	60.00	4.48	61.0	6926.13	113.54	8.47	244.0	113.54	16.03	3721	123039

32	7005.22	4459.00	26.04	72.00	6.44	61.0	6861.22	112.48	10.07	244.0	112.48	15.73	3721	127008
33	6964.31	4432.96	26.04	60.00	4.48	61.0	6844.31	112.20	8.37	244.0	112.20	15.65	3721	130977
34	6923.40	4406.92	26.04	72.00	6.44	61.0	6779.40	111.14	9.95	244.0	111.14	15.36	3721	134946
35	6882.49	4380.88	26.04	60.00	4.48	61.0	6762.49	110.86	8.27	244.0	110.86	15.28	3721	138915
36	6841.59	4354.84	26.04	72.00	6.44	61.0	6697.59	109.80	9.83	244.0	109.80	14.99	3721	142884
37	6800.68	4328.80	26.04	60.00	4.48	61.0	6680.68	109.52	8.17	244.0	109.52	14.91	3721	146853
38	6759.77	4302.76	26.04	72.00	6.44	61.0	6615.77	108.46	9.71	244.0	108.46	14.62	3721	150822
39	6718.86	4276.72	26.04	60.00	4.48	61.0	6598.86	108.18	8.07	244.0	108.18	14.55	3721	154791
40	6677.95	4250.68	26.04	72.00	6.44	61.0	6533.95	107.11	9.59	244.0	107.11	14.26	3721	158760
41	6637.04	4224.64	26.04	60.00	4.48	61.0	6517.04	106.84	7.97	244.0	106.84	14.19	3721	162729
42	6596.13	4198.60	26.04	72.00	6.44	61.0	6452.13	105.77	9.47	244.0	105.77	13.91	3721	166698
43	6555.22	4172.56	26.04	60.00	4.48	61.0	6435.22	105.50	7.87	244.0	105.50	13.84	3721	170667
44	6514.31	4146.52	26.04	72.00	6.44	61.0	6370.31	104.43	9.35	244.0	104.43	13.56	3721	174636
45	6473.40	4120.48	26.04	60.00	4.48	61.0	6353.40	104.15	7.77	244.0	104.15	13.49	3721	178605
46	6432.49	4094.44	26.04	72.00	6.44	61.0	6288.49	103.09	9.23	244.0	103.09	13.21	3721	182574
47	6391.58	4068.40	26.04	60.00	4.48	61.0	6271.58	102.81	7.67	244.0	102.81	13.14	3721	186543
48	6350.67	4042.36	26.04	72.00	6.44	61.0	6206.67	101.75	9.11	244.0	101.75	12.87	3721	190512
49	6309.76	4016.32	26.04	60.00	4.48	61.0	6189.76	101.47	7.57	244.0	101.47	12.80	3721	194481
50	6268.85	3990.28	26.04	72.00	6.44	61.0	6124.85	100.41	8.99	244.0	100.41	12.53	3721	198450
51	6227.94	3964.24	26.04	60.00	4.48	61.0	6107.94	100.13	7.47	244.0	100.13	12.46	3721	202419
52	6187.03	3938.20	26.04	72.00	6.44	61.0	6043.03	99.07	8.87	244.0	99.07	12.20	3721	206388
53	6146.12	3912.16	26.04	60.00	4.48	61.0	6026.12	98.79	7.37	244.0	98.79	12.13	3721	210357
54	6105.21	3886.12	26.04	72.00	6.44	61.0	5961.21	97.72	8.75	244.0	97.72	11.87	3721	214326
55	6064.30	3860.08	26.04	60.00	4.48	61.0	5944.30	97.45	7.27	244.0	97.45	11.81	3721	218295
56	6023.39	3834.04	26.04	72.00	6.44	61.0	5879.39	96.38	8.63	244.0	96.38	11.55	3721	222264
57	5982.48	3808.00	26.04	60.00	4.48	61.0	5862.48	96.11	7.17	244.0	96.11	11.48	3721	226233
58	5941.57	3781.96	26.04	72.00	6.44	61.0	5797.57	95.04	8.51	244.0	95.04	11.23	3721	230202
59	5900.66	3755.92	26.04	60.00	4.48	61.0	5780.66	94.76	7.07	244.0	94.76	11.16	3721	234171
60	5859.75	3729.88	26.04	72.00	6.44	61.0	5715.75	93.70	8.39	244.0	93.70	10.92	3721	238140
61	5818.84	3703.84	26.04	60.00	4.48	61.0	5698.84	93.42	6.97	244.0	93.42	10.85	3721	242109
62	5777.93	3677.80	26.04	72.00	6.44	61.0	5633.93	92.36	8.27	244.0	92.36	10.61	3721	246078
63	5737.03	3651.76	26.04	60.00	4.48	61.0	5617.03	92.08	6.87	244.0	92.08	10.54	3721	250047
64	5696.12	3625.72	26.04	72.00	6.44	61.0	5552.12	91.02	8.15	244.0	91.02	10.30	3721	254016
65	5655.21	3599.68	26.04	60.00	4.48	61.0	5535.21	90.74	6.77	244.0	90.74	10.24	3721	257985
66	5614.30	3573.64	26.04	72.00	6.44	61.0	5470.30	89.68	8.03	244.0	89.68	10.00	3721	261954
67	5573.39	3547.60	26.04	60.00	4.48	61.0	5453.39	89.40	6.67	244.0	89.40	9.94	3721	265923
68	5532.48	3521.56	26.04	72.00	6.44	61.0	5388.48	88.34	7.91	244.0	88.34	9.70	3721	269892
69	5491.57	3495.52	26.04	60.00	4.48	61.0	5371.57	88.06	6.57	244.0	88.06	9.64	3721	273861
70	5450.66	3469.48	26.04	72.00	6.44	61.0	5306.66	86.99	7.79	244.0	86.99	9.41	3721	277830
71	5409.75	3443.44	26.04	60.00	4.48	61.0	5289.75	86.72	6.47	244.0	86.72	9.35	3721	281799
72	5368.84	3417.40	26.04	72.00	6.44	61.0	5224.84	85.65	7.67	244.0	85.65	9.12	3721	285768
73	5327.93	3391.36	26.04	60.00	4.48	61.0	5207.93	85.38	6.37	244.0	85.38	9.06	3721	289737
74	5287.02	3365.32	26.04	72.00	6.44	61.0	5143.02	84.31	7.55	244.0	84.31	8.84	3721	293706
75	5246.11	3339.28	26.04	60.00	4.48	61.0	5126.11	84.03	6.27	244.0	84.03	8.78	3721	297675
76	5205.20	3313.24	26.04	72.00	6.44	61.0	5061.20	82.97	7.43	244.0	82.97	8.56	3721	301644

77	5164.29	26.04	3287.20	60.00	4.48	61.0	5044.29	82.69	244.0	6.17	82.69	3721	8.50	305613
78	5123.38	26.04	3261.16	72.00	6.44	61.0	4979.38	81.63	244.0	7.31	81.63	3721	8.28	309582
79	5082.47	26.04	3235.12	60.00	4.48	61.0	4962.47	81.35	244.0	6.07	81.35	3721	8.23	313551
80	5041.56	26.04	3209.08	72.00	6.44	61.0	4897.56	80.29	244.0	7.19	80.29	3721	8.01	317520
81	5000.65	26.04	3183.04	60.00	4.48	61.0	4880.65	80.01	244.0	5.97	80.01	3721	7.96	321489
82	4959.74	26.04	3157.00	72.00	6.44	61.0	4815.74	78.95	244.0	7.07	78.95	3721	7.75	325458
83	4918.83	26.04	3130.96	60.00	4.48	61.0	4798.83	78.67	244.0	5.87	78.67	3721	7.69	329427
84	4877.92	26.04	3104.92	72.00	6.44	61.0	4733.92	77.61	244.0	6.95	77.61	3721	7.49	333396
85	4837.01	26.04	3078.88	60.00	4.48	61.0	4717.01	77.33	244.0	5.77	77.33	3721	7.43	337365
86	4796.10	26.04	3052.84	72.00	6.44	61.0	4652.10	76.26	244.0	6.83	76.26	3721	7.23	341334
87	4755.19	26.04	3026.80	60.00	4.48	61.0	4635.19	75.99	244.0	5.67	75.99	3721	7.18	345303
88	4714.28	26.04	3000.76	72.00	6.44	61.0	4570.28	74.92	244.0	6.71	74.92	3721	6.98	349272
89	4673.37	26.04	2974.72	60.00	4.48	61.0	4553.37	74.65	244.0	5.57	74.65	3721	6.93	353241
90	4632.47	26.04	2948.68	72.00	6.44	61.0	4488.47	73.58	244.0	6.59	73.58	3721	6.73	357210
91	4591.56	26.04	2922.64	60.00	4.48	61.0	4471.56	73.30	244.0	5.47	73.30	3721	6.68	361179
92	4550.65	26.04	2896.60	72.00	6.44	61.0	4406.65	72.24	244.0	6.47	72.24	3721	6.49	365148
93	4509.74	26.04	2870.56	60.00	4.48	61.0	4389.74	71.96	244.0	5.37	71.96	3721	6.44	369117
94	4468.83	26.04	2844.52	72.00	6.44	61.0	4324.83	70.90	244.0	6.35	70.90	3721	6.25	373086
95	4427.92	26.04	2818.48	60.00	4.48	61.0	4307.92	70.62	244.0	5.27	70.62	3721	6.20	377055
96	4387.01	26.04	2792.44	72.00	6.44	61.0	4243.01	69.56	244.0	6.23	69.56	3721	6.02	381024
97	4346.10	25.04	2766.40	60.00	4.48	61.0	4226.10	69.28	244.0	5.17	69.28	3721	5.97	384993
98	4305.19	26.04	2740.36	72.00	6.44	61.0	4161.19	68.22	244.0	6.11	68.22	3721	5.79	388962
99	4264.28	26.04	2714.32	60.00	4.48	61.0	4144.28	67.94	244.0	5.07	67.94	3721	5.74	392931
100	4223.37	26.04	2688.28	72.00	6.44	61.0	4079.37	66.87	244.0	5.99	66.87	3721	5.56	396900
101	4182.46	26.04	2662.24	60.00	4.48	61.0	4062.46	66.60	244.0	4.97	66.60	3721	5.51	400869
102	4141.55	26.04	2636.20	72.00	6.44	61.0	3997.55	65.53	244.0	5.87	65.53	3721	5.34	404838
103	4100.64	26.04	2610.16	60.00	4.48	61.0	3980.64	65.26	244.0	4.87	65.26	3721	5.29	408807
104	4059.73	26.04	2584.12	72.00	6.44	61.0	3915.73	64.19	244.0	5.75	64.19	3721	5.12	412776
105	4018.82	26.04	2558.08	60.00	4.48	61.0	3898.82	63.92	244.0	4.77	63.92	3721	5.08	416745
106	3977.91	26.04	2532.04	72.00	6.44	61.0	3833.91	62.85	244.0	5.63	62.85	3721	4.91	420714
107	3937.00	26.04	2506.00	60.00	4.48	61.0	3817.00	62.57	244.0	4.67	62.57	3721	4.87	424683
108	3896.09	26.04	2479.96	72.00	6.44	61.0	3752.09	61.51	244.0	5.51	61.51	3721	4.70	428652
109	3855.18	26.04	2453.92	60.00	4.48	61.0	3735.18	61.23	244.0	4.57	61.23	3721	4.66	432621
110	3814.27	26.04	2427.88	72.00	6.44	61.0	3670.27	60.17	244.0	5.39	60.17	3721	4.50	436590
111	3773.36	26.04	2401.84	60.00	4.48	61.0	3653.36	59.89	244.0	4.47	59.89	3721	4.46	440559
112	3732.45	26.04	2375.80	72.00	6.44	61.0	3588.45	58.83	244.0	5.27	58.83	3721	4.30	444528
113	3691.54	26.04	2349.76	60.00	4.48	61.0	3571.54	58.55	244.0	4.37	58.55	3721	4.26	448497
114	3650.63	26.04	2323.72	72.00	6.44	61.0	3506.63	57.49	244.0	5.15	57.49	3721	4.11	452466
115	3609.72	26.04	2297.68	60.00	4.48	61.0	3489.72	57.21	244.0	4.27	57.21	3721	4.07	456435
116	3568.82	26.04	2271.64	72.00	6.44	61.0	3424.82	56.14	244.0	5.03	56.14	3721	3.92	460404
117	3527.91	26.04	2245.60	60.00	4.48	61.0	3407.91	55.87	244.0	4.17	55.87	3721	3.88	464373
118	3487.00	26.04	2219.56	72.00	6.44	61.0	3343.00	54.80	244.0	4.91	54.80	3721	3.73	468342
119	3446.09	26.04	2193.52	60.00	4.48	61.0	3326.09	54.53	244.0	4.07	54.53	3721	3.70	472311
120	3405.18	26.04	2167.48	72.00	6.44	61.0	3261.18	53.46	244.0	4.79	53.46	3721	3.55	476280
121	3364.27	26.04	2141.44	60.00	4.48	61.0	3244.27	53.18	244.0	3.97	53.18	3721	3.52	480249

122	3323.36	26.04	2115.40	72.00	6.44	61.0	3179.36	52.12	4.67	244.0	52.12	3.38	3721	484218
123	3282.45	26.04	2089.36	60.00	4.48	61.0	3162.45	51.84	3.87	244.0	51.84	3.34	3721	488187
124	3241.54	26.04	2063.32	72.00	6.44	61.0	3097.54	50.78	4.55	244.0	50.78	3.21	3721	492156
125	3200.63	26.04	2037.28	60.00	4.48	61.0	3080.63	50.50	3.77	244.0	50.50	3.17	3721	496125
126	3159.72	26.04	2011.24	72.00	6.44	61.0	3015.72	49.44	4.43	244.0	49.44	3.05	3721	500094
127	3118.81	26.04	1985.20	48.00	2.86	61.0	3022.81	49.55	2.96	244.0	49.55	3.09	3721	504063
128	3077.90	26.04	1959.16	40.00	1.99	60.2	2997.90	49.82	2.48	240.7	49.82	3.09	3622	507929
129	3036.99	26.04	1933.12	48.00	2.86	59.4	2940.99	49.54	2.96	237.4	49.54	3.05	3524	511694
130	2996.08	26.04	1907.08	40.00	1.99	58.5	2916.08	49.81	2.48	234.2	49.81	3.08	3427	515359
131	2955.17	26.04	1881.04	48.00	2.86	57.7	2859.17	49.54	2.96	230.9	49.54	3.05	3332	518926
132	2914.26	26.04	1855.00	40.00	1.99	56.9	2834.26	49.81	2.48	227.6	49.81	3.08	3238	522395
133	2873.35	26.04	1828.96	48.00	2.86	56.1	2777.35	49.52	2.96	224.3	49.52	3.05	3145	525768
134	2832.44	26.04	1802.92	40.00	1.99	55.3	2752.44	49.81	2.48	221.0	49.81	3.08	3054	529047
135	2791.53	26.04	1776.88	48.00	2.86	54.4	2695.53	49.51	2.95	217.8	49.51	3.05	2964	532233
136	2750.62	26.04	1750.84	40.00	1.99	53.6	2670.62	49.81	2.48	214.5	49.81	3.08	2875	535326
137	2709.71	26.04	1724.80	48.00	2.86	52.8	2613.71	49.50	2.95	211.2	49.50	3.05	2788	538329
138	2668.80	26.04	1698.76	40.00	1.99	52.0	2588.80	49.80	2.48	207.9	49.80	3.08	2702	541243
139	2627.89	26.04	1672.72	48.00	2.86	51.2	2531.89	49.49	2.95	204.6	49.49	3.04	2617	544069
140	2586.98	26.04	1646.68	40.00	1.99	50.3	2506.98	49.80	2.48	201.4	49.80	3.08	2534	546809
141	2546.07	26.04	1620.64	48.00	2.86	49.5	2450.07	49.48	2.95	198.1	49.48	3.04	2452	549463
142	2505.16	26.04	1594.60	40.00	1.99	48.7	2425.16	49.80	2.48	194.8	49.80	3.08	2372	552033
143	2464.26	26.04	1568.56	48.00	2.86	47.9	2368.26	49.46	2.95	191.5	49.46	3.04	2292	554521
144	2423.35	26.04	1542.52	40.00	1.99	47.1	2343.35	49.79	2.48	188.2	49.79	3.08	2215	556928
145	2382.44	26.04	1516.48	48.00	2.86	46.2	2286.44	49.45	2.95	185.0	49.45	3.04	2138	559255
146	2341.53	26.04	1490.44	40.00	1.99	45.4	2261.53	49.79	2.48	181.7	49.79	3.08	2063	561504
147	2300.62	26.04	1464.40	48.00	2.86	44.6	2204.62	49.43	2.95	178.4	49.43	3.04	1989	563676
148	2259.71	26.04	1438.36	40.00	1.99	43.8	2179.71	49.79	2.48	175.1	49.79	3.08	1917	565771
149	2218.80	26.04	1412.32	48.00	2.86	43.0	2122.80	49.41	2.95	171.8	49.41	3.04	1846	567793
150	2177.89	26.04	1386.28	40.00	1.99	42.1	2097.89	49.78	2.48	168.6	49.78	3.08	1776	569741
151	2136.98	26.04	1360.24	48.00	2.86	41.3	2040.98	49.39	2.95	165.3	49.39	3.03	1707	571618
152	2096.07	26.04	1334.20	40.00	1.99	40.5	2016.07	49.78	2.48	162.0	49.78	3.08	1640	573424
153	2055.16	26.04	1308.16	48.00	2.86	39.7	1959.16	49.37	2.95	158.7	49.37	3.03	1575	575161
154	2014.25	26.04	1282.12	40.00	1.99	38.9	1934.25	49.77	2.48	155.4	49.77	3.08	1510	576831
155	1973.34	26.04	1256.08	48.00	2.86	38.0	1877.34	49.35	2.95	152.2	49.35	3.03	1447	578434
156	1932.43	26.04	1230.04	40.00	1.99	37.2	1852.43	49.77	2.48	148.9	49.77	3.08	1385	579972
157	1891.52	26.04	1204.00	48.00	2.86	36.4	1795.52	49.33	2.94	145.6	49.33	3.03	1325	581447
158	1850.61	26.04	1177.96	40.00	1.99	35.6	1770.61	49.76	2.47	142.3	49.76	3.08	1266	582859
159	1809.70	26.04	1151.92	48.00	2.86	34.8	1713.70	49.30	2.94	139.0	49.30	3.08	1208	584210
160	1768.79	26.04	1125.88	40.00	1.99	33.9	1688.79	49.76	2.47	135.8	49.76	3.08	1152	585502
161	1727.88	26.04	1099.84	48.00	2.86	33.1	1631.88	49.27	2.94	132.5	49.27	3.02	1097	586735
162	1686.97	26.04	1073.80	40.00	1.99	32.3	1606.97	49.75	2.47	129.2	49.75	3.08	1043	587912
163	1646.06	26.04	1047.76	48.00	2.86	31.5	1550.06	49.24	2.94	125.9	49.24	3.01	991	589033
164	1605.15	26.04	1021.72	40.00	1.99	30.7	1525.15	49.74	2.47	122.6	49.74	3.08	940	590099
165	1564.24	26.04	995.68	48.00	2.86	29.8	1468.24	49.20	2.94	119.4	49.20	3.01	890	591113
166	1523.33	26.04	969.64	40.00	1.99	29.0	1443.33	49.74	2.47	116.1	49.74	3.08	842	592075

167	1482.42	943.60	26.04	48.00	2.86	28.2	1386.42	49.16	2.93	112.8	49.16	3.01	795	592988
168	1441.51	917.56	26.04	40.00	1.99	27.4	1361.51	49.73	2.47	109.5	49.73	3.07	750	593851
169	1400.60	891.52	26.04	48.00	2.86	26.6	1304.60	49.12	2.93	106.2	49.12	3.00	705	594666
170	1359.70	865.48	26.04	40.00	1.99	25.7	1279.70	49.72	2.47	103.0	49.72	3.07	663	595436
171	1318.79	839.44	26.04	48.00	2.86	24.9	1222.79	49.07	2.93	99.7	49.07	2.99	621	596161
172	1277.88	813.40	26.04	40.00	1.99	24.1	1197.88	49.70	2.47	96.4	49.70	3.07	581	596842
173	1236.97	787.36	26.04	48.00	2.86	23.3	1140.97	49.01	2.92	93.1	49.01	2.99	542	597481
174	1196.06	761.32	26.04	40.00	1.99	22.5	1116.06	49.69	2.47	89.8	49.69	3.07	504	598079
175	1155.15	735.28	26.04	48.00	2.86	21.6	1059.15	48.94	2.92	86.6	48.94	2.98	468	598638
176	1114.24	709.24	26.04	40.00	1.99	20.8	1034.24	49.68	2.47	83.3	49.68	3.07	433	599159
177	1073.33	683.20	26.04	48.00	2.86	20.0	977.33	48.87	2.92	80.0	48.87	2.97	400	599643
178	1032.42	657.16	26.04	40.00	1.99	19.2	952.42	49.66	2.47	76.7	49.66	3.07	368	600091
179	991.51	631.12	26.04	48.00	2.86	18.4	895.51	48.77	2.91	73.4	48.77	2.96	337	600506
180	950.60	605.08	26.04	40.00	1.99	17.5	870.60	49.64	2.47	70.2	49.64	3.06	308	600888
181	909.69	579.04	26.04	48.00	2.86	16.7	813.69	48.67	2.90	66.9	48.67	2.94	280	601238
182	868.78	553.00	26.04	40.00	1.99	15.9	788.78	49.61	2.47	63.6	49.61	3.06	253	601559
183	827.87	526.96	26.04	48.00	2.86	15.1	731.87	48.53	2.90	60.3	48.53	2.93	227	601850
184	786.96	500.92	26.04	40.00	1.99	14.3	706.96	49.58	2.47	57.0	49.58	3.06	203	602115
185	746.05	474.88	26.04	48.00	2.86	13.4	650.05	48.37	2.89	53.8	48.37	2.91	181	602353
186	705.14	448.84	26.04	40.00	1.99	12.6	625.14	49.54	2.46	50.5	49.54	3.05	159	602567
187	664.23	422.80	26.04	48.00	2.86	11.8	568.23	48.16	2.87	47.2	48.16	2.88	139	602757
188	623.32	396.76	26.04	40.00	1.99	11.0	543.32	49.48	2.46	43.9	49.48	3.04	121	602926
189	582.41	370.72	26.04	48.00	2.86	10.2	486.41	47.88	2.86	40.6	47.88	2.85	103	603074
190	541.50	344.68	25.04	40.00	1.99	9.3	461.50	49.41	2.46	37.4	49.41	3.04	87	603202
191	500.59	318.64	26.04	48.00	2.86	8.5	404.59	47.49	2.83	34.1	47.49	2.80	73	603313
192	459.68	292.60	26.04	40.00	1.99	7.7	379.68	49.31	2.45	30.8	49.31	3.02	59	603407
193	418.77	266.56	26.04	48.00	2.86	6.9	322.77	46.91	2.80	27.5	46.91	2.74	47	603486
194	377.86	240.52	26.04	40.00	1.99	6.1	297.86	49.15	2.44	24.2	49.15	3.00	37	603551
195	336.95	214.48	26.04	48.00	2.86	5.2	240.95	45.98	2.74	21.0	45.98	2.63	27	603603
196	296.04	188.44	26.04	40.00	1.99	4.4	216.04	48.88	2.43	17.7	48.88	2.97	20	603644
197	255.14	162.40	26.04	48.00	2.86	3.6	159.14	44.20	2.64	14.4	44.20	2.43	13	603676
198	214.23	136.36	26.04	40.00	1.99	2.8	134.23	48.28	2.40	11.1	48.28	2.90	8	603699
199	173.32	110.32	26.04	48.00	2.86	2.0	77.32	39.45	2.35	7.8	39.45	1.93	4	603714
200	132.41	84.28	26.04	40.00	1.99	1.1	52.41	45.97	2.29	4.6	45.97	2.63	1	603724
201	91.49	58.24	26.04	45.74	2.60	(ONLY 4 CORNER STONES)							4	603728

CAP STONE, BASE=50.58IN., HEIGHT=32.20IN, WEIGHT=3.93 TONS

31

III Quarrying Of The Blocks Of Stones

Stones Used In The Great Pyramid (See Figure No. 8)

Most of the pyramid is built with poor quality limestone blocks cut right on the spot and/or in the near by local quarry, just south of the pyramid, on the west side of the Nile. The better quality blocks of the pyramid's casing, a finer grain pure white limestone, were cut at the Tura quarries. These are located in the Arabian Hills, 30 miles to the south, on the eastern side of the Nile.

The small amount of granite in the chambers of the pyramid and the basalt pavement of the Mortuary Temple came from the Aswan quarries. These are located 600 miles to the south, on the eastern side of the Nile.

Hardness Of Various Materials

It is meaningful to discuss, at this point, the hardness of limestone, granite and compare these to other materials. That is, what martials were used by the ancient Egyptians to cut these three types of stones with different hardness.

Hardness as applied to solids has various interpretations. Commonly, it refers to the resistance of surface abrasion, so that two solids, the one that will scratch the other, as diamond scratches glass is the harder. One such scale is the Mohs Scale which rates substances on a scale of 1 to 10 as shown in Table No. 3. From this table it can be seen that limestone (dolomite) has a hardness of 3.5-4.0. Granite (formed of quartz, orthoclase and microcline) has a hardness of 6.0-6.5. Basalt (formed of augite and magnetite) has a hardness of 6.0-6.5.

Tools And Abrasive Used To Quarry These Stones

One method of quarrying loose blocks of granite was the use of heavy dolerite balls (2 to 22 inches in diameter). A dolerite ball was found resting on an unfinished obelisk at an Aswan granite quarry. This method is a heart stopping task.

A second method made use of harden copper tools: saws, chisels of various length and thickness, and drills. Saw marks have been hound on Khufu's red granite sarcophagus in the king's chamber, and in the basalt pavement blocks of the Mortuary Temple of the Great Pyramid.

A third method for cutting hard stone made use of hard abrasive powders. The Egyptians had quartz sand, flint and other hard substances. In one case, sand was found at the bottom of a drill hole in a piece of alabaster. So it can be concluded that such abrasive powders, with harden copper drills, chisels, and saws were used to cut all types of stones.

The Egyptians, by accident, must have developed a way to temper and make copper very hard. Beryl, Mohs hardness of 7.8, is found in granite rock and in beryl of gem quality in Africa. That is, in working with copper tools, to cut granite, Egyptians found that some material in the granite, Beryl, together with the heat developed, enabled these materials to be precipitation harden, which today is known to reach the hardness of heat-treated steels. These (Ni-Moyl) steels have a Brinell hardness of 350, same as beryllium-copper cold rolled sheets. Therefore, it can be concluded that the Egyptians used harden copper tools, quartz sand, flint and other hard powders with water to cut, shape, and polish all the stones that went into building the pyramid and its temples.

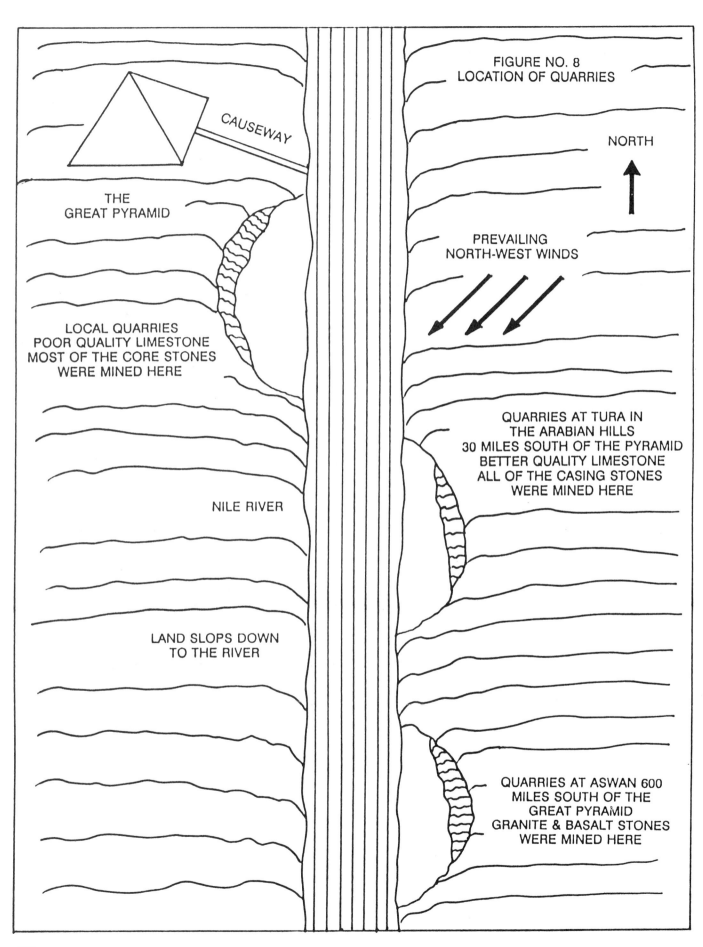

CAUSEWAY

THE
GREAT PYRAMID

LOCAL QUARRIES
POOR QUALITY LIMESTONE
MOST OF THE CORE STONES
WERE MINED HERE

NILE RIVER

LAND SLOPS DOWN
TO THE RIVER

FIGURE NO. 8
LOCATION OF QUARRIES

NORTH

PREVAILING
NORTH-WEST WINDS

QUARRIES AT TURA IN
THE ARABIAN HILLS
30 MILES SOUTH OF THE PYRAMID
BETTER QUALITY LIMESTONE
ALL OF THE CASING STONES
WERE MINED HERE

QUARRIES AT ASWAN 600
MILES SOUTH OF THE
GREAT PYRAMID
GRANITE & BASALT STONES
WERE MINED HERE

TABLE NO. 3
MOHS SCALE OF HARDNESS
COMPARISON OF HARDNESS VALUES OF VARIOUS MATERIALS

SUBSTANCE	MOHS VALUE
AGATE	6.0-7.0
ALABASTER	1.7
ALUMINA	9.0
AUGITE	6.0
BASALT (DOLERITE)	6.0-6.5
BERYL	7.8
BERYLLIUM CARBIDE	9.0
BRASS	3.0-4.0
CALCITE	3.0
CARBORUNDUM	9.0-10.0
CHROMIUM	9.0
COPPER	2.5-3.0
CORUNDUM	9.0
DIAMOND	10.0
DOLOMITE (LIMESTONE)	3.5-4.0
EMERY	7.0-9.0
FELDSPAR (ORTHOCLASE)	6.0
FLINT	7.0
GARNET	6.5-7.0
GLASS	4.5-6.5
GRANITE	6.0-6.5
GOLD	2.5-3.0
SILVER	2.5-4.0
IRON	4.0-5.0
MAGNETITE	6.0
MARBLE	3.0-4.0
PUMICE	6.0
PYRITE	6.3
QUARTZ	7.0
SILICON	7.0
STEEL	5.0-8.5
TOPAZ	8.0
TOURMALINE	7.3

DESITY OF LIMESTONE AND GRANITE IS ABOUT 165 POUNDS PER CUBIC FOOT

Two Methods Were Used To Quarry Limestone Blocks

The First Method

Is called Surface or Open-Cast (See Figure No. 9). It is the simplest method and was used to cut most of the pyramid's stones. The selection of the 100 foot high plateau was a very wise choice for the pyramid's site. That is, it was possible to quarry most of the limestone blocks needed, right on the spot. Also, a sizable core of bedrock could be left in the center, lower section of the pyramid to give it stability. Cutting the blocks of stone right on the pyramid's site and/or in the local quarries near by, reduced considerably the torturous effort to drag them from distance quarries.

An example that this surface quarrying was done is the Sphinx which was cut out of the same plateau, just south of the pyramid (See Figure No. 10).

An other example that this surface quarrying was done is the waste chips of the stone cutters thrown over the cliffs, on the north and south sides of the pyramid. These chips formed banks stretching out a few hundred yards, occupying a space more than half the volume of the pyramid. The qualities of refuse, thrown away on different days, varied from large chips to just sweepings. In pits dug into parts of these heaps revealed layers of desert flint and sand. Among the rubbish were found pieces of worker's water jugs, food vessels, chips of wood, charcoal, and a piece of ancient string.

The Second Method

Is called Mining. It was used to obtain the better quality, white-fine-grain, limestone blocks used for the pyramid's casing which were cut in the Tura quarries. When the Egyptians mined limestone, they first cut a hollow in the side of the cliff (See Figure No. 11). This hollow would be large enough for a few men to work in. The floor of the hollow would be the top of the first stone to be cut free from the bedrock. The stone cutters then crawled into this hollow and cut all sides of the first block of stone with long harden-copper chisels. They used wooden mallets to hammer down the chisels. The block would then be free on all sides except the bottom.

Holes would then be cut at the bottom of the block and wedges were driven in to make the blocks split away from the bedrock. Sometimes the wedges were made of wood which swelled up when soaked with water, causing the rock to split along the bottom holes. Great care had to be taken, at this stage, or the rock might split in the wrong direction spoiling all their previous hard work.

The block was moved out of the way and work started on the next block of stone. This time the stone cutters had plenty of headroom. When they reached floor level, they would have to start all over again, at the top, and at the same time going further into the cliff. This type of mining left huge holes in the cliffs which still can be see today.

Quarrying Of Hard Stones Like Granite And Basalt

First Method

Quarrying of hard rocks like granite and basalt was far more difficult than mining of limestone. Use was made of any loose blocks lying on the quarry surfaces. Stone cutters flattened the surfaces of these blocks by bruising them with balls of dolerite held in their hands. Balls were from 5 to 22 inches in diameter and had an average weight of 12 pounds. This difficult method took a very long time.

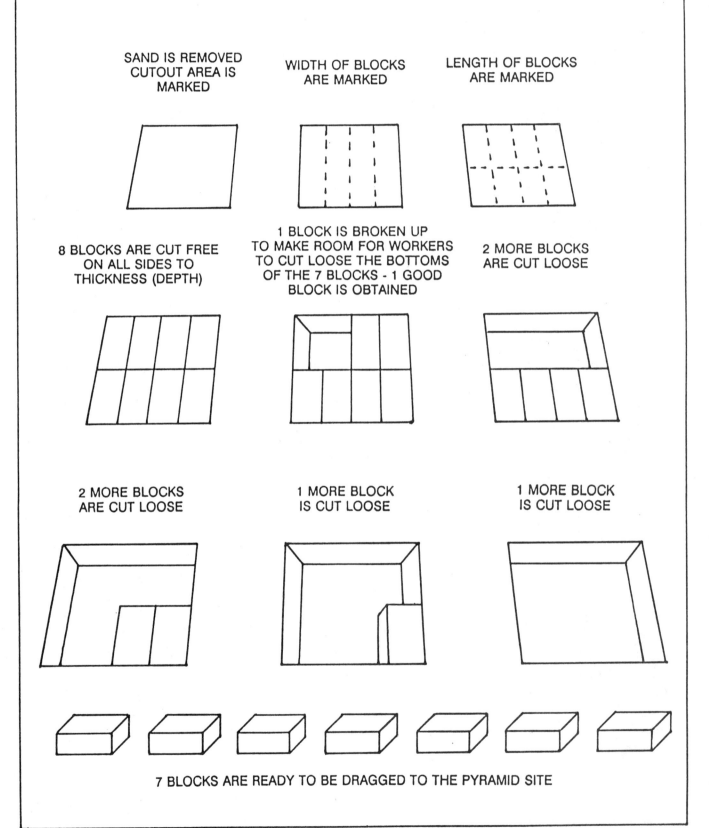

FIGURE NO. 9
SURFACE (OPEN-CAST) METHOD OF QUARRYING LIMESTONE

SAND IS REMOVED
CUTOUT AREA IS
MARKED

WIDTH OF BLOCKS
ARE MARKED

LENGTH OF BLOCKS
ARE MARKED

8 BLOCKS ARE CUT FREE
ON ALL SIDES TO
THICKNESS (DEPTH)

1 BLOCK IS BROKEN UP
TO MAKE ROOM FOR WORKERS
TO CUT LOOSE THE BOTTOMS
OF THE 7 BLOCKS - 1 GOOD
BLOCK IS OBTAINED

2 MORE BLOCKS
ARE CUT LOOSE

2 MORE BLOCKS
ARE CUT LOOSE

1 MORE BLOCK
IS CUT LOOSE

1 MORE BLOCK
IS CUT LOOSE

7 BLOCKS ARE READY TO BE DRAGGED TO THE PYRAMID SITE

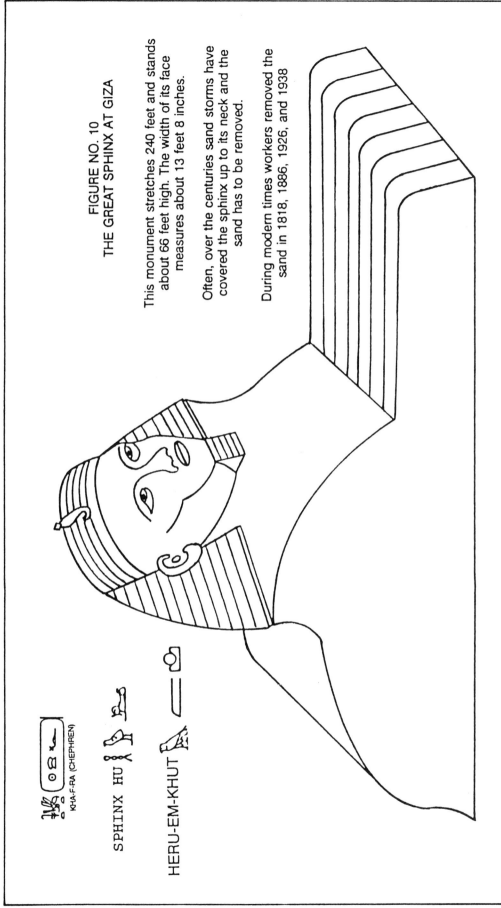

FIGURE NO. 10
THE GREAT SPHINX AT GIZA

This monument stretches 240 feet and stands about 66 feet high. The width of its face measures about 13 feet 8 inches.

Often, over the centuries sand storms have covered the sphinx up to its neck and the sand has to be removed.

During modern times workers removed the sand in 1818, 1886, 1926, and 1938

KHA-F-RA (CHEPHREN)

SPHINX HU

HERU-EM-KHUT

The age of the Sphinx is unknown and few facts connected with its history have come down to the present. When the stele was found, which recorded the repairs made to the temple of the Sphinx by Thothmes IV, about 1466 B.C., it also, recorded that one day the god Harmachis appeared to Thothmes IV, and promised to bestow upon him the crown of Egypt if he would dig his image out of the sand. At the end of the inscription on this stele the name of Kha-f-Ra (Chephren) 3050 B.C., builder of the second largest pyramid at Giza, appears. Hence, some have thought that this king was the maker of the Sphinx as his statue was subsequently found in the temple close by. This theory was generally adopted.

Egyptian called the Sphinx, "hu" and it represented the god Harmachis, "Heru-em-khut", "horus in the horizon", or the rising sun, the conqueror of darkness, the god of the morning.

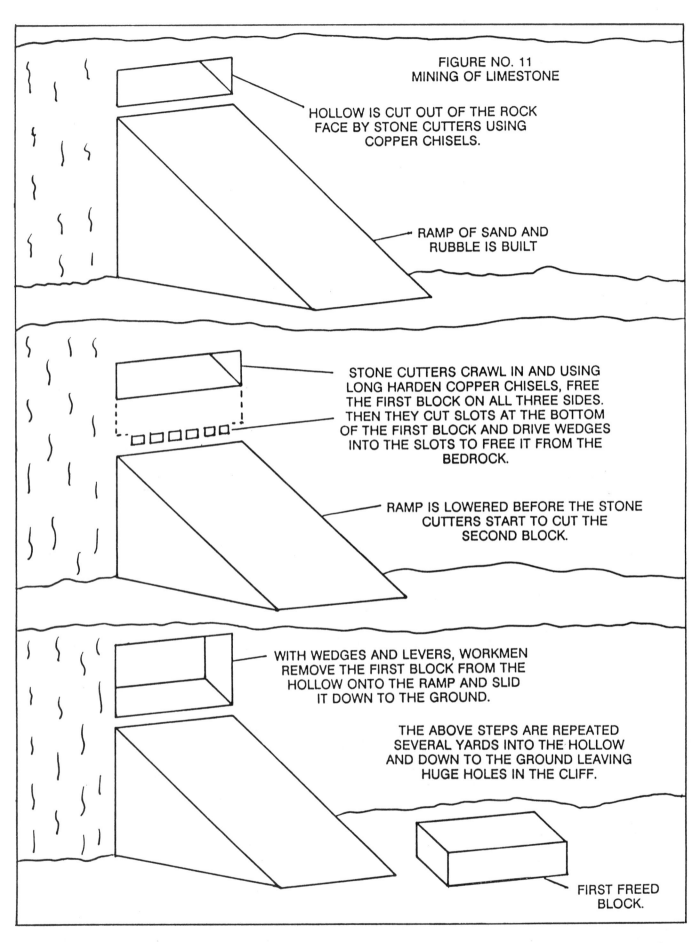

FIGURE NO. 11
MINING OF LIMESTONE

HOLLOW IS CUT OUT OF THE ROCK
FACE BY STONE CUTTERS USING
COPPER CHISELS.

RAMP OF SAND AND
RUBBLE IS BUILT

STONE CUTTERS CRAWL IN AND USING
LONG HARDEN COPPER CHISELS, FREE
THE FIRST BLOCK ON ALL THREE SIDES.
THEN THEY CUT SLOTS AT THE BOTTOM
OF THE FIRST BLOCK AND DRIVE WEDGES
INTO THE SLOTS TO FREE IT FROM THE
BEDROCK.

RAMP IS LOWERED BEFORE THE STONE
CUTTERS START TO CUT THE
SECOND BLOCK.

WITH WEDGES AND LEVERS, WORKMEN
REMOVE THE FIRST BLOCK FROM THE
HOLLOW ONTO THE RAMP AND SLID
IT DOWN TO THE GROUND.

THE ABOVE STEPS ARE REPEATED
SEVERAL YARDS INTO THE HOLLOW
AND DOWN TO THE GROUND LEAVING
HUGE HOLES IN THE CLIFF.

FIRST FREED
BLOCK.

Second And Third Methods

With one exception, these are the same as the surface and mining methods used for cutting limestone blocks. That is, first the face of the bedrock has to be cleared of all loose layers since granite does separate in layers with age. This is accomplished by fire to crack the poor granite layers. Then dolerite balls with harden copper chisels are used to clear the loose layers down to the solid granite.

An example of cutting granite blocks is the following. A very large block of unfinished granite was found at the Aswan quarry with dolerite balls resting on it. This block was obtained as follows. First the block was cut free on all sides except the bottom side. Next, several large slots were cut on the bottom side and beams of wood were slid into these slots. Then other smaller slots were cut and wooden or hardened copper wedges were driven into these slots, and water or heat was used to swell the wedges, thus bursting the block free from its bed. After all freed sides were finished the block was turned over on to wooden beams and flattening of the slots was continued. The size of this rough cut granite block was immense. Its length is 137 feet with a base of 14 feet square. Had it been extracted, its weight would have been about (137 x 14 x 14 x 165)/2000 = 2,215 tons.

Names Of Stone Cutting Gangs

There were many stone cutting gangs working in the quarries. As these gangs finished cutting a block of stone, they painted, in red, their names on these blocks. Some of these marking are still visible today. Shown below are four blocks with gang names in hieroglyphics on them. Their English translation are to the right of each block.

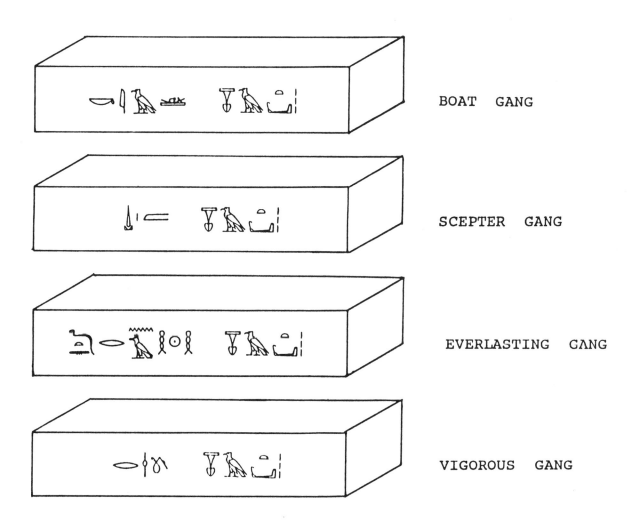

BOAT   GANG

SCEPTER   GANG

EVERLASTING   GANG

VIGOROUS   GANG

IV Transporting Blocks Of Stone

Moving Blocks Of Stone Over The Ground

The largest blocks in the pyramid are the core stones behind the casing stones in Step No. 1. Each weighs (5ft.x12.12ft.x12.12ft.x165)/2000 = 60.59 tons. Depending on ground conditions, a combination of three methods were used to move these stones: (1) stone on a sled was dragged over the ground; (2) stone on logs was rolled over the ground; and (3) stone was moved by a row of men, on each side of the block, using levers and wedges.

An example of the sled method is the wall relief at Der Al-Bahari showing one of queen Hatshepsut's obelisk being dragged. An other example of the same method is a wall painting at Al-Barshah (Figure No. 12 below), wherein 164 men are dragging an alabaster colossus of the twelfth dynasty provincial governor, Dhtihotep, from the quarries of Hatnub to near by Al-Barshah in Middle Egypt. These men were trained to pull in rhythm to a beat from the leader shown standing on the leg of the statue, and to songs they sang. The statue measured about 22 feet high and weighs over 25 tons. The scene also shows men carrying levers, pots and another pouring liquid from one of these pots, in front of the sled, to prevent the wooden runners from catching fire as a result of the friction. Out front of each line is a man holding the end of each rope.

FIGURE NO. 12
DRAGGING A 25 TON COLOSSAL

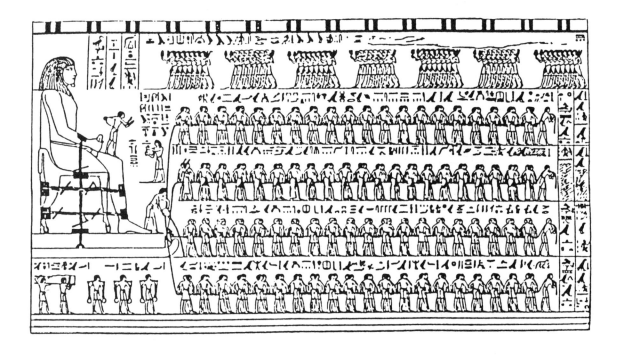

Blocks Of Granite From Quarry To Loading Them On A Boat

Large blocks were raised by means of levers and ropes to a height sufficient to enable them to clear the edge of the quarry onto a ramp of polished stone, the end of which was slightly higher than the deck of the boat anchored at the river's edge (See Figure No. 13). This ramp was steep enough so that the block, with lubrication, would slide freely by itself. Then three crews of men with ropes, wedges, and levers would slowly let the block slide down the ramp onto the ship.

The level of the boat's deck was controlled to be slightly lower than the end of the ramp by taking on and or getting rid of water ballast, just like ocean going ships do today.

Design Of Boats By The Ancient Egyptians

We know from the Palermo Stone that in the reign of Seneferu (father of Cheops), the Egyptians were able to build sea-going boats of great length, beam, and carrying capacity. At a later period they found no difficulty in building boats that were able to transport blocks of stone weighing 900 tons. The granite colossal statue of Rameses II at the Ramesseum weighed nearly 900 tons. An inscription of Anna, who flourished in the first half of the XVIIIth. Dynasty, throws much light on the style of boat that was used in the transport of obelisks. He says:

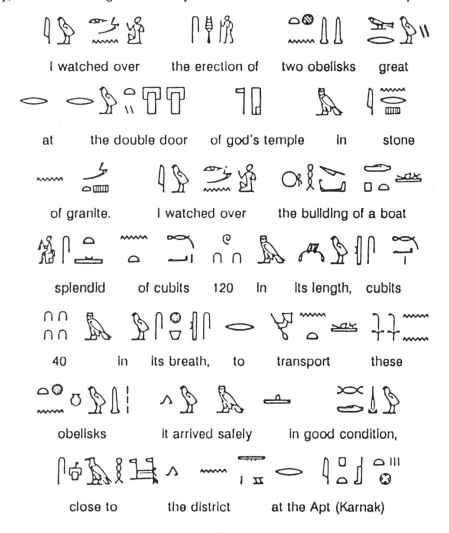

I watched over	the erection of	two obelisks	great
at	the double door	of god's temple	in	stone
of granite.	I watched over	the building of a boat
splendid	of cubits	120	in	its length,	cubits
40	in	its breath,	to	transport	these
obelisks	it arrived safely	in good condition,
close to	the district	at the Apt (Karnak)

The boat built by Anna, was 120 cubits long and 40 cubits broad. If we reckon the cubit at 20 inches, we obtain 200 feet and 67 feet as the dimensions of the boat. The two obelisks in the inscription weighed 600 tons.

41

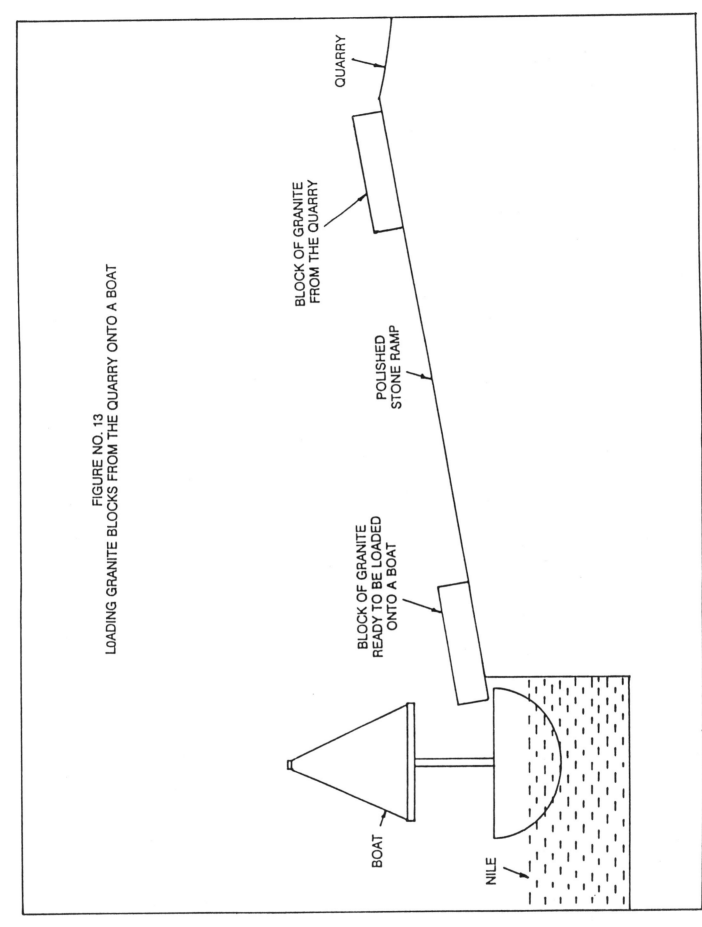

FIGURE NO. 13
LOADING GRANITE BLOCKS FROM THE QUARRY ONTO A BOAT

QUARRY

BLOCK OF GRANITE
FROM THE QUARRY

POLISHED
STONE RAMP

BLOCK OF GRANITE
READY TO BE LOADED
ONTO A BOAT

BOAT

NILE

Calculation Of The Carrying Capacity Of Anna's Boat

If it is assumed that the bottom of the boat has the ideal shape of a semi-circle, and that only the main buoyancy force, FB, is taken into consideration, the maximum carrying capacity of Anna's boat is calculated as follows:

FB = weight of displaced water acting at the centroid of the boat.
y = specific weight of water which is 62.43 pounds per cubic foot.
v = the volume of water displaced in cubic feet.
FB = yv = (62.43x3.14x33.5x33.5x200)/(2000x2) = 10,999.7 tons.

This value of 10,999.7 tons is the ideal maximum because the boat bottom was assumed to be in the shape of a semi-circle. However, even if it had some other shape that would reduce the carrying capacity, it can be concluded that Ann's boat was well designed with more than enough capacity to carry the two obelisks which together weighed 600 tons.

Once the boat was loaded with blocks of stone, it was now ready for the long 600 mile trip down the Nile, against the prevailing north-west winds. Even though the swollen river current would help, at times these winds were very strong requiring the use of many rowers. A leader would beat out the rowing time to a monotonous rhythm. They would row in time to this rhythm and probably chant out well known songs at the same time. This help them to put up with the hard, strenuous work of rowing under the hot Egyptian sun. A foreman would be watching the rowers to see that they did not slack in their work. The man at the helm had a job which required both skill and knowledge of the river. If he made a mistake the boat could easily run aground on one of the many sand bars in the Nile.

When the boat arrived at the pyramid's site, the stones would be unloaded on to the short ramp. Then they were dragged up the ramp, across the Valley Temple's floor, up the Causeway, and across the Mortuary Temple's floor to the pyramid (See Figure No. 14). The boat would not be travelling empty, back to the quarry. Fresh supplies of equipment and food for the workers at the quarry would be on board. On a regular basis there would be a gang of workers to relieve the quarry gangs who had finished their tour of duty. At times fresh instructions to the chief overseer at the quarry would be sent in the form of a papyrus roll. Once a month a government inspector would travel on the boat to see for himself how the quarrying was progressing. When the boat reached the quarry, it was unloaded of its cargo of men and supplies. Then preparations got under way to load an other cargo of stones for the pyramid.

Short Ramp, Valley Temple, Causeway, Mortuary Temple

These structures will be briefly mentioned here because they play an important part in the conveyance of all types of stone blocks that arrive at the pyramid's site (See Figure No.14). Herodotus stated that the causeway was 3,051 ft. long, 60 ft. wide and 48 ft. high. Since the SR, VT, and MT no longer exist they will be assumed to have had the dimensions shown in the calculations below. Also, it will be assumed that they are built entirely with limestone blocks, 8 ft. by 8 ft. by 2.5 ft. Then the quantities of blocks needed are:

SR = (50ft.x48ft.x10ft.)/(8ft.x8ft.x2.5ft.) = 150.
VT = (100ft.x100ft.x20ft.)/(8ft.x8ft.x2.5ft.) = 1,250.
CW = (3,051ft.x60ft.x48ft.)/(8ft.x8ft.x2.5ft.) = 54,918.
MT = (100ft.x100ft.x20ft.)/(8ft.x8ft.x2.5ft.) = 1,250.
Total blocks needed = 57,568.

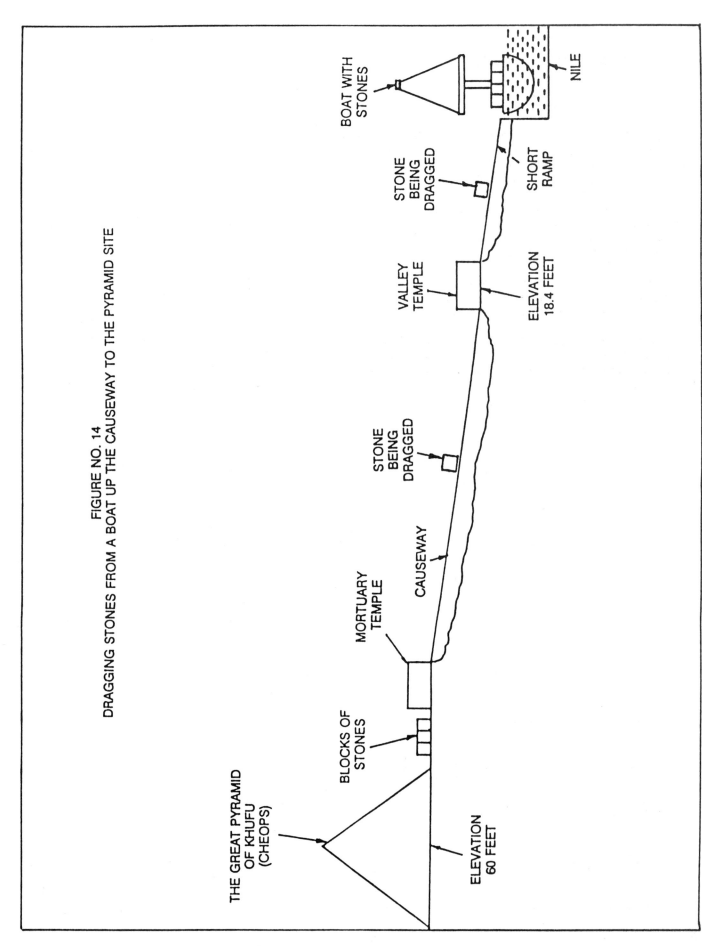

FIGURE NO. 14

DRAGGING STONES FROM A BOAT UP THE CAUSEWAY TO THE PYRAMID SITE

V SHAPING AND POLISHING THE BLOCKS OF STONE

Once the stones were brought to the pyramid site, they were cut and shaped so that all joints fit tightly and over lap, just like a well built brick building.

When all blocks had been placed, then the 51·51' face angles were cut, on the outer casing blocks, using harden copper saws and chisels. Next, the rough slant faces were polished by rubbing them with small hand held flat blocks of granite using abrasive. This finishing was done top to bottom, step by step, using the pyramid's steps to stand on and do the work. No scaffolding was needed, (See Figures No's 15 and 16).

It is estimated that two years was spent in finishing the pyramid's faces. What a wonderful period this was for these Egyptian workers. Finally, here they are, after 18 years of heart stopping labor, standing hundreds of feet above the hot desert, under clear blue skies, seeing this magnificent structure reflect the rays of the bright sun. What a rare, spectacular sight this must have been.

During this period there was a large number of workers, with baskets, just below the stone cutters, moving up and down the pyramid's steps carrying away pieces of stone, chips, and fine grains of limestone and abrasive, depositing them over the cliffs of the bluff.

This period of two years seems reasonable, because, as the work progressed downward, the length of each Step-Level increased, allowing more room for additional workers. That is, by the time the first Step-Level was reached, at the platform, its length became a maximum of 755 feet. If ten feet is allowed for each worker, then 75 workers can be cutting, chipping and finishing the blocks on each face. This means that (4x75) = 300 men were shaping the blocks at the same time, singing their songs of a job well done.

FIGURE NO. 15
SIDE VIEW SHOWING THE 51·51' FACE ANGLE OF THE PYRAMID
(DASHED LINE) MARKED FOR CUTTING AND FINISHING OF THE END CASING
BLOCKS OF THE FIRST FOUR STEP-LEVELS

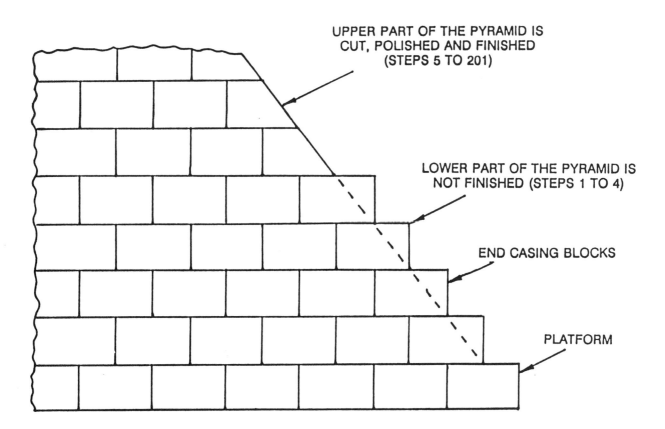

UPPER PART OF THE PYRAMID IS
CUT, POLISHED AND FINISHED
(STEPS 5 TO 201)

LOWER PART OF THE PYRAMID IS
NOT FINISHED (STEPS 1 TO 4)

END CASING BLOCKS

PLATFORM

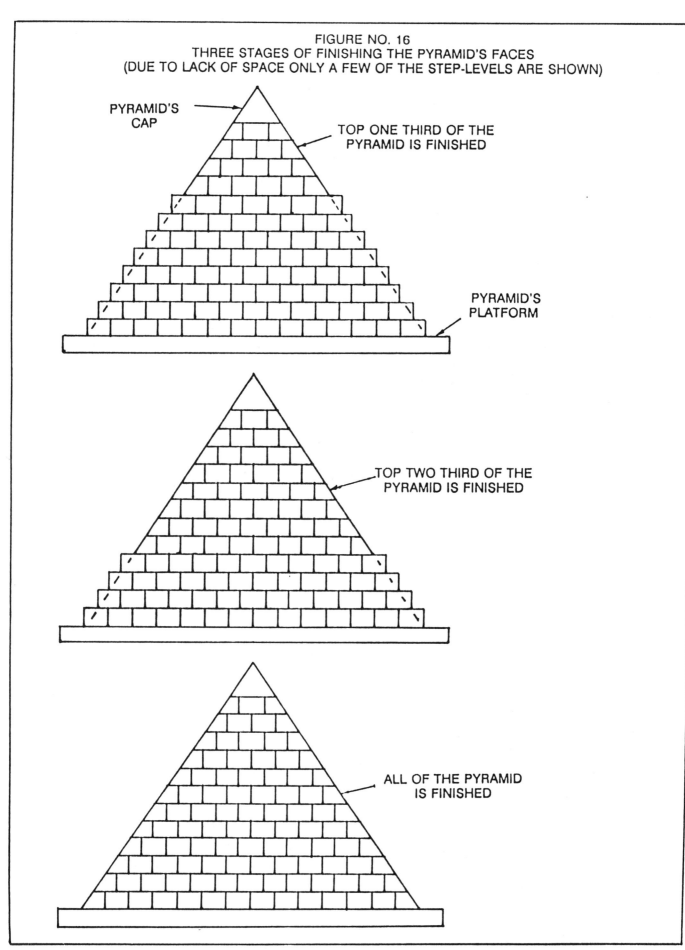

FIGURE NO. 16
THREE STAGES OF FINISHING THE PYRAMID'S FACES
(DUE TO LACK OF SPACE ONLY A FEW OF THE STEP-LEVELS ARE SHOWN)

PYRAMID'S CAP

TOP ONE THIRD OF THE PYRAMID IS FINISHED

PYRAMID'S PLATFORM

TOP TWO THIRD OF THE PYRAMID IS FINISHED

ALL OF THE PYRAMID IS FINISHED

Check Out Receipt

RCLS - Palm Desert Library
760-346-6552
www.rivlib.net

Wednesday, May 15, 2019 12:07:56 PM

Item: 0000127230407
Title: Ancient Egypt
Due: 05/29/2019

Item: 0000118902543
Title: Back in time, 3104 B.C. to the Great
Pyramid : Egyptians broke their backs to bu
ild it : how the Great Pyramid was really bui
lt
Due: 05/29/2019

Total items: 2

You just saved $18.50 by using your library
card!

Thank you!

288

VI Building The Pyramid - Three Methods (a), (b), and (c)

Method (a) - Pyramid Slides, Levers, Wedges, Rollers And Ropes

All of the work has been completed for the site, planning the building and the cutting of the blocks of stone are on schedule. The builders are now ready to start constructing the pyramid. First the pyramid's platform is set in place. Then the blocks of stones are piled upon it in the shape of the pyramid. Three methods will be studied. Due to the relatively small size of the pages of this book, it is not possible to draw dimensions to scale. therefore, all drawings in this book are used only to show approximate relationships.

Forces Involved In Moving Heavy Blocks Of Stone

Before proceeding to build the pyramid, it is important that the forces involved in handling large heavy blocks of stone be discussed. It is not known if the ancients calculated these forces. However, they knew how to use them to their advantage. It is this practical knowledge of forces that was the secret of how they moved blocks weighing in the hundreds of tons, with simple tools and much labor. The readers will gain a greater insight on how these ancients build their huge projects of stones.

Figure No. 17 diagrams the forces acting on a 20.62 ton platform block of stone, lying on a horizontal surface and on an incline plane of 30°. AW represents the force of gravity pulling the block towards the center of the earth with a pull equal to the weight of the stone. Its components are AB parallel to the plane, and BW perpendicular to the plane. AB denotes the force tending to pull the block down the plane. Then the length of AB tells the magnitude of the smallest braking force that will keep the block from moving downward. If angle Θ is the angle of inclination, AW is the weight of the 20.62 ton block of stone, then the components, AB, BW are calculated to the nearest hundredth of a ton, for angles 0° to 90°, in increments of 10°. The results are tabulated in Table No. 4.

FIGURE NO. 17
FORCES ACTING ON A 20.62 TON BLOCK OF STONE

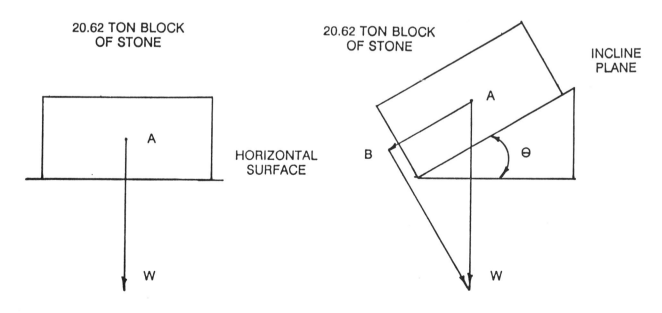

20.62 TON BLOCK
OF STONE

HORIZONTAL
SURFACE

A

W

20.62 TON BLOCK
OF STONE

INCLINE
PLANE

A

B

Θ

W

Typical Calculations For Table No. 4

AB/AW = sine Θ = sine 30°, AB = 20.62 tons x sine 30° = 10.31 tons.

BW/AW = cosine Θ = cosine 30°, BW = 20.62 tons x cosine 30° = 17.86 tons.

Note: Forces AW and BW act through the centroid of the mass of the block of stone. That is, if it were possible to throw this block, it would rotate about its centroid point as though all the mass of the block were concentrated at this point.

TABLE NO. 4
FORCES ACTING ON A 20.62 TON BLOCK OF STONE

ANGLE Θ DEGREES	FORCE AW TONS	FORCE AB TONS	FORCE BW TONS
0	20.62	0.00	0.00
10	20.62	3.58	20.31
20	20.62	7.05	19.38
30	20.62	10.31	17.86
40	20.62	13.25	15.80
50	20.62	15.80	13.25
60	20.62	17.86	10.31
70	20.62	19.38	7.05
80	20.62	20.31	3.58
90	20.62	20.62	0.00

Balanced And Unbalanced Forces

Figure No. 18 shows a block, weighing 20.62 tons, with its center-line-of-mass (M) resting on fulcrum, F, perfectly balanced, (Position No. 1). If end A is lightly pushed, in the arrow's direction, it will easily move downward. At the same time edge B will move upward. It takes very little force to do this, when the block is so balanced, (Position No. 2).

FIGURE NO. 18
BALANCED AND UNBALANCED FORCES

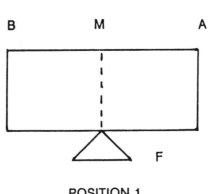

POSITION 1

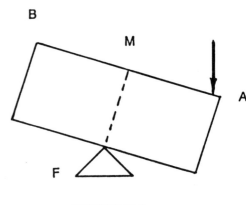

POSITION 2

Figure No. 19 uses this principle of balanced and unbalanced forces to lift a 20.62 ton platform block of stone onto another one as follows:

Position 1: Wedges, levers, and small pivots blocks of stone are used to slid block D so that its center-line-of-mass (M) rests on the edge, E, of block G. Using the same tools, block D can now be easily rotated in a counter clock direction, see Positions 2 and 3. This rotation is continued until block D softly comes to rest on top of block G, see Position 4. It is this principle of balanced and unbalanced forces that was used by the ancient Egyptians to lift one heavy block onto another one.

FIGURE NO. 19
LIFTING ONE 20.62 TON BLOCK OF STONE ONTO ANOTHER ONE
(USING BALANCED AND UNBALANCED FORCES)

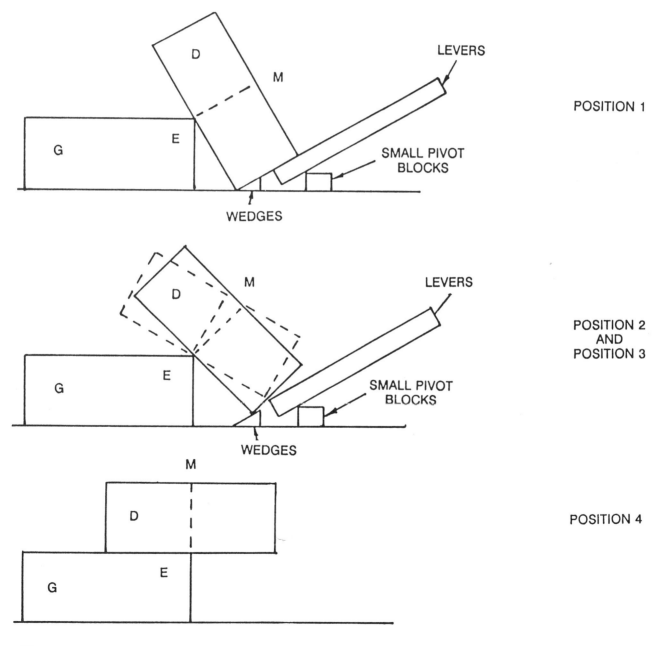

POSITION 1

POSITION 2
AND
POSITION 3

POSITION 4

Friction

It is important that Friction be discussed briefly because it plays a major role in the magnitude of forces needed to move large, heavy, blocks of stone. Friction is the resistance to sliding, a property of the interface between two solids in contact. In stationary systems, friction manifests itself as a force equal and opposite to the shear force applied to the interface. Thus, in Figure No. 20, if a small force S is applied, a friction force P will be generated, equal and opposite to S, so that the surfaces remain at rest. P can take on any magnitude up to a limiting value F, and can therefore prevent sliding whenever S is less than F. If the shear force S exceeds F, slipping occurs. During sliding, the friction force remains approximately equal to F (though often it is smaller by about 20%) and always acts in a direction opposing the relative motion.

FIGURE NO. 20
COEFFICIENT OF FRICTION

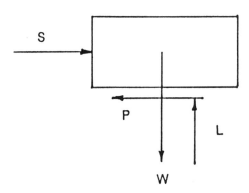

The friction force is proportional to the normal force L, which is equal to the weight of the block. The constant of proportionality is defined as the friction coefficient f, this is expressed by the equation $F = fL = fW$.

The modern theory of friction attributes friction to adhesion between surface atoms which accounts for more than 85% of the total force. Besides the adhesion mechanism there are a few minor mechanisms that act so as to increase the friction: (1) a plowing mechanism, (2) the roughness effect, (3) elastic compression, and (4) electrostatic attraction between the surfaces.

Almost all the friction energy appears as heat at the interface between the sliding surfaces. This frictional heat was used by humans in prehistoric times to light fires. This survives today in the striking of matches, with chemical combustion initiated by the temperature rise produced by striking. However, frictional heat usually is a nuisance, and sliding surfaces must often be cooled to prevent heat damage.

Friction Angle Θ_f

Closely related to the friction coefficient is the concept of friction angle. The friction angle Θ_f is the largest angle relative to the horizontal at which a surface may be tilted, so that an object on the surface does not slide down. Leonard Euler was the first to show that tangent Θ_f is equal to the friction coefficient.

Friction Coefficients

It should be emphasized that the friction coefficient values shown in Table No. 5 are typical ones, and that in any specific case, friction values differing by as much as 30% are quite likely to be found. Indeed, it is not yet possible for an expert in the field, to be able to estimate the friction coefficient in any given case to within 10%. Actually, the friction coefficient is primarily a property of the contacting material and lubricants at the interface.

TABLE NO. 5
FRICTION COEFFICIENT VALUES

TYPICAL SYSTEM	VALUES
CAR ON DRY ROAD	0.8
CAR ON WET ROAD	0.5
TRAIN ON DRY RAILS	0.3
TRAIN ON WET RAILS	0.2
CAR ON ICY ROAD	0.1
METAL ON METAL (CAREFULLY CLEANED)	0.3 - 1.0
METAL ON METAL (NOT CLEANED)	0.15 - 0.3
METAL ON METAL (WELL LUBRICATED)	0.12 - 0.5
NONMETAL ON NONMETAL (NOT LUBRICATED)	0.3 - 0.8
NONMETAL ON NONMETAL (WELL LUBRICATED)	0.1 - 0.15
BALL ROLLING ON A FLAT SURFACE	0.001
BALL BEARINGS	0.002 - 0.005
STONE ON FLAT STONE SURFACE	0.5
STONE ON LOGS ON FLAT STONE SURFACE	0.2 - 0.3
STONE ON 51·51' INCLINE STONE SURFACE	1.0
STONE ON 51·51' INCLINE STONE SURFACE (LUBRICATED)	0.3 - 0.5
STONE ON 51·51' INCLINE STONE SURFACE ON LOGS	0.2 - 0.3

THE NORTH WIND WAS CALLED QEBUI

NORTH WIND

NORTH WIND

Building The Great Pyramid With 590,712 Blocks Of Stone

The information in the two sections on this page came from Table No. 2 which contains the computer's detailed calculations for all of the blocks of stone needed to build the pyramid. The passageways and chambers were ignored because their volume is very small compared to the huge volume of the pyramid. As stated by Herodotus, the time of twenty years and pools of 100,000 workers rotated every three months were used.

The sizes of the blocks, in Table No.2, are based on the chance discovery in 1837 by Howard Vyse. He found two of the original side casing blocks at the base of the pyramid, 5 ft. by 8 ft. by 12 ft., with an angle of 51°51' cut on one of the 12 ft. sides. Each of these stones weighed $(5 \times 8 \times 12 \times 165)/2000 = 39.9$ tons before the face angle was cut. These original dimensions were used for the side casing stones of Step No. 1, in Table No. 2. The sizes of all the other blocks were scaled from these two original blocks for the remaining Steps No.'s 2 to 201.

Number Of Various Blocks Of Stone Used To Build The Great Pyramid

The number of platform blocks, 2.5 ft. by 10 ft. square, equals $((759.3 \times 759.3) - (412.7 \times 412.7))/(10 \times 10) = 4,062$.

The number of corner casing stones where the pyramid faces meet equals $(201 \times 4) = 804$.

The number of side casing stones equals $((244 \times 127) + 8,953) = 39,941$.

Due to the bedrock core, in the center of Steps No.'s 1 to 10, the total number of blocks needed is reduced by 13,016. Therefore, the total number of blocks for the pyramid equals $(603,728 - 13,016) = 590,712$.

The number of all blocks behind the casing stones equals $(590,712 - 804 - 39,941) = 549,967$.

The average number of blocks that have to be placed each day equals $(590,712)/(20 \times 364.25) = 81$. If 10 crews of 300 men work on each of the four sides of the pyramid, then the totals of 40 crews and 12,000 men will be needed. Each of the crews will be responsible to place $81/40 = 2$ blocks per day.

The work load passes through three phases of decreasing difficulty which are determined by the weights of the heaviest blocks: (1) Steps No.'s 1 to 21, (60.59 to 27.24 tons; (2) Steps No.'s 22 to 126, (17.66 to 6.44 tons); and (3) Steps No.'s 127 to 201, (3.05 to 2.63 tons).

As the weights of the blocks decrease, Step to Step, the sizes of drag crews will decrease. However, when this happens the number of blocks needed to be dragged each day can be reduced because one large block can be dragged and cut into several smaller blocks that are needed.

As the pyramid rises there is less space for the crews to work in and fewer blocks to be placed. In other words, the number of workers that will be needed depends on three factors of: weight of blocks, number of blocks to be placed, and the working space available.

The Great Pyramid's Platform

The first Step of the pyramid rests on a platform of finely finished limestone blocks. These blocks are approximately 2.5 ft. by 10 ft. by 10 ft. They project beyond the outer edges of the first Step's casing stones an average of 2 feet on all sides.

This platform is so flat that the official survey of the Egyptian government found that it was less than 1/2 of an inch from being level. The removal of several platform stones showed that the bedrock had been cut and leveled to receive each individual stone, sometimes as deep as 1 to 2 inches. On the north side the platform stones have been laid at an irregular angle, each socket being carefully cut to receive the next stone. One explanation for this irregularity of stone placement is that these northern platform stones will have a greater resistance to sliding from the downward and horizontal pressure, caused by the super imposed loads and the prevailing north-west winds that exert huge pressures on the pyramid's faces.

Placement Of The Platform Blocks

During the surface mining of the bluff for the pyramid's site, its core, and in local quarry, most of the blocks of stone needed for the pyramid were cut and stored close to the pyramid site. Only the casing, granite and basalt stones came from distant quarries across the Nile.

Sections of all four corners of the low wall surrounding the pyramid are removed to allow space for sleds to pass through. Then it is only a short task in time, effort, and distance to load the blocks on the sleds, and drag them to the platform grid for placement (see Figures No.'s 21 and 22).

The bedrock core is about 412.7 feet square and 46.25 feet high. The platform extends from the core edges to about 2 feet beyond the pyramid's edges. The pyramid is 755.3 feet square. With these dimensions the number of platform blocks required (2.5 ft. by 10 ft.square) = $((755.3+2+2)(755.3+2+2) - (412.7 \times 412.7))/(10 \times 10)$ = 4,062.2. The weight of each block = $((2.5 \times 10 \times 10)(165)/2000$ = 20.62 tons.

If it is assumed that a man of 150 pounds can pull twice his weight in short rhythmic jerks, then it will take $(20.62 \times 2000)/(150 \times 2)$ = 138 men per sled to move this block of stone. Two additional men will be needed to lubricate the sled's runners and to call out the rhythm. If 8 crews of 140 men per sled are assigned to each of the four sides of the pyramid, and each crew is required to place 2 blocks per day, then it will take $(4,062.2)/(8 \times 2 \times 4)$ = 63.47 days to complete the laying of all the platform blocks. The movement of all of these blocks will require a total of $(140 \times 8 \times 4)$ = 4,480 men, going back and forth, between the platform site and the block storage areas.

Method For Raising A Platform Block

Figure No. 23 shows one platform block being raised from the horizontal ground position, to the vertical position. The step sequences are:

Position 1 - A crew of ten men drive one wedge, underneath the block, on sides opposite each other, at the centerline-of-mass (M). Then they push down on the top of the left side (S1) to raise the right side (S2).

Position 2 - Levers are set, underneath the right raised side (S2) to lift this side at least 12 inches above the ground, then larger wedges are set at the centerline-of-mass (M) and the levers are removed.

Position 3 - A crew of 140 men place two-2 inch ropes around the top face of the block, near the raised edge (S2); then around the bottom face where each of the two lengths of each rope are twisted twice around themselves; and then brought up over the top raised edge near the corners C1 and C2. Now each of the four lengths of rope are extended to the left of the block and held tightly by four groups of 35 men, respectively along these lengths.

Positions 4, 5, and 6 - The four groups of 35 men, working together, in rhythm slowly rotate the block counter clockwise until it stands vertical on its side (S1), and the ropes are removed.

53

FIGURE NO. 21
PLATFORM LAYOUT

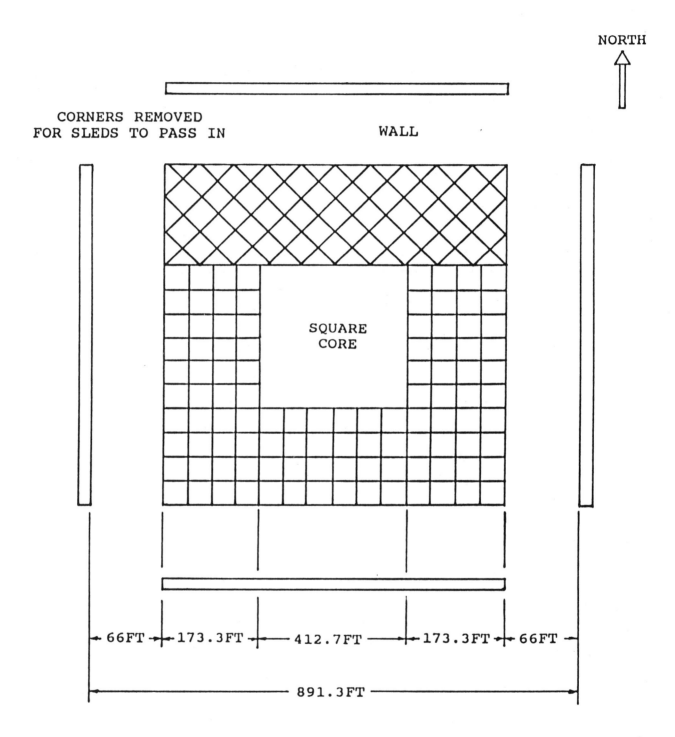

PLAN VIEW

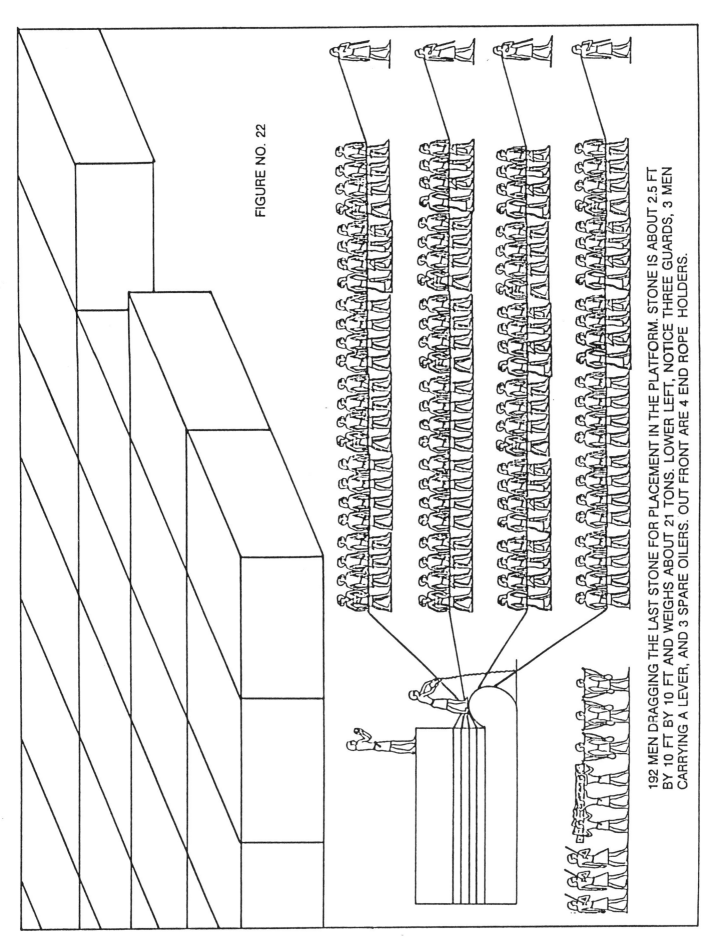

FIGURE NO. 22

192 MEN DRAGGING THE LAST STONE FOR PLACEMENT IN THE PLATFORM. STONE IS ABOUT 2.5 FT BY 10 FT BY 10 FT AND WEIGHS ABOUT 21 TONS. LOWER LEFT, NOTICE THREE GUARDS, 3 MEN CARRYING A LEVER, AND 3 SPARE OILERS. OUT FRONT ARE 4 END ROPE HOLDERS.

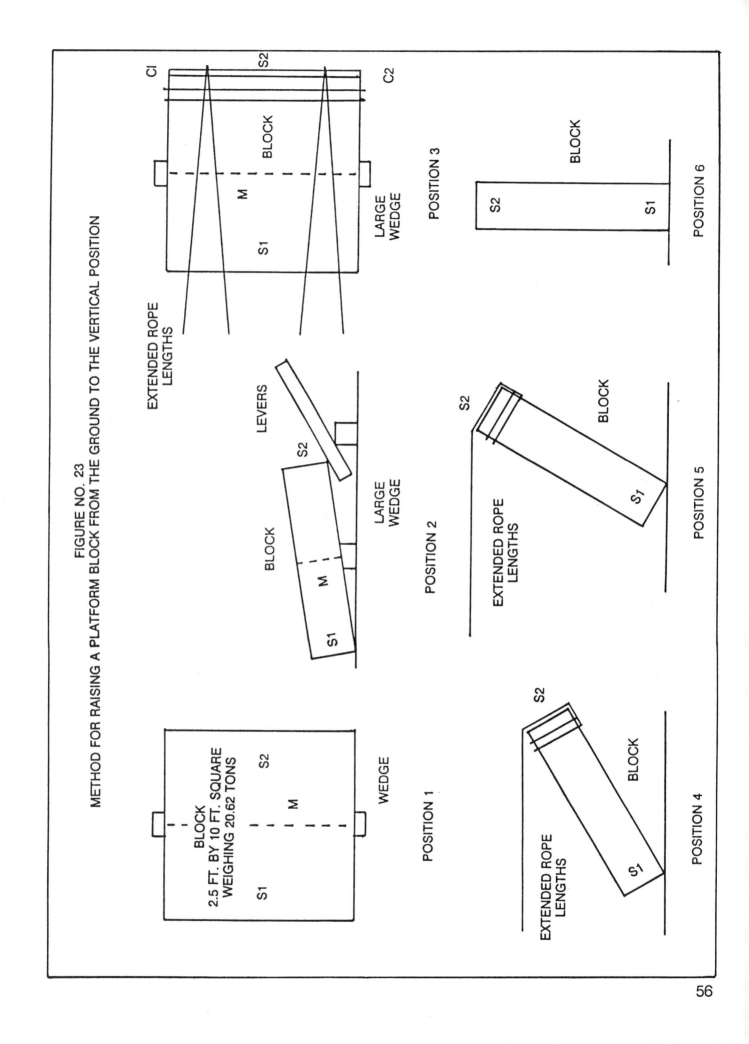

FIGURE NO. 23

METHOD FOR RAISING A PLATFORM BLOCK FROM THE GROUND TO THE VERTICAL POSITION

56

Method For Loading A Platform Block Onto A Sled

Figure No. 24 shows the same block from Figure No. 23 raised from the ground to the vertical position. This block is now going to be placed on a sled and dragged to the pyramid site for placement in the platform grind pattern. The sequences of block movements are:

Position 1 - The sled is brought along side the block, leaving a gap between them, which will make it possible for the sled's top edge, TS1, to touch P1 of the block when it is rotated onto the sled. Also, that the sled's top edge, TS2, will touch P2 of the block. Thus leaving even lengths of block overhangs, E1-P1 equals E2-P2. This results in half of the block's length, P1-P2, coming to rest on the sled.

Position 2 - A crew of 140 men place two-2 inch ropes around and near the top edge, E2, of the block. Then the two lengths of each rope are twisted twice around themselves, and each length is held tightly, by 4 groups of 35 men, to the right of the sled.

Position 3 - A crew of ten men drive wedges and set levers along the block's edge, E1, to start to title the block towards the sled.

Position 4 - The four rope groups, working in rhythm with the wedge-lever groups, slowly rotate the block towards the sled.

Position 5 - As the block rotates in the direction of the sled, its points P1 and P2 will touch the sled's edges TS1 and TS2 respectively coming to rest on top of the sled.

Position 6 - The block is now resting well balanced on the sled. The crews remove the two ropes, wedges and levers and they start to drag the sled to the pyramid's site by pulling the heavy duty ropes attached to the block and sled as shown.

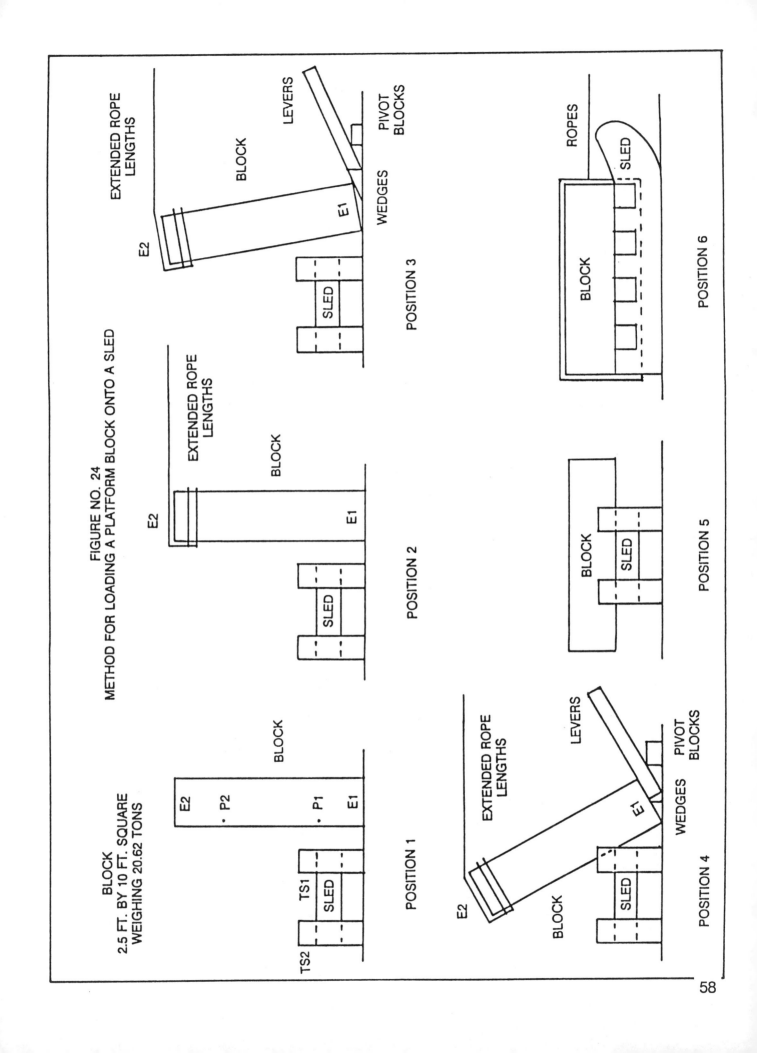

FIGURE NO. 24
METHOD FOR LOADING A PLATFORM BLOCK ONTO A SLED

58

Method For Taking A Block Off A Sled And Placing It In The Platform

Figure No. 25 shows the same block from Figure No. 24 laying on a sled. It was dragged to the pyramid's platform site where it will be unloaded and placed in the platform's block pattern. The sequence of block movements are:

Position 1 - Two-2 inch ropes are placed around the top surface of the left end of the block. The two lengths of each rope are brought down, around the bottom of the left end of the block. Then the two lengths of each rope are twisted twice around themselves, brought up over the left end of the block and each of the four rope lengths are extended to the right and held tightly by four crews of 35 men respectively.

Position 2 - A crew of ten men set levers underneath the roped end of the block, on top of small lever blocks, ready for raising the block's left end.

Position 3 - Then all together, in rhythm, levers are pushed, ropes are pulled, until the sled tips over onto the right runner and the block slides off the sled, and comes to rest on its edge E1. The block is held in this position until a fine texture of mortar is spread on the block's left 10 foot square surface, which will come in contact with the platform surface.

Position 4 - The sled is removed. The holding crews, slowly allow the block to rotate, counter clockwise, until it comes to rest on wedges.

Position 5 - The ropes are removed and mortar is spread on all the sides of the block with the exception of the top surface and the wedges are removed.

Position 6 - The block is now pushed, and due to the mortar, will slid easily into its assigned place among the other blocks already in place.

These sequences of moves are repeated until all of the 4,062 blocks have been placed in the platform pattern (See Figures No's 21 and 22).

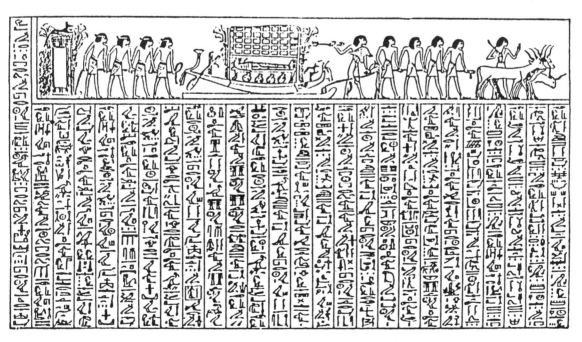

AN EGYPTIAN FUNERAL PROCESSION - THE HIEROGLYPHIC TEXT IS THE FIRST BOOK OF THE DEAD
(FROM THE BRITISH MUSEUM PAPYRUS NO. 9901)

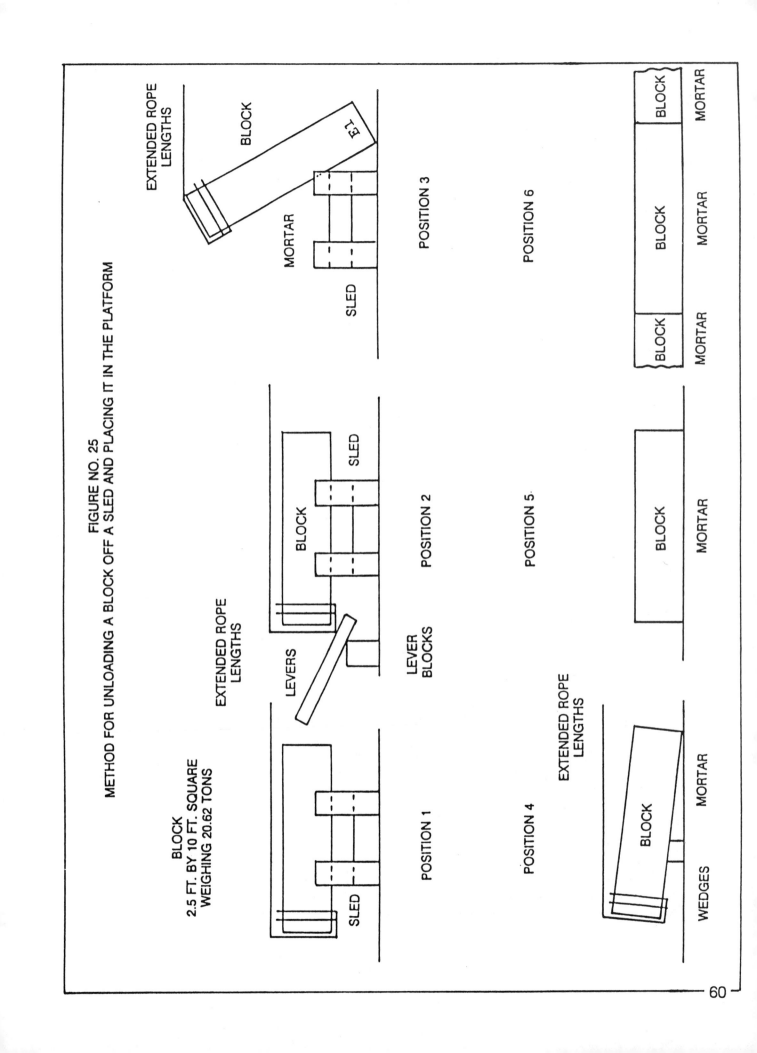

FIGURE NO. 25
METHOD FOR UNLOADING A BLOCK OFF A SLED AND PLACING IT IN THE PLATFORM

BLOCK
2.5 FT. BY 10 FT. SQUARE
WEIGHING 20.62 TONS

EXTENDED ROPE LENGTHS

BLOCK

MORTAR

SLED

POSITION 3

EXTENDED ROPE LENGTHS

BLOCK

SLED

LEVERS

LEVER BLOCKS

POSITION 2

POSITION 1

SLED

POSITION 4

POSITION 5

POSITION 6

MORTAR

BLOCK

MORTAR

MORTAR

BLOCK

MORTAR

BLOCK

MORTAR

BLOCK

MORTAR

BLOCK

MORTAR

EXTENDED ROPE LENGTHS

BLOCK

MORTAR

WEDGES

Dragging Heavy Sarcophagi Up A Steep Rocky Slide

In western Aswan is a very interesting flight of steps in the side of a steep, rocky hill, with a slid down the middle. Sarcophagi, weighing up to six tons, were dragged up this slide from the river bank. In the sides of this hill, tombs were hewn out of the solid rock, tier above tier. These tombs were very popular in Egypt among high military and priestly officials from the XXVIth dynasty downward. A body carefully buried therein would be extremely difficult to find once the opening of the tomb had been blocked up. To this day these tombs remain complete, and are one of the most interesting antiquities in Egypt.

Slides For Dragging Blocks Of Stone Up The Pyramid's Faces

Two short and one long slides, with tapering sides, are cut in the casing stones with an incline close to the final 51°51' slant of the pyramid's faces. These were used for dragging blocks of stone upward. The cutting of the slides is done after the last block is placed in Step No. 201. The taper of the slides is determined by the largest block in each Step. Shorter slides start at Step No. 1 and end at Step No. 128. Longer slides start at Step 1 and end at Step No. 201 (see Figures NO.'s 26 and 27.)

FIGURE NO. 26
PLAN VIEW OF THE PYRAMID'S SLIDES
(DUE TO SMALL PAGE SIZE - ONLY A FEW OF THE 201 STEPS ARE SHOWN)

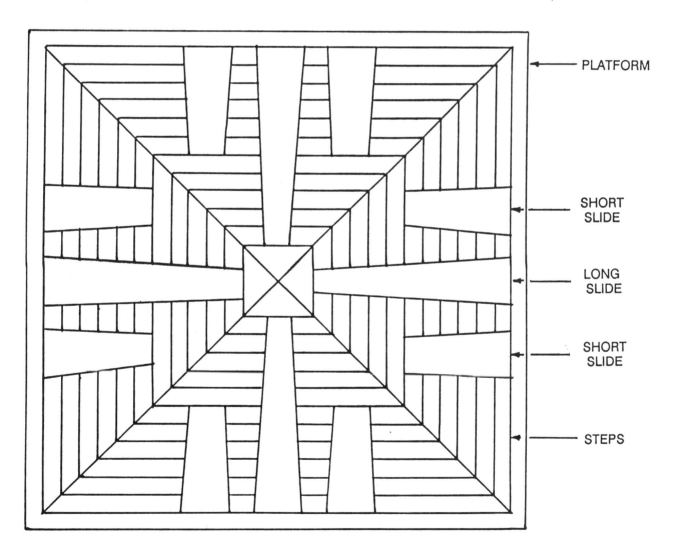

PLATFORM

SHORT SLIDE

LONG SLIDE

SHORT SLIDE

STEPS

FIGURE NO. 27
ELEVATION VIEW OF THE PYRAMID'S SLIDES
(DUE TO SMALL PAGE SIZE - ONLY A FEW OF THE 201 STEPS ARE SHOWN)

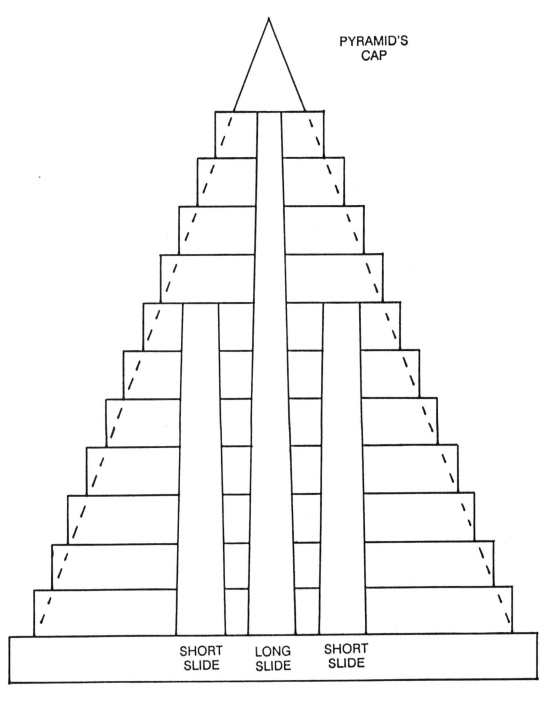

PYRAMID'S
CAP

SHORT
SLIDE

LONG
SLIDE

SHORT
SLIDE

PLATFORM

Forces Acting When Heavy Blocks Of Stone Are Dragged Up The Slides On The Pyramid's Face

It is critical to know these forces because they determine the number of men and ropes needed to move the blocks. Table No. 6 below contains this information and typical calculations follow it. A sketch of the forces is shown in Figure No. 28. A coefficient of friction of 1.00 was assumed even though lubricants and or log rollers were used. This results in a greater safety factor for the ropes used.

TABLE NO. 6
FORCES ACTING WHEN HEAVY BLOCKS OF STONE ARE DRAGGED UP
THE PYRAMID'S 51·51' FACE

WEIGHT OF BLOCK AW	FORCE NEEDED TO DRAG THE BLOCK UP AB	NUMBER OF MEN IN THE DRAG CREW	NUMBER OF ROPES NEEDED
TONS	TONS	(f = 1.00)	(f = 1.00)
60	47.18	400	5
50	39.32	333	4
40	31.45	266	4
35	27.52	233	3
30	23.59	200	3
25	19.65	166	2
20	15.72	133	2
15	11.79	100	2
10	7.86	66	1
5	3.93	33	1
4	3.14	26	1
3	2.35	20	1
2	1.57	13	1
1	0.78	7	1

Typical Calculations For Table No. 6

AW = Weight of block in tons. AB = Force, in tons, tending to pull the block down the face of the pyramid.
AD = Force needed to drag the block up the steps, (AD must be slightly greater than AB).
BW = Force of the block against the pyramid, in tons. For a 60 ton block the calculations are:

AB/AW = sine 51·51'. AB = 60 x sine 51·51' = 47.18 tons.
Number of men needed to pull the 60 ton block up = (60 x 2000)/(300 lbs. per man) = 400.
Number of 2 inch diameter ropes needed = (60 x 2000)/25,000 = 5.

(Note: The rope's tensile strength is 75,000 lbs. per square inch. A safety factor of 3 to 1 was used for the rope. The actual safety factor is greater because the full block weight of 60 tons was used instead of the component value, AB = 47.18 tons. A friction coefficient of 1.00 was assumed even though lubricants and log rollers were used which reduces the AB component, thus increasing the rope's safety factor further.)

NECHEBT   THE   PATRON   GODDESS   OF   KINGS

FIGURE NO.28
FORCES ACTING WHEN HEAVY BLOCKS OF STONE ARE DRAGGED UP THE PYRAMID'S SLIDES

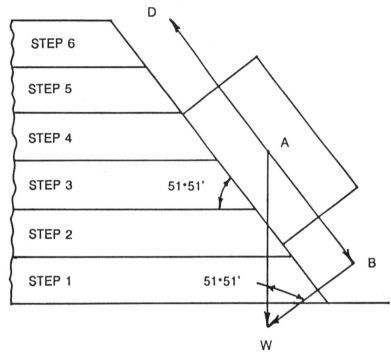

STEP 6

STEP 5

STEP 4

STEP 3 51·51'

STEP 2

STEP 1 51·51'

D

A

B

W

AW = Weight of block in tons.

AB = Force, in tons, tending to pull the block downward.

AD = Force, in tons, needed to drag the block upward which must be slightly greater than AB.

BW = Force, in tons, of the block against the pyramid.

KING RAMSES II RECEIVES FROM AMON RA, "THE LORD OF KARNAK," WHO IS SEATED IN A CHAPEL, THE SIGN OF MANY FESTIVAL WHICH HE SHOULD YET LIVE TO SEE;

THE GOD SAYS: " MY BELOVED SON OF MY BODY, LORD OF THE TWO COUNTRIES, USER-MA-RA, CHOSEN OF RA, I GIVE THEE THE TWO COUNTRIES IN PEACE, I GIVE THEE MANY FESTIVALS IN LIFE, DURATION, AND PURITY." NUT, THE MATE OF AMON, THE LADY OF HEAVEN AND THE RULER OF THE GODS, "SAYS: "I PLACE THE DIADEM OF RA ON THY HEAD, AND GIVE THEE YEARS OF FESTIVALS, WHILE ALL THE BARBARIANS LIE BENEATH THY FEET." THE MOON GOD AAH-TEHUTI, THE CHILD OF THE TWO GODS, SAYS: "I GIVE THEE MY STRENGTH."

Two Methods Were Used For Raising Blocks Of Stone Up The Pyramid's Slides

Method No. 1 - Wedges, Levers, and Ropes

Figure No. 29 shows a core (backing) stone, 60 inches, by 142 inches square, weighing 56 tons being raised to the top of Step No. 2 for placement as the first stone in Step No. 3. Water was used as a lubricant between the block and the slide's surface, SS. The sequences for the stone's movements are:

Position 1 - A stone is unloaded from a sled as was previously explained, standing vertically with its edge E3, of the longest side, touching the slide's base edge SBE.

Position 2 - Two-2 inch ropes are placed near the top, around the stone, twisted tightly around each other and each of the 4 free ends are held tightly by 4 crews of 46 men extending to the right of the stone.

Position 3 - A crew of 10 men drive wedges and push levers along edge E4 to tilt the stone, on its edge E3, in a counter clockwise direction towards the pyramid's slide surface, SS. These crews working together, in rhythm, continue to slowly rotate the block on its E3, allowing the stone to softly come to rest on the slide's surface, SS. The two ropes are removed and all of the slide's surface, in front of the block is wet with water to be used as a lubricant.

Position 4 - Four-2 inch ropes are set around the stone and the eight ends are twisted together forming a tight, secure attachment to the stone around its ends E1-E2 and E3-E4.

Position 5 - Eight crews of 44 men standing on Step No. 2 slowly pull on rope ends until the stone's centerline-of-mass, CLM, is opposite Step No. 2's edge, SE.

Position 6 - These same crews continue to move the stone upward until its centerline-of-mass, CLM, is just past the edge SE of Step No.2 and then the stone will rotate until it comes to rest on the end of Step No.2. Water as a lubricant was now poured on Step No.2, in front of the stone, which is then dragged to it place to start filling in Step No.3.

Method No. 2 - Wedges, Levers, Rollers, and Ropes

Figure No. 30 shows the same core stone, in Method No. 1, being raised to the top of Step No. 2 as in Method No. 1. The sequences for the stone's movements are:

Position No. 1 - Four-2 inch ropes are set around the stone and the eight ends are twisted together forming a tight secure attachment to the stone. The stone rests on no more than three logs, No's. 1, 2, and 3. Eight crews of 44 men, standing on Step No. 2, slowly pull on the eight extended ends of the rope until the stone reaches the surface of the pyramid's slide, SS.

Position No. 2 - These crews proceed to pull on the ropes until the stone rolls up the slide and log No. 1 rolls free from underneath the stone.

Position No. 3 - The pulling motion is carry on as the stone mounts the slide and log No. 4 is placed underneath the front end of the stone as log No. 2 rolls free of the stone.

Positions No's. 4, 5, and 6 - The pulling motion is slowly continued, while replacing each log that comes free, until the stone tips downward onto the horizontal surface of Step No. 2 when the centerline-of-mass, CLM, moves past the Step's edge, SE. During these moves no more than three logs are use under the stone. The stone is then rolled to its place to start filling in Step No. 3.

(Note: The block movements are repeated for Methods No's. 1 and 2 until all of the 201 Steps are filled in with stones and the pyramid is in its unfinished Step Shape (see Figures No's. 31, 32, and 33). The pyramids slides are not shown in these Figures. All of the stones in each Step are cut and fitted. Mortar is used and then the stones are slid into place. All joints are overlapped just like a well built brick wall.

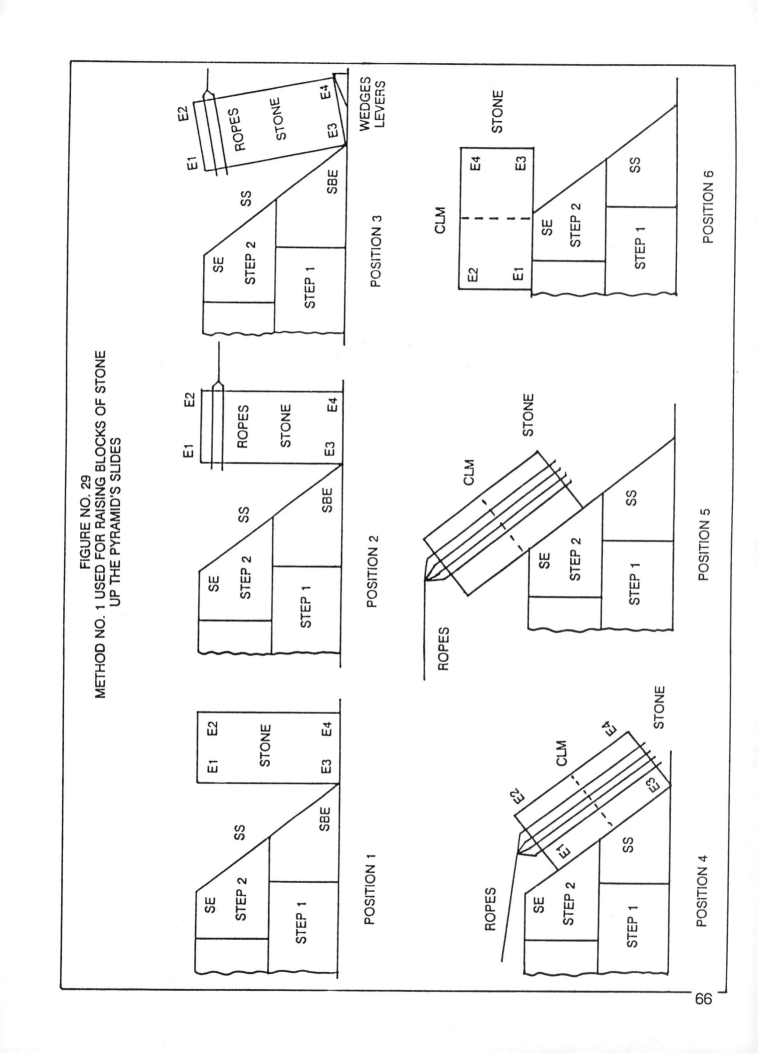

FIGURE NO. 29
METHOD NO. 1 USED FOR RAISING BLOCKS OF STONE
UP THE PYRAMID'S SLIDES

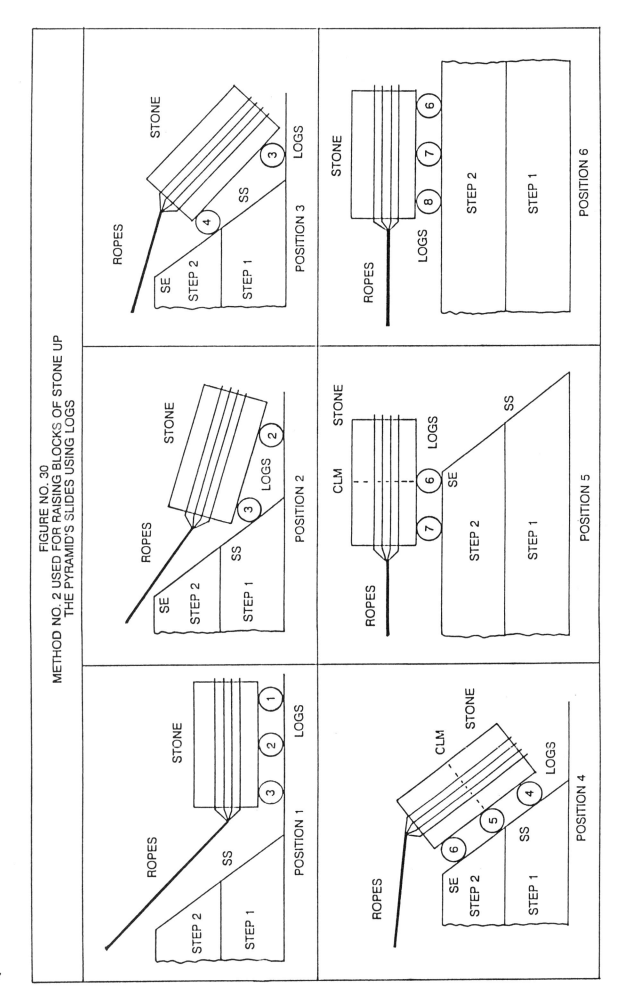

FIGURE NO. 30
METHOD NO. 2 USED FOR RAISING BLOCKS OF STONE UP
THE PYRAMID'S SLIDES USING LOGS

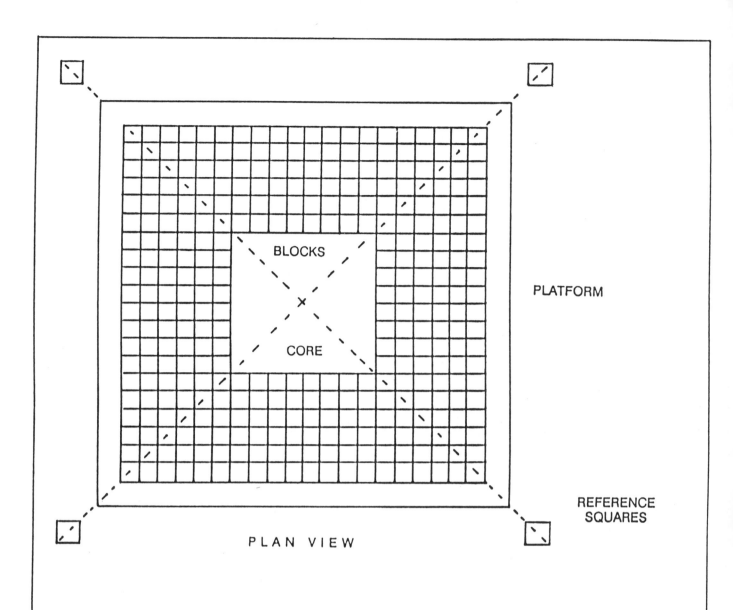

PLATFORM

REFERENCE
SQUARES

PLAN VIEW

FIGURE NO. 31
LAYING OF BLOCKS OF STONE FOR STEP NO. 1
(NOTE: BLOCKS ARE NOT TO SCALE - ALL JOINTS ACTUALLY OVER LAP)

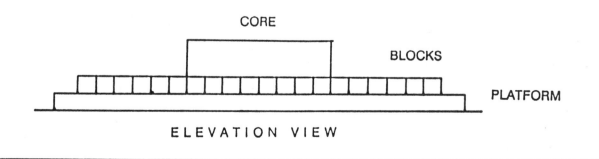

CORE

BLOCKS

PLATFORM

ELEVATION VIEW

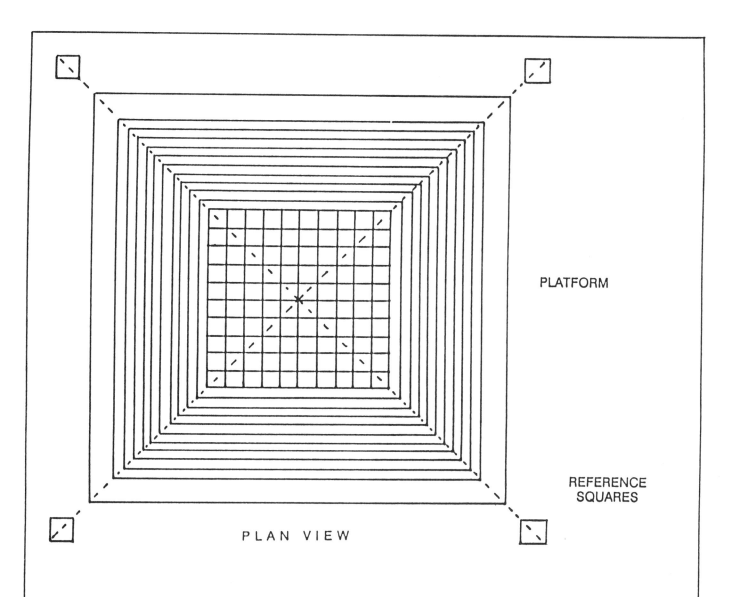

PLATFORM

REFERENCE
SQUARES

PLAN VIEW

FIGURE NO. 32
LAYING OF BLOCKS OF STONE FOR SEVERAL STEPS
(NOTE: BLOCKS ARE NOT TO SCALE - ALL JOINTS ACTUALLY OVER LAP)

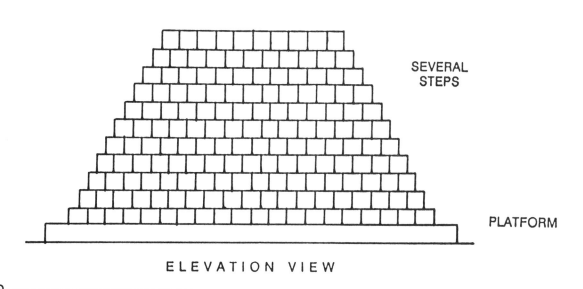

SEVERAL
STEPS

PLATFORM

ELEVATION VIEW

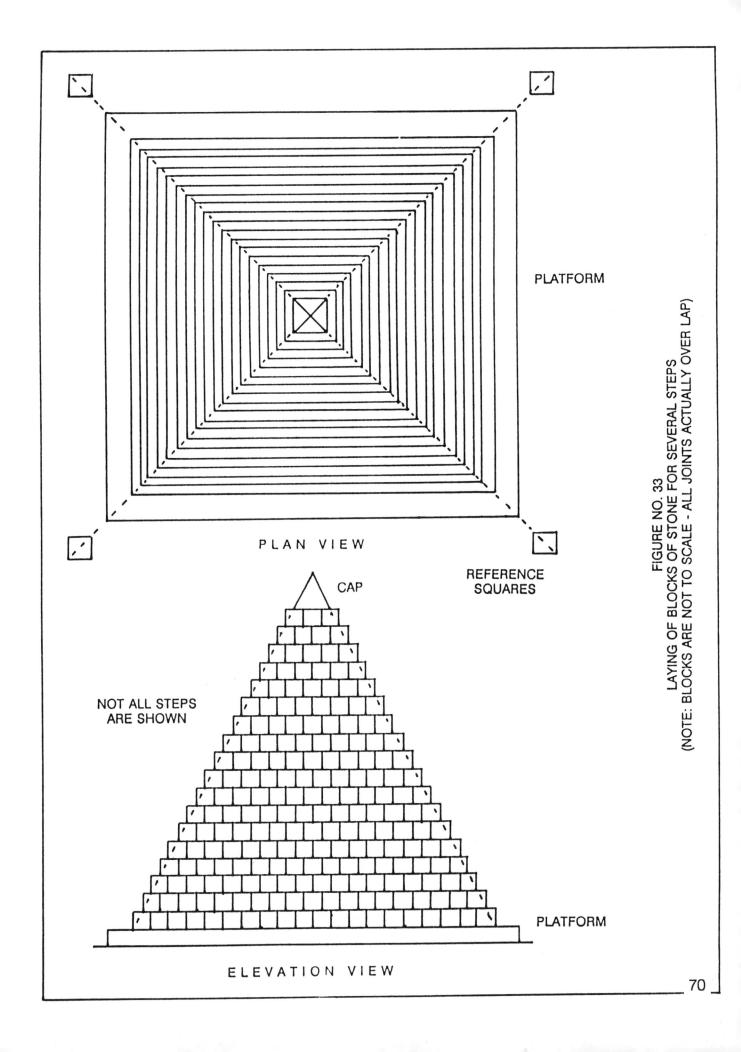

PLATFORM

PLAN VIEW

REFERENCE
SQUARES

CAP

NOT ALL STEPS
ARE SHOWN

PLATFORM

ELEVATION VIEW

FIGURE NO. 33
LAYING OF BLOCKS OF STONE FOR SEVERAL STEPS
(NOTE: BLOCKS ARE NOT TO SCALE - ALL JOINTS ACTUALLY OVER LAP)

Available Width Of Pyramid's Steps At Its Face For The Towing Crews To Use

As the blocks of stone are moved upward Step by Step, it is important that the available width of each Step at the pyramid's face, be wide enough for the towing crews to stand on. The space on each Step varies between Steps No's. 1 to 21 because the block thickness for these Steps were successively reduced by one inch. From Steps No's. 22 to 201 this space remains constant because the block thickness remains constant at 20.46 inches. Table No. 7 below lists these available Step spaces.

For these two Methods of using Wedges, Levers, Rollers and Ropes, I have stuck to the Egyptian way of doing things. That is, what ever they built, they did it in a simple way, with simple tools, and much labor. This Chapter will be concluded by discussing in detail the Ramp Methods and then the entrance to the pyramid, its passageways, and chambers will be described.

TABLE NO. 7
AVAILABLE STEP WIDTHS FOR THE TOWING CREWS TO USE

PYRAMID'S STEP NUMBER	WIDTH OF PYRAMID'S FACE COLUMN (2) TABLE NO. 2 INCHES	THICKNESS OF BLOCK AT STEP COLUMN (4) TABLE NO.2 INCHES	AVAILABLE WALKING STEP WIDTH INCHES
1	9063.85	60.00	47.10
2	8969.64	59.00	46.34
3	8876.95	58.00	45.56
4	8785.83	57.00	44.77
5	8696.28	56.00	43.99
6	8608.30	55.00	43.20
7	8521.90	54.00	42.42
8	8437.06	53.00	41.63
9	8353.80	52.00	40.85
10	8272.10	51.00	40.06
11	8191.98	50.00	39.27
12	8113.43	49.00	38.49
13	8036.45	48.00	37.70
14	7961.04	47.00	36.92
15	7887.20	46.00	36.13
16	7814.93	45.00	35.34
17	7744.24	44.00	34.56
18	7675.11	43.00	33.73
19	7607.56	42.00	32.99
20	7541.57	41.00	32.20
21	7477.16	40.00	31.42
22	7414.32	26.04	20.46
23	7373.41	26.04	20.46
...	....	.....	.....
200	132.41	26.04	20.46
201	91.49	26.04	20.46

Typical Calculations For Available Working Step Width

For Step No. 1 = (9063.85 - 8969.64)/2 = 47.10 inches.
For Step No. 2 = (8969.64 - 8876.95)/2 = 46.34 inches.
For Step No. 22 = (7414.32 - 7373.41)/2 = 20.46 inches.
For Step No. 200 = (132.41 - 91.49)/2 = 20.46 inches.

Method (b) One Long Ramp, Levers, Wedges, And Ropes

The main problem with the ramp method is to determine what materials can be used to construct it and this depends on: (1) their availability in Egypt; (2) they must not crack, distort and break under the ramp's own superimposed load and blocks of stone that weigh over 60 tons which will be dragged up the ramp; (3) can mortar be used with these materials; (4) they can't be dissolved by the flood water of the Nile; and (5) they must not erode by weather conditions. Table No. 8 contains a list of materials and their suitability to construct the ramp.

TABLE NO. 8
MATERIALS AVAILABLE FOR CONSTRUCTING THE RAMP

MATERIAL	AVAILABLE IN EGYPT	SUITABILITY FOR USE	OBJECTION
LOGS	NO	NO	WILL WEAR DOWN
RUBLE	YES	NO	WILL NOT KEEP ITS SHAPE
SAND	YES	NO	WILL NOT KEEP ITS SHAPE
SUN BAKED BRICK	YES	NO	WILL BREAK & WATER DISSOLVES THEM
KILN BAKED BRICK	YES	YES	SEE THE FOLLOWING DISCUSSION
STONE	YES	YES	SEE THE FOLLOWING DISCUSSION

Stone would be the best material to use for constructing the ramp, however, the huge ramp's volume would be close to 88 percent of the pyramid's volume which means that twice the number of stone would have to be cut and transported to the pyramid site. Also, once the pyramid is completed the ramp would have to be torn down and the blocks of stone hauled away which means that the effort and time to build the pyramid would be more than doubled. Therefore, stone has to be ruled out.

For this study large kiln baked bricks (1 ft. by 1 ft. by 6 inches) will be used even though it is not known if the ancient Egyptians were skilled in their production. The millions of bricks needed would require very large kilns and many of them. The enormous amount of wood for the brick molds and heat for the kilns must come from outside Egypt. Corn stalks could be used to supplement the fuel requirements. In spite of all these unknowns let's proceed to built the ramp and see what problems may develop.

Number Of Kiln Baked Bricks Needed To Build The One Ramp

This ramp will be built with brick and mortar just like a well built brick wall with all joints over lapping. It will extend from the center of the east face of the pyramid base at elevation of 60 feet down onto the Nile's flood plain at elevation 18.4 feet. The ramp will have a gradient of 1 to 12, that is, for every foot it rises, its length will be extended 12 feet. This enormous ramp will have a height of 517.5 feet, a width of 50 feet, and a length of 6210 feet (See Figure No. 34 and Table No's. 2 and 9).

Typical Calculations For Table No. 9 At Step No. 201

Height of ramp above the flood plain = (5769.40 - 58.24)/12 + (60.0 - 18.4) = 517.5 feet (See Table No. 2 for the pyramid's dimensions).

Width of step = 91.49/12 = 8 feet (rounded off).

Horizontal length of ramp = 517.5 x 12 = 6210 feet (one mile has 5,280 feet).

Volume of ramp = (517.5 x 6210 x 50)2 = 80,341,875 cubic feet volume of the pyramid = (755.32 x 755.32 x 480.78)/3 = 91,429,661 cubic feet).

Number of bricks needed = 80,341,875 /(1 x 1 x 6/12) = 160,068,000.

The number of stones in columns 7 and 8 came from Table No. 2. As mentioned before the total number of stones is slightly lower due to the bedrock core.

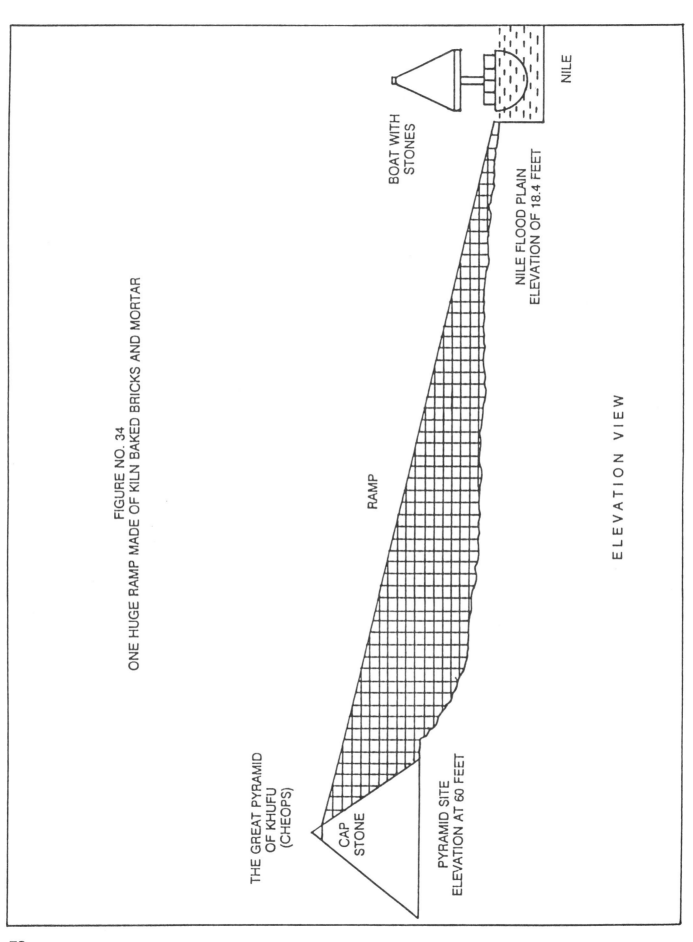

FIGURE NO. 34
ONE HUGE RAMP MADE OF KILN BAKED BRICKS AND MORTAR

THE GREAT PYRAMID
OF KHUFU
(CHEOPS)

CAP
STONE

PYRAMID SITE
ELEVATION AT 60 FEET

RAMP

BOAT WITH
STONES

NILE FLOOD PLAIN
ELEVATION OF 18.4 FEET

NILE

ELEVATION VIEW

ONE RAMP METHOD FOR BUILDING THE GREAT PYRAMID
50 FOOT WIDE RAMP - REQUIREMENTS FOR BRICKS AS THE PYRAMID RISES

STEP	HEIGHT ABOVE FLOOD PLAIN FEET	WIDTH OF STEP FEET	HORIZONTAL LENGTH OF RAMP FEET	VOLUME OF BRICK CUBIC FEET	NUMBER OF BRICK (1'X 1'X 6")	NUMBER OF STONES LEFT TO PLACE (TABLE NO.2)	TOTAL STONES PLACED IN PYRAMID (TABLE NO.2)
12	92.0	676	1104	2,539,200	5,078,400	559,100	47,628
28	142.1	597	1705	6,057,013	12,114,025	492,596	111,132
74	241.9	441	2903	17,555,893	35,111,785	310,022	293,706
120	341.7	284	4100	35,024,250	70,048,500	127,448	476,280
166	441.6	127	5299	58,500,960	117,000,000	11,653	592,075
189	491.5	49	5898	72,471,675	144,940,000	654	603,074
190	493.7	45	5924	73,116,970	146,230,000	526	603,202
195	504.5	28	6054	76,356,075	152,710,000	125	603,603
200	515.4	11	6185	79,693,725	159,390,000	4	603,724
201	517.5	8	6210	80,341,875	160,068,000	4	603,728

NOTES: At step No. 189, the ramp's width of 50 feet starts to exceed the pyramid's step width, and therefore, the ramp has to be narrowed to the width of the remaining steps, which results in less space to work on for these steps.

The number of bricks above is high because no corrections were made for the facts that the ramp over laps the pyramid's face and has to be narrowed above Step No. 189. Also, volume of the mortar joints has to be taken into consideration. These corrections are estimated to be about 10 percent, and therefore, the number of total bricks needed is about (160,068,000 - 16,006,800) = 144,061,200.

Disadvantages Of The One Ramp Method

(1) Table No. 9 shows that the number of bricks needed to build the ramp increases very rapidly as the pyramid rises, while at the same time the number of stones remaining to be placed in the pyramid decrease very rapidly. Therefore, it is difficult to justify the millions of bricks needed near the top of the pyramid for increasing the ramp when only a few stones remain to be placed.

(2) As the ramp rises, the distance that the stones have to be dragged increases to more than one mile. This long up hill distance puts a tremendous load on the crews of men dragging the blocks which results in back, legs and arm injuries taking their toll on these men.

(3) The 144,061,200 bricks needed for the ramp would require that more than ((144,061,200)/(20 years x 364.25 days)) = 19,775 bricks have to be formed and baked each day. Wood for the forms and fuel for the kilns must come from outside Egypt.

(4) Time needed to increase the length and height of the ramp results in constant delays in its use and it becomes increasingly difficult to maintain a smooth 1 to 12 gradient so that the sled friction can be kept to a minimum.

(5) When the teams of men dragging the sleds loaded with stones reach the top of the ramp there is no room left to continue to pull, so the sleds have to be pushed from behind.

(6) During the finishing of the pyramid's faces, it will be necessary to tear down the ramp and remove this huge amount of material.

(7) All stones have to be loaded onto the ramp's east lower end, at the flood plain elevation. This means that stones quarried close to the pyramid can't be brought directly to the pyramid site but have to use the ramp. If the ramp was built opposite any of the other three faces then the stones from the quarries across the Nile first have to be dragged up the causeway, then around the pyramid, along the ramp's length, to it's lower end before they can be loaded onto the ramp. This results in an enormous waste of time and effort.

Conclusions On The One Ramp Method

Considering the above disadvantages, it is concluded that one huge ramp was never used to build The Pyramid of Khufu (Cheops).

Even though the recent discovery of the unfinished pyramid of king Sekhem-khem at Sakkarah shows that ramps were used, which still can be seen, one must keep in mind that this pyramid is small, uses brick, as other small pyramids that show remains of ramps. They are not true, large pyramids as the three at Giza, which were built entirely of large stones.

There has never been reported by historians and other visitors, down through the thousands of years that these large pyramids have been standing, that ramps were used in their construction. Also, there exists no remains of ramps in and around the sites of these large pyramids built with huge blocks stone.

THE GODS HAP (NILE), HEKAU (WORDS OF POWER) AND HORUS (MORNING SUN) PRESENTING THE ROYAL CHILD
AMEN-HETEP III AND HIS KA (DOUBLE) TO AMEN-RA (KING OF THE GODS)
FROM A BASE REFIEF IN THE TEMPLE OF LUXOR

Method (c) Side Ramps, Levers, Wedges, And Ropes

The same remarks made on materials for the One Ramp Method apply here. That is, kiln baked bricks with mortar will be used. In Table No. 10 are tabulated the number of side ramps that can be built when a 1 to 12 gradient is used for these ramps (See Figures No. 35).

Typical Calculations For Ramps No. 1 and No. 2 Shown In Table No. 10

For Ramp No. 1: The length of the base of the first step (horizontal length of Ramp No. 1) = 9063.85 inches (See Table No. 2). The distance to the base of Ramp No. 1 (base of Step No. 1), from the top of the pyramid = 5769.40 inches. Therefore, the height of Ramp No. 1 = 9063.85/12 = 755.32 inches. Total Horizontal Length Of Ramps = 9063.85 inches.

For Ramp No. 2: Distance To Base of Ramp No. 2 from the top of the pyramid = 5769.40 - 755.32 = 5014.08 inches (See Table No. 2). The horizontal length of Ramp No. 2 = (5014.08 x 2)/tangent 51°51' = 7877.22 inches. The height of Ramp No. 2 = 7877.22/12 = 656.43 inches. Total Horizontal Length Of Ramps = 9063.85 + 7877.22 = 16,941.07 inches.

The causeway will be used to transport the stones up to the pyramid's site. From there they will be dragged up Ramp No. 1 located at the base of the east face of the pyramid.

Disadvantages Of The Side Ramps Method

(1) 38 side ramps are required (See Table No. 10). The time needed to build these ramps will result in constant delays in their used. Also, it becomes increasingly difficult to maintain the 1 to 12 gradient with a smooth surface so that the sled friction can be kept to a minimum.

(2) The ramps have to be at least 40 feet wide to allow space for dragging the stones upward, moving ramp materials, empty sleds returning downward, walkway for workers, and supplies. However, the projection of the supporting brick work for ramp No. 15 will over lap ramp No. 11 at 118 feet from the top of the pyramid (See Tables No's. 2, 7, and 10). Therefore, ramps No's. 15 to 38 must have reduced widths leaving smaller spaces to work on. Also, between these ramps their lengths decrease very rapidly again leaving very little spaces to work on. The net reduction of ramp widths means that the remaining stones have to be lifted up using levers, wedges, and ropes.

(3) At all four corners where the pyramid's faces and the ramps meet large platforms are needed to allow room to turn the sleds loaded with stones around the corners onto the next rising ramps. This corner turning will be very difficult and dangerous because sleds have to be pushed and turned from behind. Also, due to the large size needed for these corner platforms their vertical projection downward will start to over lap other platforms below them somewhere between ramps No's. 10 and 15. It is estimated that about 2,000,000 bricks will be needed for these platforms.

(4) The number of bricks needed for these ramps is estimated at (40 x 478 x 68,900/12)/(4)(1 x 1 x 0.5) = 54,890,333. Several large kilns will be needed to produce these bricks. Also, the huge amount of wood for brick forms and fuel for the kilns have to be shipped in from outside of Egypt.

(5) During the finishing of the pyramid's faces, it will be necessary to tear down these ramps and dispose of the huge amount of ramp material.

(6) As the pyramid rises the total length of all ramps increases to more than one mile. This long up hill distance , around the faces of the pyramid, puts a tremendous load on the men dragging the blocks of stones which results in back, legs and arm injuries taking their toll on these men.

Conclusions On The Side Ramps Method

The conclusions on The Side Ramp Method are the same as those for The One Ramp Method.

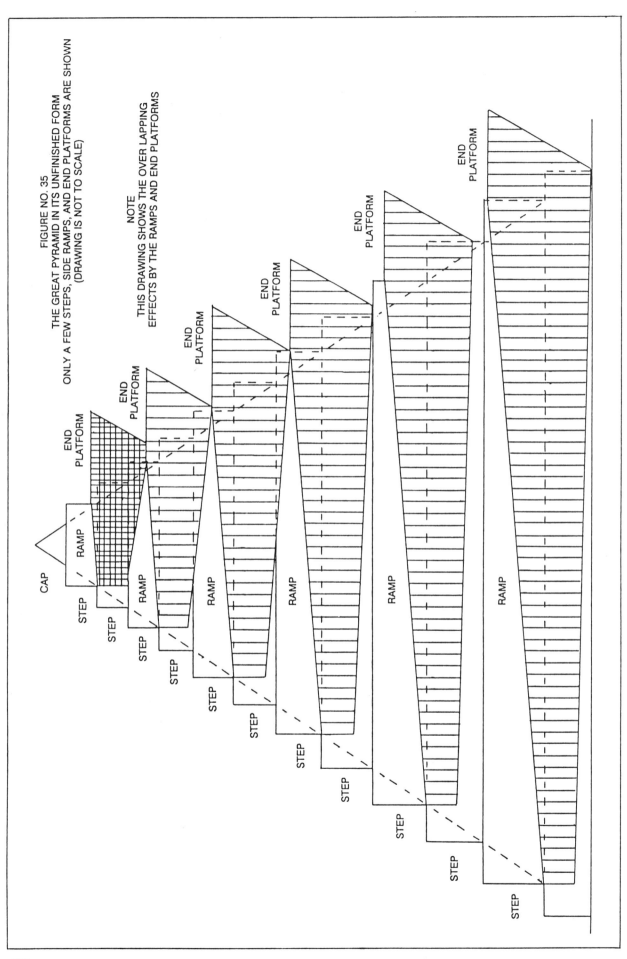

FIGURE NO. 35
THE GREAT PYRAMID IN ITS UNFINISHED FORM
ONLY A FEW STEPS, SIDE RAMPS, AND END PLATFORMS ARE SHOWN
(DRAWING IS NOT TO SCALE)

NOTE
THIS DRAWING SHOWS THE OVER LAPPING
EFFECTS BY THE RAMPS AND END PLATFORMS

TABLE NO. 10
SIDE RAMP METHOD FOR BUILDING THE GREAT PYRAMID
(40 FOOT WIDE RAMPS - 1 TO 12 GRADIENTS)

RAMP NUMBER	HORIZONTAL LENGTH OF RAMP	HEIGHT OF RAMP	DISTANCE TO RAMP BASE FROM THE TOP OF THE PYRAMID	TOTAL LENGTH OF RAMPS HORIZONTAL DISTANCE
	INCHES	INCHES	INCHES	INCHES
1	9063.85	755.32	5769.40	9,063.85
2	7877.22	656.43	5014.08	16,941.07
3	6845.95	570.49	4357.65	23,787.02
4	5949.70	495.80	3787.16	29,736.72
5	5170.79	430.89	3291.36	34,907.51
6	4493.85	374.48	2860.47	39,401.36
7	3905.54	325.46	2485.99	43,306.90
8	3394.23	282.85	2160.53	46,701.13
9	2949.87	245.82	1877.68	49,651.00
10	2563.68	213.64	1631.86	52,214.68
11	2228.05	185.67	1418.22	54,442.73
12	1936.36	161.36	1232.55	56,379.09
13	1682.86	140.23	1071.19	58,061.95
14	1462.55	121.87	930.96	59,524.50
15	1271.09	105.92	809.09	60,795.59
16	1104.69	92.05	703.17	61,900.28
17	960.08	80.00	611.12	62,860.36
18	834.40	69.53	531.12	63,694.76
19	725.16	60.43	461.59	64,419.92
20	630.23	52.51	401.16	65,050.15
21	547.73	45.64	348.65	65,597.88
22	476.03	39.66	303.01	66,073.91
23	413.72	34.49	263.35	66,487.63
24	359.54	29.96	228.85	66,847.17
25	312.46	26.03	198.89	67,159.63
26	271.56	22.62	172.85	67,431.18
27	236.01	19.66	150.23	67,667.19
28	205.12	17.09	130.59	67,872.31
29	178.27	14.85	113.48	68,050.58
30	154.94	12.91	98.63	68,205.52
31	136.36	11.36	85.72	68,341.88
32	116.82	9.73	74.36	68,458.70
33	101.53	8.46	64.63	68,560.23
34	88.24	7.35	56.17	68,648.47
35	76.69	6.39	48.82	68,725.16
36	66.65	5.55	42.43	68,791.81
37	57.93	4.82	36.88	68,849.74
38	50.36	4.19	32.06	68,900.10

Final Conclusions On The Three Methods For Building The Great Pyramid

In this book extensive studies were presented on the three methods suggested by: Herodotus (using the Pyramid itself, levers, wedges, rollers and ropes); and Egyptologists (one large, long ramp and many side ramps using levers, wedges and ropes). Analyses, calculations, Tables, and Figures were made for a thorough investigation of these three methods. The method reported by Herodotus proved to be in tune with the ancient Egyptian way of building their enormous works of stone. Also, this method proved to be practical and matched the ancient requirements that only a few simple tools and much labor be used.

The builder of this pyramid was a genius for he used the Pyramid itself (Slides and Steps) to raise the heavy blocks of stone upward, level by level. He demonstrated tremendous creativity by using the Steps to finish the Pyramid thus, eliminating the need for scaffolding. He chose Limestone as the building material which has the property of not eroding with the passing of time. If the casing stones hadn't been removed, the faces of the pyramid would still be smooth and shinny today after thousands of years of weathering.

In the final analysis, the two ramp methods proved to have too many disadvantages and their use results in delays during the building of The Great Pyramid. Over the thousands of years that the pyramid has been standing no evidence has ever surfaced that ramps were used. As was concluded in the detailed studies, ramps are not practical for building large, true pyramids made of heavy blocks of stone. The wood needed for making the bricks to build these ramps does not exists in Egypt. Many other books have been written supporting the ramp methods, but unfortunately the authors of these books didn't justify these techniques.

These studies unraveled the mystery of "How" the Great Pyramid was built. It is truly mind boggling to learn that such a super intellect existed, way back there more than 5,000 years ago, capable of designing and building a huge magnificent structure like The Great Pyramid. This ancient Egyptian architect was unique for his creation still stands out there on the Libyan plateau after thousands of year. It has endured just about everything that man has ever built.

KING KHUFU MAKING OFFERINGS TO THE SPHINX

Description Of The Inside Of The Great Pyramid

See Figure No. 36 for the descriptions that follows. The entrance to this pyramid is on the north face at Step No. 16, 70 feet above the pyramid's platform. The passage A B C is 345 feet long, 3.5 feet high, 4 feet wide and descends into the center of the pyramid at an angle of 26.5 °. From C the passage becomes level for 25 feet and then enters the subterranean chamber D which measures 46 x 27 x 10.5 feet and is about 600 feet below the apex of the pyramid. This chamber was to be the final resting place for king Khufu's body, which was the customary way of burial in the "Old Kingdom" for deceased rulers. However, this chamber D was abandon and never used. From the end of the chamber a narrow 50 foot passage, E, leads to a blank wall.

B F is a passage sloping 26.5 ° upward, 4 feet high, 3.5 feet wide, and 125 feet long ending at the large Hall, F G. This Hall slopes upward at 26.5°, and is 28 feet high, by 155 feet long. The Hall's walls are raised vertically in seven courses of polished limestone, each off-set 3 inches towards the center of the Hall making it about 5 feet wide at the base and 42 inches wide at the top. The first course is 7 feet high.

Along each side of the Hall's 2 foot wide upward sloping central passage are two ramps 1.5 feet wide and 2 feet high with a series of notches cut in the top of these ramps along the wall line. It is speculated that the main purpose of the Hall was to store enough limestone blocks and three granite blocks that were released by some mechanism using these notches to seal the passage B F after the king's body was placed in his sarcophagus. That is, when the passage B F was first opened it had three granite blocks plugging the lower end at B and the rest of the passage was plugged tight with limestone blocks.

From the Hall, FG, a low 22 foot long passage, G I, leads through an antechamber, H, which was originally closed by four granite doors, remains of which are still visible today. This passage leads into the King's Chamber, J, which is lined with red granite, and measures about 35 x 17 x 19 feet. Inside this chamber, J, lies the uncovered broken, polish red granite sarcophagus of king Khufu (Cheops), measuring 6.5 x 3.25 x 3.33 feet. Air shafts P and Q measure 174 feet x 8 inches x 6 inches and 234 feet x 8 inches x 6 inches respectively. Above the King's Chamber, J, are five shallow Chambers, K, L, M, N, and O which it is believed serve to lighten the pressure on the king's chamber from the superincumbent load above of almost 200 feet of stone. Written on the walls of the two top chambers are three variations of Khufu's name and the number 17 indicating that the pyramid's construction reached this level in 17 years.

It is also believed that these shallow chambers were to be used as storage areas for jewelry, gold, silver, food, furniture, tools, utensils and other necessities for a good life in the hereafter.

The vertical shaft, F R, 3.5 feet square, leads, first to the horizontal passage, S T, which connects with the Queen's Chamber, U. Second, the shaft then drops downward making a connection at, V, with the passage A B C. It is believed that the small crew of men who released the blocks of stone from Hall F G used Shaft F R V to escape out the entrance of the pyramid. Now in retrospect, if the Shaft F R V and passages F B and A B C were completely sealed with the same limestone blocks they were built with, then the pyramid would have been a safe place for Khufu's body and the items buried therein. If Khufu's sarcophagus had a solid gold cover, it could be broken up and the pieces taken out by this escape route.

The Queens Chamber, U, measures about 17 x 19 x 20 feet with walls of finished limestone and is placed beneath the apex of the pyramid. The floor of the Chamber, U, is roughly dressed. There is an empty niche in the east wall probably for placing a large statue. It is 3.5 feet deep, 16 feet high, with four off-set courses making the niche about 5 feet wide at the base and 3.25 feet wide at the top. There are two unfinished air shafts, W and X, leading from the north and south walls.

It is speculated that the three Chambers D, U, and J represent three design changes for locating a safe place for placement of the king's body. There is the belief among some Egyptologists that Khufu's body was never placed in the pyramid because of the fear of robbers. Even the kings that followed Khufu to the throne might rob his final resting place.

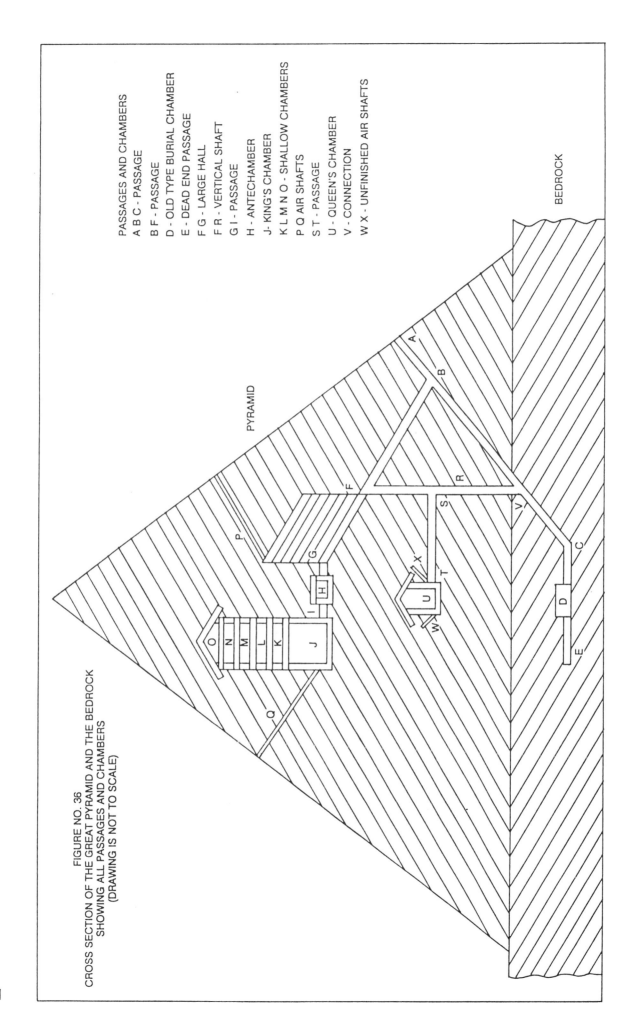

FIGURE NO. 36
CROSS SECTION OF THE GREAT PYRAMID AND THE BEDROCK
SHOWING ALL PASSAGES AND CHAMBERS
(DRAWING IS NOT TO SCALE)

PASSAGES AND CHAMBERS

A B C - PASSAGE
B F - PASSAGE
D - OLD TYPE BURIAL CHAMBER
E - DEAD END PASSAGE
F G - LARGE HALL
F R - VERTICAL SHAFT
G I - PASSAGE
H - ANTECHAMBER
J - KING'S CHAMBER
K L M N O - SHALLOW CHAMBERS
P Q AIR SHAFTS
S T - PASSAGE
U - QUEEN'S CHAMBER
V - CONNECTION
W X - UNFINISHED AIR SHAFTS

PYRAMID

BEDROCK

81

CHAPTER 2

NILE RIVER AND ITS VALLEY IN ANCIENT TIMES

THE NILE VALLEY

Geologists tells us that Egypt consists of a series of sedimentary deposits of the Cretaceous and Tertiary ages. These layers were laid down upon the eroded surface at the eastern edge of the Shara desert. The direction of the Nile Valley is north and south, and is due to the great movements of the earth's plates which took place in Miocene times.

The Nile valley was formed by a fracture of the earth's crust that extends 750 miles from the sea to the first cataract at Aswan. A subsequent rise of the area converted this fault into a river valley, and with the deposition of the Nile mud began the formation of cultivable land. Today this mud averages about 18 meters in thickness throughout the Nile valley. Crystalline rocks occurs, at the surface, at Aswan and other points further south forming cataracts and gorges. The best known of these rocks are the red granites of Aswan, which were mostly used by the Egyptians for temples, statues, and obelisks. From Luxor to Cairo is an immense thickness of white limestone, which form the cliffs of the Nile valley and is the source of most of the building stone in Egypt. The valley is about 30 miles wide at Aswan and narrows northward to about 15 miles at Cairo.

The Nile River

Ancient Egyptians called the Nile, Hap,   . Since they divided their country into north and

south, they believed in the existence of two Niles. The South Nile they called, "Hap Reset",

, and the North Nile they called, "Hap Mehet",   . Both Niles were represented by men having female attributes, and wearing on their heads the plants which were characteristic of the region through which they flowed.

Thus: , the papyrus plant, represented the country of the south where the papyrus grew; and ,the lotus plant, typified the country of the north, that is the Delta where the lotus grew.

The ancient Egyptians appeared to have no knowledge of the sources of the Nile, and in later times it was thought that the river sprang out from two mountains which lay between the islands of Elephantine and Philae near Aswan. In the temple at Philae is a very interesting relief in which an attempt is made to depict the sources of the Nile of the South. Here we see a huge pile of rocks and standing on the top of it are a vulture and a hawk. At the bottom of this pile is a serpent, within its coils kneels the Nile god of the South with a cluster of papyrus plants on his head. In his hands he holds two vases, out of which he is pouring water. See Figure No. 37 for representations of the Nile God.

FIGURE NO. 37
THREE REPRESENTATIONS OF THE NILE GOD BRINGING FORTH WATER
(THE NILE GOD IS REPRESENTED BY MEN WITH FEMALE ATTRIBUTES)

Information About The Nile River (See Figure No. 38)

The main sources of the Nile are Lake Victoria and Lake Albert. Lake Victoria is situated on the Equator in a region of perpetual rains. It is fed by several springs and tributaries like the Kagera river.

Two great tributaries called the Blue Nile (eastern branch), and the White Nile (western branch), join together at Khartoum to form the true Nile river. The White Nile gets its color from a fine whitish clay that it picks up along its course. It is broader and deeper than the eastern branch, and it brings down a much larger volume of water. However, the true makers of Egypt are the Sobat, Blue Nile, and the Atbara rivers. For during their rapid courses from the eastern mountains they carry down with them all the rich mud which, during the lapse of ages, has been spread over the land on each side of its course, forming the fertile land of Egypt.

Lake Victoria is about 3,675 feet above the sea, and 1,425 feet higher than Lake Albert. It is 160 miles long, 200 miles wide, with an area of about 27,000 square miles. When the Nile river leaves the lake it is about 1,300 feet wide. At Ripon Falls it drops about 13 feet, then it flows 242 miles through a number of swamps and then into the N.E. corner of Lake Albert. Next it flows in a broad, deep, and almost a level stream for a distance of 125 miles to the Fola Falls. At this point it is just 300 feet wide, and becomes a torrent.

Flowing on to Lado, about 125 miles, the river becomes only 6.5 feet deep in the Winter at low water, and 15 feet in flood. From Lado to Bohr, a distance of about 102 miles the river has a rapid fall and keeps to one channel. From Bohr to the mouth of the Bahr Al-Ghazal river (a distance of about 350 miles) the stream passes through many channels. Here are large masses of living vegetation which are called, "Sadd", and they form barriers to navigation. Then the Bahr Al-Ghazal flows into the Nile's west bank, and 60 miles further on the Sobat river flows into the Nile's east bank.

From this latter river to Khartoum, a distance of about 598 miles, the White Nile flows in a stream about 6.5 feet deep, and more than a mile wide. At Khartoum, where the 960 mile long Blue Nile from the eastern mountains joins the White Nile, the river is about 1,270 feet above sea level. The blue Nile is almost clear in the Winter, but from June to October its water is of a reddish-brown color, and is highly charged with alluvium. The greenish color which is some time observed in the Nile, far to the north, is due to the decaying vegetation which is brought down by the White Nile.

About 56 miles below Khartoum is the Sixth Cataract, and 145 miles lower down the 700 mile long Atbara river flows into the Nile's east bank. About 32 miles below the Atbara is the Fifth Cataract, 100 miles in length, and the Nile drops about 205 feet. 60 miles lower down begins the Fourth Cataract, 66 miles long, and the Nile drops 160 feet. 195 miles down begins the Third Cataract, which is 45 miles long and river drops 36 feet. The Second Cataract begins about 70 miles lower down, is 125 miles long, and the river drops 213 feet.

The distance between the Second Cataract and the First Cataract is about 210 miles, and the stream is usually 1,630 feet wide. The First Cataract is about three miles long, and between Philae Island at the southern end and Aswan at the northern end the river drops 16 feet. From Aswan to Cairo, the length of the river is about 600 miles, and its mean width is 3,000 feet.

Just to the north of Cairo, the Nile splits into the Rosetta and Danuetta branches, each of which is about 145 miles long. The mean width of the former is 1,630 feet, and that of the latter is 870 feet. In ancient days the Nile emptied its waters into the sea by seven mouths, the is; the Pelusiac, Tanitic, Mendesian, Phatnitic, Sebennytic, Bolbitic and the Canopic.

In Egypt the width of the Nile Valley varies from 15 to 30 miles. The width of the strip of cultivated land in Egypt is about 8 to 9 miles. The Delta is about 90 miles across from east to west, and about the same distance of the Apex from the sea.

In summary: from Lake Victoria to Khartoum is 1,560 miles; Khartoum to Aswan is 1,165 miles; and from Aswan to the sea about 748 miles. So the Nile's total course is about 3,473 miles.

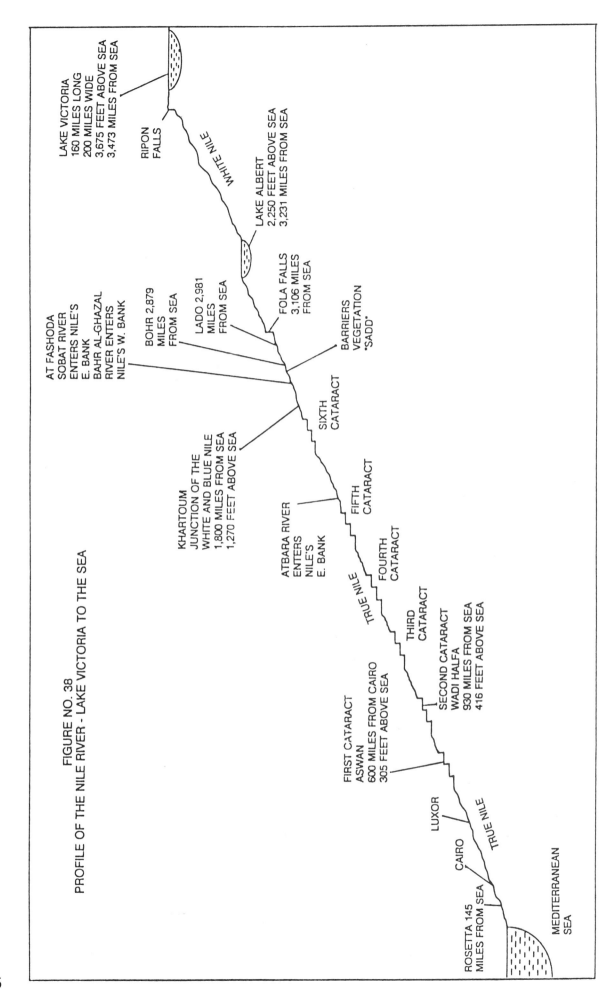

FIGURE NO. 38
PROFILE OF THE NILE RIVER - LAKE VICTORIA TO THE SEA

Inundation (Flooding Of The Nile River)

Results by the rains which fall in the country around Lake Victoria and in the eastern mountains. In the former, the rainy seasons lasts from February to November, with one maximum in April and another in October. In the latter there are light rains in January and February, and heavy rains from the middle of April to September, with a maximum in August.

In April the heavy rains, near Lado on the White Nile, force down the green waters of the swamps, and about April 15 the Nile has begun to rise at this place. This rise is felt at Khartoum about May 20, and at Aswan about June 10. The green water announcing this rise is seen at Cairo about June 20.

About June 5 the Blue Nile begins to rise quickly, and it reaches its maximum by August 25. Its red, muddy water reaches Aswan about July 15, and Cairo 10 days later. When once the red water has appeared the rise of the Nile is rapid, for the Atbara river is in flood shortly after the Blue Nile. The Atbara flood begins early in July and is at its highest about August 20.

The Nile continues to rise until the middle of September, when it remains stationary for a period of about three weeks, sometimes a little less. In October it rises again, and attains its highest level.

From this period it begins to subside, and though it rises yet once more, and reaches occasionally it former point, it sinks steadily until the month of June, when it is again at its lowest level. Thus it is clear that the Sobat, Blue Nile, and the Atbara Rivers supply the waters of the inundation, and the White Nile supplies Egypt for the rest of the year.

In flood time the waters of the Nile use to take 50 days to flow from Lake Victoria to the sea, and at low water 90 days. From Lake Victoria to Lake Albert 8 days, Lake Albert to Lado 5 days, Lado to Khartoum 20 days, Khartoum to Aswan 10 days, Aswan to Cairo 5 days, Cairo to the sea 2 days. At low water the times were 8,5,36,26,12, and 3 day respectively.

The above, natural, annual rhythm of the Nile's flood waters that went on for thousands of years was plugged up by the construction of the Aswan High Dam which began in 1960 and went into operation in 1970.

Irrigation

In Ancient Egypt was determined by the height of the river level indicated on the Nile flood Gauges like the one on the east side of the Island of Elephantine opposite Aswan. When the maximum rise of the river at Aswan is only 21 cubits (1 cubit = 20.62 inches) there will be famine in parts of Upper Egypt. When the rise is between 21 and 23 cubits much of the land of Upper Egypt will not be completely watered. When the rise is between 23.5 cubits and 25 cubits certain lands will only be watered with difficulty in Upper Egypt. If the rise is between 25 and 26.5 cubits the whole country can be watered. When the rise is between 26.5 cubits and 28 cubits the country will be flooded. Any rise beyond the last figure will spell misery and ruin for many.

If the statements made by ancient writers be compared with facts ascertained in modern times, it will be seen that the actual height of the inundation is the same now (before 1960) as it always was. It maintains the same proportion to the land it irrigates. Before the Aswan High Dam was built the Nile was depositing in its bed mud at the rate of 12 centimeters per 100 years. The thickness of the Nile mud averages about 18 meters in all of Egypt.

Measuring The Nile's Flood Levels

From the first Cataract, just north of Aswan, Nile Flood Gauges were built to keep track of the Nile's flood levels, northward to within a few hundred miles of the sea. There were mainly two types in use: a high well connected with the Nile by a channel and open stairs built right on the steep rocky cliffs of the Nile. In 1799 Napoleon's savants discovered the main Egypt stair type Nile Flood Gauge on the Island of Elephantine just north of the foot of the First Cataract. It consisted of two sets of stairs and from the markings and inscriptions on them it is clear that about 100 A.D. the Nile often rose 24 cubits and sometimes 25 cubits. According to Plutarch the Nile rose at Elephantine to the height of 28 cubit. A very interesting text at Edfu states that if the river rises 24 cubits 3-1/4 hands at Elephantine, it will water the country satisfactorily. See Figure No. 39 for a sketch of the Nile-Meter Gauge at Elephantine.

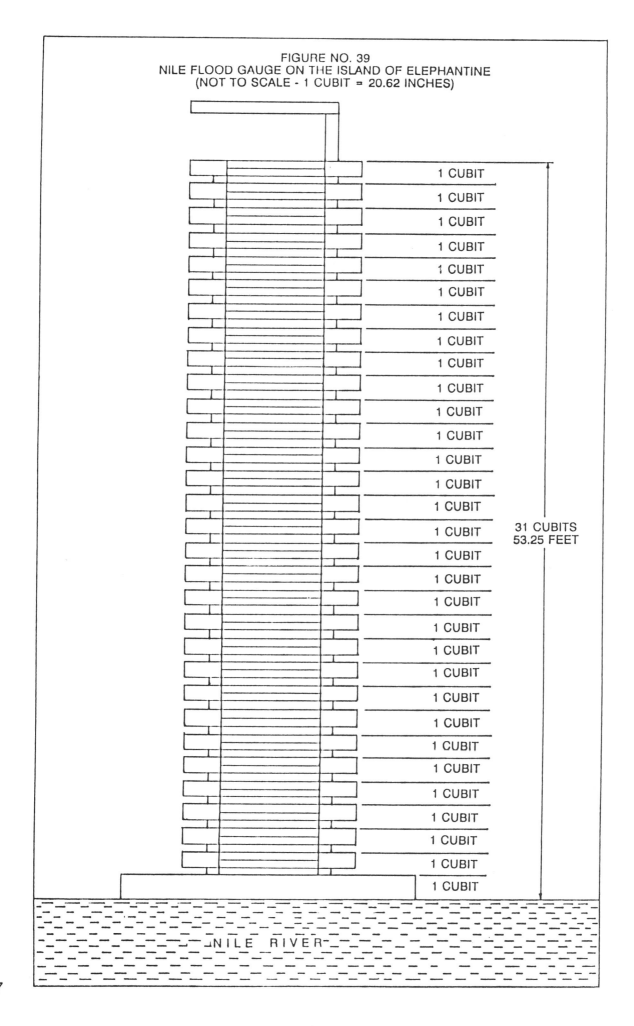

FIGURE NO. 39
NILE FLOOD GAUGE ON THE ISLAND OF ELEPHANTINE
(NOT TO SCALE - 1 CUBIT = 20.62 INCHES)

1 CUBIT
1 CUBIT
1 CUBIT
1 CUBIT
1 CUBIT
1 CUBIT
1 CUBIT
1 CUBIT
1 CUBIT
1 CUBIT
1 CUBIT
1 CUBIT
1 CUBIT
1 CUBIT
1 CUBIT
1 CUBIT
1 CUBIT
1 CUBIT
1 CUBIT
1 CUBIT
1 CUBIT
1 CUBIT
1 CUBIT
1 CUBIT
1 CUBIT
1 CUBIT
1 CUBIT
1 CUBIT
1 CUBIT
1 CUBIT
1 CUBIT

31 CUBITS
53.25 FEET

NILE RIVER

Egyptian Measuring Scale

The Royal Cubit was used by the ancient Egyptians to keep track of the flood levels of the Nile River. This Unit Of Measure is seven hand-widths, or 28 finger-widths or 0.524 meters, and/or 20.62 inches.

To the left is Figure No. 40 is an Egyptian Scale located in the Turin Museum in Turin, Italy. This Scale has five columns of Hieroglyphic Figures which are briefly translated as follows, reading each Column from bottom to top, and left to right:

Column 1 - It starts out by extending eternal life to the last king of Dynasty XVIII as is noticed by his royal ovals (cartouches) which contain his "Prenomen" and "Nomen" names that are explained below. The rest of this column list his achievements in beautiful everlasting monuments and events.

Column 2 - This one continues much the same as Column 1.

Column 3 - These Figures are the Phonetic Hieroglyphic representations of the Cubit Measures shown in each of the 28 rectangles in Columns 4 and 5.

Column 4 - The first 13 rectangles contain the Hieroglyphic figures for 1 Cubit, 2 Cubits, 3 Cubits, and so on up to 13 Cubits. Rectangle 14 contains the Hieroglyphic figures and numerals for 1 Cubit divided into 16 parts. Rectangles 15 to 28 contain the Hieroglyphic figures and numerals for dividing 1 Cubit into 15 parts to 2 parts respectively.

Column 5 - The first 13 blank rectangles represent 1 Cubit respectively. Rectangles 14 to 28 contain the actual spaces for dividing 1 Cubit into 16 to 2 parts respectively.

The Egyptian word for a Cubit is, Meh, and the following are several different variations of its Hieroglyphic representation:

FIGURE NO. 40 - TO THE LEFT
EGYPTIAN SCALE
KING'S NAME - LAST KING OF DYNASTY XVIII
(1490 - 1231 B.C.)

TCHESER-KHEPERU-RA
SETEP-EN-RA

SON OF
THE SUN

AMEN--MERI-EN HERU
EM-HEB

CHAPTER 3

KINGS OF EGYPT

Names Of Egyptian Kings

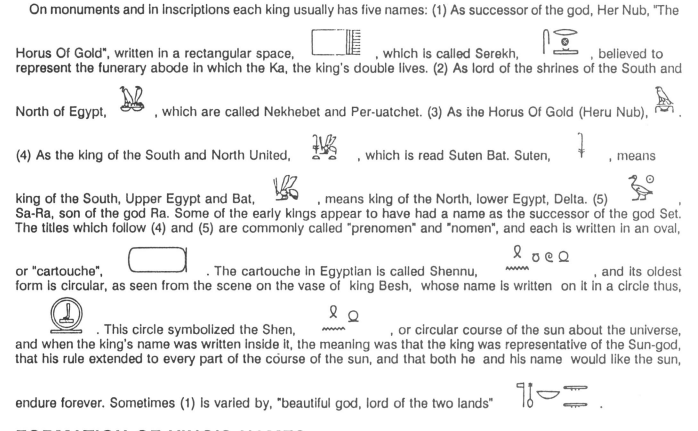

On monuments and in inscriptions each king usually has five names: (1) As successor of the god, Her Nub, "The Horus Of Gold", written in a rectangular space, ⬜️ , which is called Serekh, , believed to represent the funerary abode in which the Ka, the king's double lives. (2) As lord of the shrines of the South and North of Egypt, , which are called Nekhebet and Per-uatchet. (3) As the Horus Of Gold (Heru Nub), .

(4) As the king of the South and North United, , which is read Suten Bat. Suten, , means king of the South, Upper Egypt and Bat, , means king of the North, lower Egypt, Delta. (5) , Sa-Ra, son of the god Ra. Some of the early kings appear to have had a name as the successor of the god Set. The titles which follow (4) and (5) are commonly called "prenomen" and "nomen", and each is written in an oval, or "cartouche", ⬭ . The cartouche in Egyptian is called Shennu, , and its oldest form is circular, as seen from the scene on the vase of king Besh, whose name is written on it in a circle thus, . This circle symbolized the Shen, , or circular course of the sun about the universe, and when the king's name was written inside it, the meaning was that the king was representative of the Sun-god, that his rule extended to every part of the course of the sun, and that both he and his name would like the sun, endure forever. Sometimes (1) is varied by, "beautiful god, lord of the two lands" .

FORMATION OF KING'S NAMES

Names of kings were influenced by: (1) name of the city of their residences (Thebes, Heliopolis, etc.); (2) the religious system practice in these cities (gods worshipped); and (3) the names of their predecessors (Rameses I, Rameses II, etc.). King's names may contain the name of a single god and or a combination of the names of more than one god. Kings were considered to be gods and therefore, the priests used the names of the gods prevalent in their cults. These gods had certain characteristics like living forever, son of the Sun, etc. which certainly were impossible for kings to have. However, some of the god qualities like love, trust, good, etc. were characteristic for some kings and their names, therefore, gave an insight to their personalities. See the long list of kings names at the end of this chapter to see how many god-name combinations were used to name the kings from Dynasty I to Dynasty XXX.

Ra the sun god. Set (Setesh=Sutekh), god of evil. Amen-Ra, king of the gods, lord of heaven and earth (there are many forms of these gods). Nefer-hetep, a god of Thebes. Nefer-hat, god of learning and one of the seven divine sages. Maat, goddess of law. Meri-Maat, a god in the Tuat (land of the dead). Ptah, a god of Memphis, he is called the "Blacksmith", father of gods. Amen a god of Thebes. Horus (Heru) is the morning sun (there are many forms of him). Mer, means like, as Mer-en-Ra means like the god Ra. Ka is the double of the king. Sa means son of. See Figure No. 40 for the images and names of some of the principle gods of ancient Egypt.

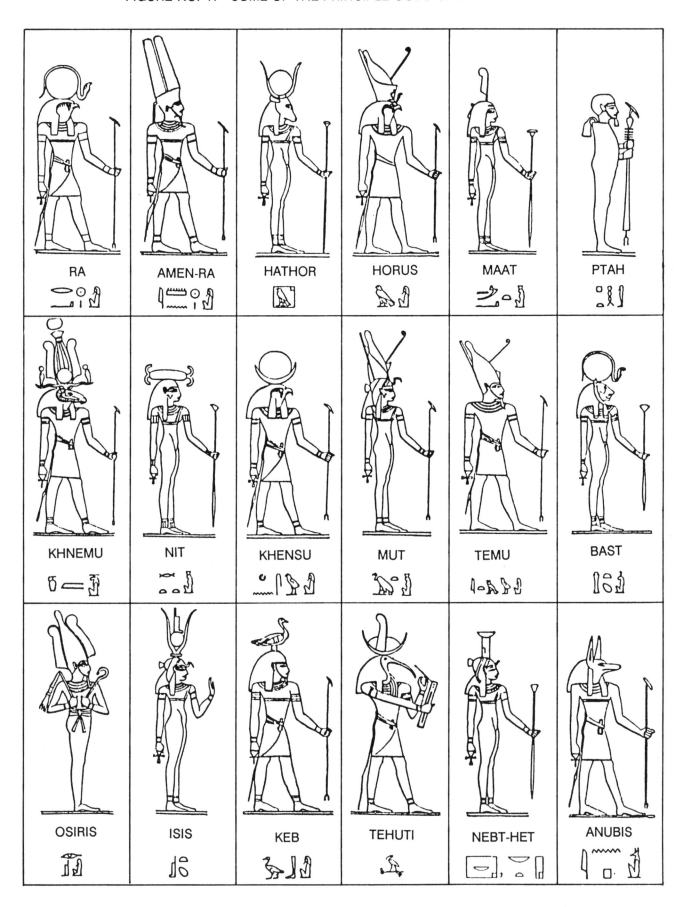

Ra the sun-god was the creator of gods, kings (pharaohs), queens, and men. His emblem was the sun's disk. His worship was very ancient, and he was said to be the offspring of Nut (the sky). He assumed the forms of several other gods, and is at times represented by the lion, cat, and hawk. These gods, kings, and queens, held in their hands various scepters:

rule,   power,   life,   dominion,   stability

They wore the following crowns most commonly seen on monuments, etc.

Details Of The Rameses II Name

Rameses II was the third king of Dynasty XIX and below are the details of his name in English and Egyptian Hieroglyphic figures:

The Horus Of Gold, Mighty Bull: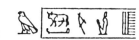

Mighty conqueror of two sides of the mountainous Syrian country:

Fought strongly for six years: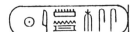

King of the South and North of Egypt: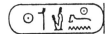

Egyptian "Prenomen" name: Ra   user Maat   setep en Ra.
English translation: Ra   strong in truth approved of Ra.

Son of: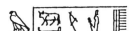

Egyptian "Nomen" name: Ra mes su Mer   Ra.
English translation: Ra son of beloved of Ra.

His condensed Egyptian Name: User-maat-Ra I setep-en-Ra Rameses II; and his full Hieroglyphic name,

List Of Kings

As stated at the bottom of Table No. 1, the tablets of Sakkarah, Karnak, Abydos don't contain a complete listing of the kings of Egypt. The Tablet of Abydos contains only 56 names (see Figure No. 41). Other sources of king's names are: the multitude of monuments, the Pyramid Text, the Abbott Papyrus, the Turin Papyrus and the Cuneiform Tablets. At the end of this chapter is a complete list of kings from Dynasty I to Dynasty XXX, which ends with Hellenic kings and their Queens about 30 B.C.

FIGURE NO. 42
THE KING LIST ON THE TABLET OF ABYDOS

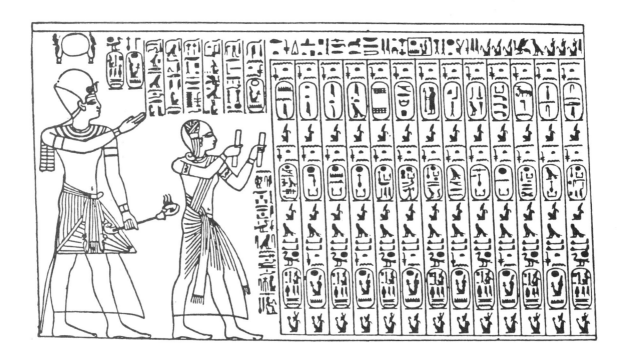

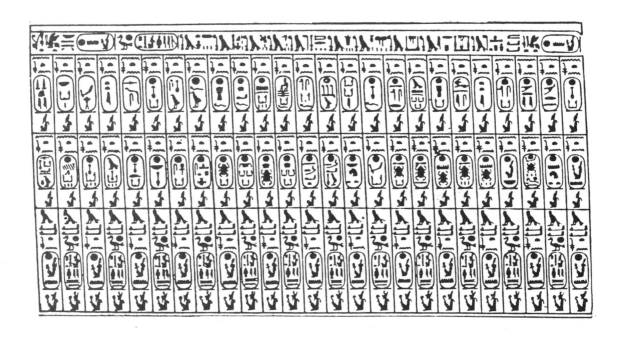

KING'S LIST BY DYNASTIES

DYNASTY I

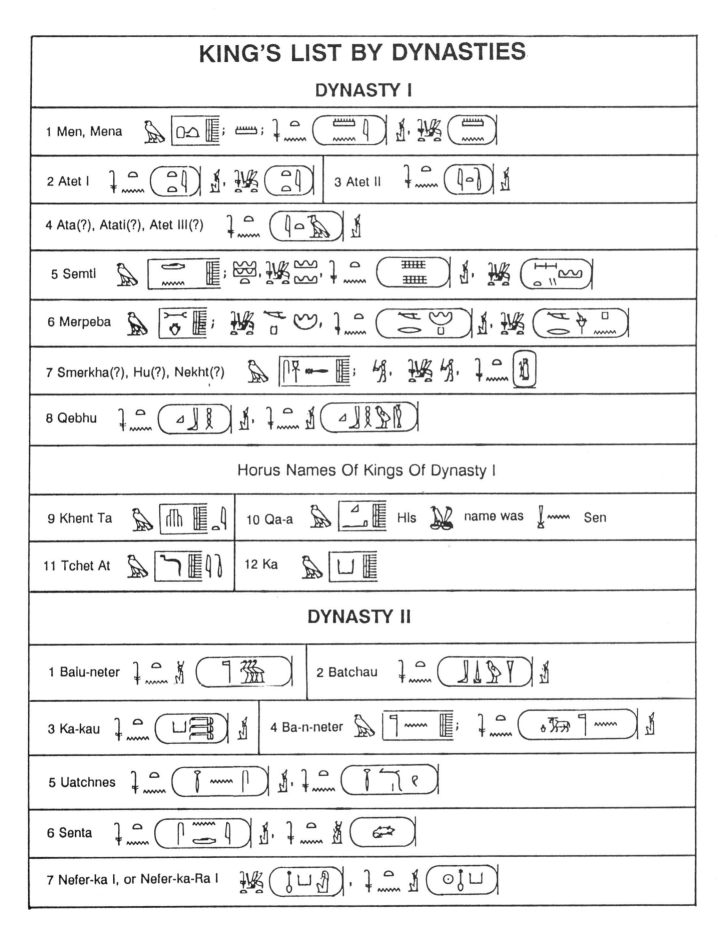

1 Men, Mena

2 Atet I | 3 Atet II

4 Ata(?), Atati(?), Atet III(?)

5 Semti

6 Merpeba

7 Smerkha(?), Hu(?), Nekht(?)

8 Qebhu

Horus Names Of Kings Of Dynasty I

9 Khent Ta | 10 Qa-a   His   name was   Sen

11 Tchet At | 12 Ka

DYNASTY II

1 Balu-neter | 2 Batchau

3 Ka-kau | 4 Ba-n-neter

5 Uatchnes

6 Senta

7 Nefer-ka I, or Nefer-ka-Ra I

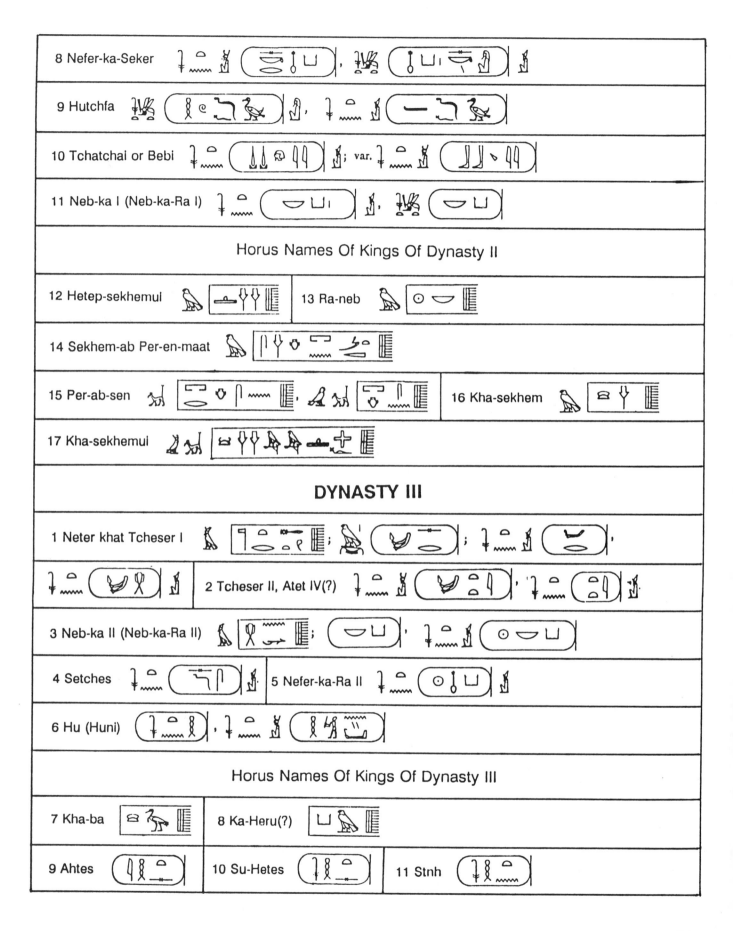

8 Nefer-ka-Seker			
9 Hutchfa			
10 Tchatchai or Bebi			
11 Neb-ka I (Neb-ka-Ra I)			

Horus Names Of Kings Of Dynasty II

12 Hetep-sekhemui		13 Ra-neb	
14 Sekhem-ab Per-en-maat			
15 Per-ab-sen		16 Kha-sekhem	
17 Kha-sekhemui			

DYNASTY III

1 Neter khat Tcheser I			
(cartouche)	2 Tcheser II, Atet IV(?)		
3 Neb-ka II (Neb-ka-Ra II)			
4 Setches		5 Nefer-ka-Ra II	
6 Hu (Huni)			

Horus Names Of Kings Of Dynasty III

7 Kha-ba		8 Ka-Heru(?)	
9 Ahtes		10 Su-Hetes		11 Stnh	

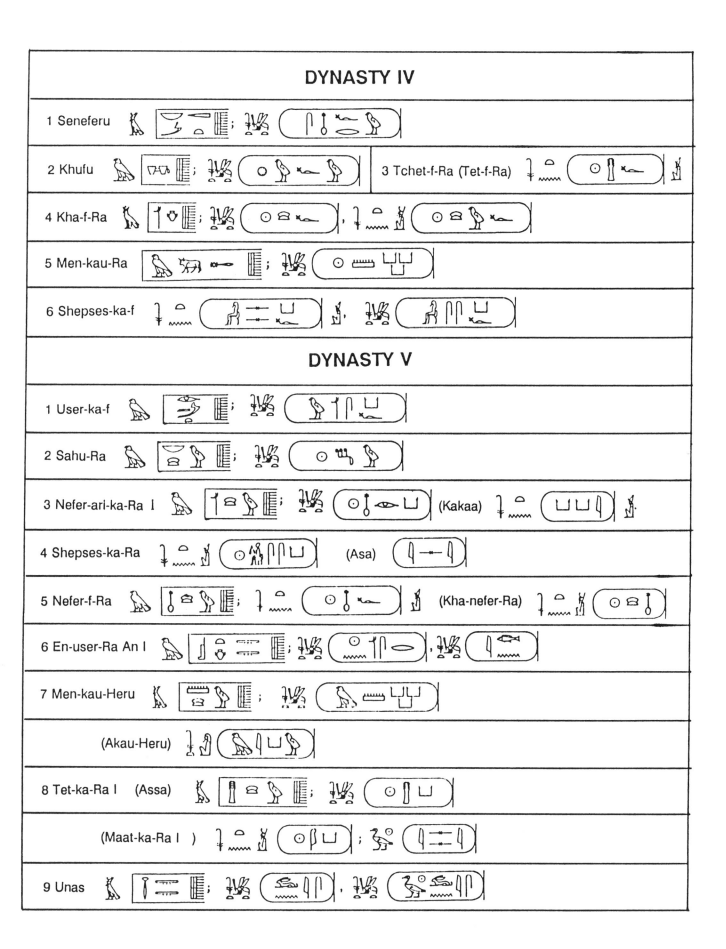

DYNASTY IV

1 Seneferu	
2 Khufu	3 Tchet-f-Ra (Tet-f-Ra)
4 Kha-f-Ra	
5 Men-kau-Ra	
6 Shepses-ka-f	

DYNASTY V

1 User-ka-f	
2 Sahu-Ra	
3 Nefer-ari-ka-Ra I	(Kakaa)
4 Shepses-ka-Ra	(Asa)
5 Nefer-f-Ra	(Kha-nefer-Ra)
6 En-user-Ra An I	
7 Men-kau-Heru	
(Akau-Heru)	
8 Tet-ka-Ra I (Assa)	
(Maat-ka-Ra I)	
9 Unas	

DYNASTY VI

1 Teta (Atet V)	
2 User-ka-Ra I (Ati I)	
3 Meri-Ra (Pepi I)	
4 Mer-en-Ra I (Mehti-em-sa-f I)	
5 Nefer-ka-Ra III (Pepi II)	
6 Mer-en-Ra II (Meht-em-sa-f II)	
7 Neter-ka-Ra	8 Net-aqerti
9 Nefer-ka II	

DYNASTIES VII AND VIII

1 Men-ka-Ra	2 Nefer-ka-Ra IV
3 Nefres(?)	4 Ab(?)
5 Nefer-ka-Ra V Nebi	
6 Tet-ka-Ra II Maa...	
7 Nefer-ka-Ra VI Khentu	
8 Mer-en-Her I	
9 Senefer-ka I (Senefer-ka-Ra I)	
10 En-ka-Ra I	11 Nefer-ka-Ra VII (Terri (?))

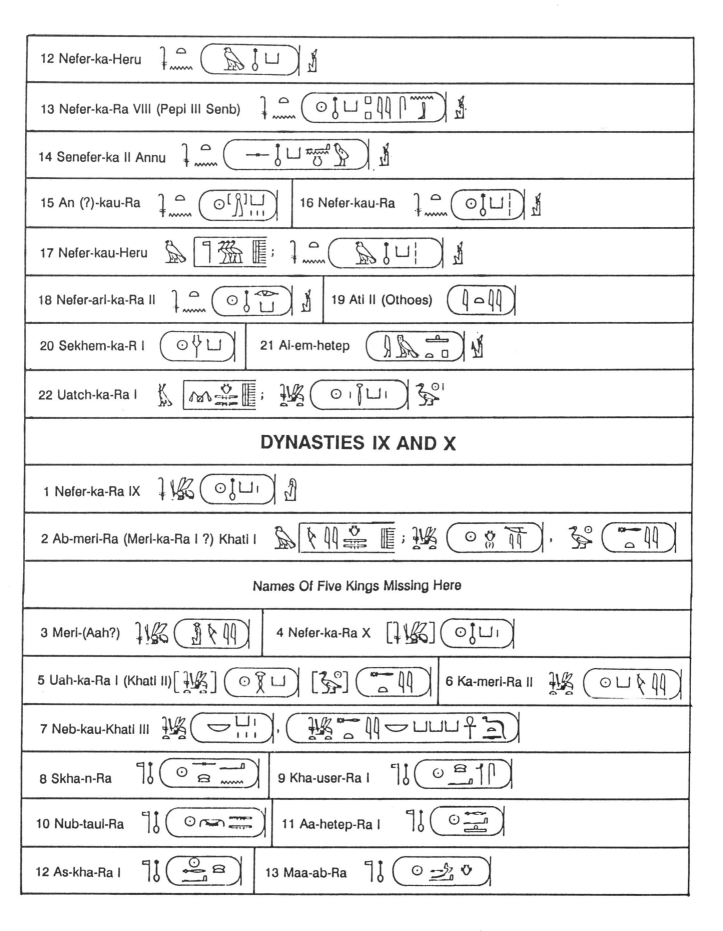

12 Nefer-ka-Heru	
13 Nefer-ka-Ra VIII (Pepi III Senb)	
14 Senefer-ka II Annu	
15 An (?)-kau-Ra	16 Nefer-kau-Ra
17 Nefer-kau-Heru	
18 Nefer-ari-ka-Ra II	19 Ati II (Othoes)
20 Sekhem-ka-R I	21 Ai-em-hetep
22 Uatch-ka-Ra I	

DYNASTIES IX AND X

1 Nefer-ka-Ra IX	
2 Ab-meri-Ra (Meri-ka-Ra I ?) Khati I	

Names Of Five Kings Missing Here

3 Meri-(Aah?)	4 Nefer-ka-Ra X
5 Uah-ka-Ra I (Khati II)	6 Ka-meri-Ra II
7 Neb-kau-Khati III	
8 Skha-n-Ra	9 Kha-user-Ra I
10 Nub-taul-Ra	11 Aa-hetep-Ra I
12 As-kha-Ra I	13 Maa-ab-Ra

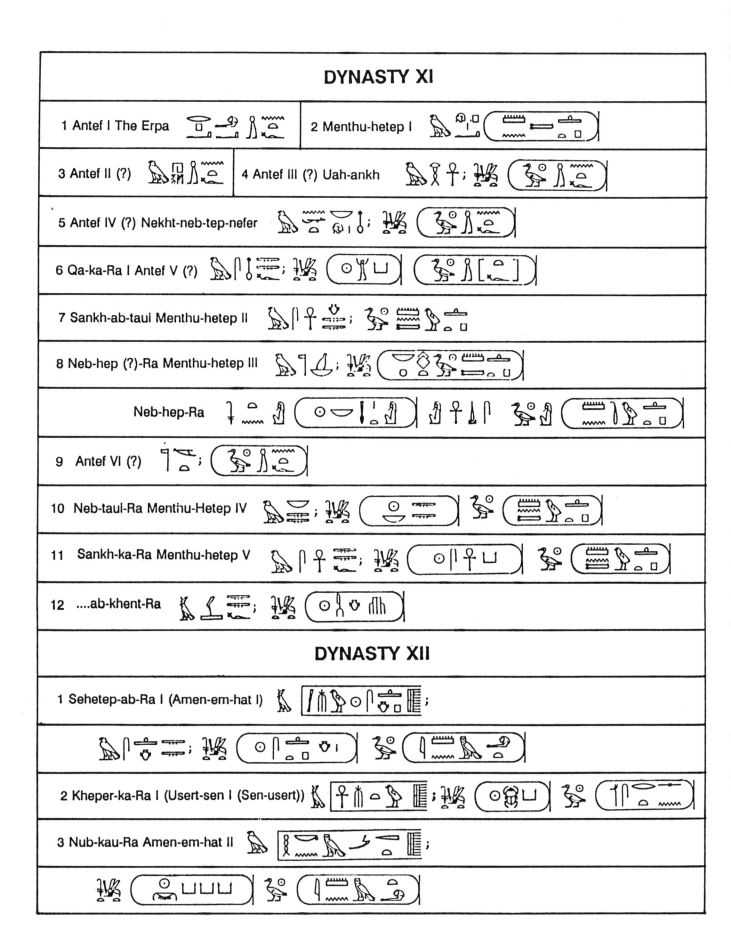

DYNASTY XI	
1 Antef I The Erpa	2 Menthu-hetep I
3 Antef II (?)	4 Antef III (?) Uah-ankh
5 Antef IV (?) Nekht-neb-tep-nefer	
6 Qa-ka-Ra I Antef V (?)	
7 Sankh-ab-taui Menthu-hetep II	
8 Neb-hep (?)-Ra Menthu-hetep III	
Neb-hep-Ra	
9 Antef VI (?)	
10 Neb-taui-Ra Menthu-Hetep IV	
11 Sankh-ka-Ra Menthu-hetep V	
12 ....ab-khent-Ra	

DYNASTY XII

1 Sehetep-ab-Ra I (Amen-em-hat I)

2 Kheper-ka-Ra I (Usert-sen I (Sen-usert))

3 Nub-kau-Ra Amen-em-hat II

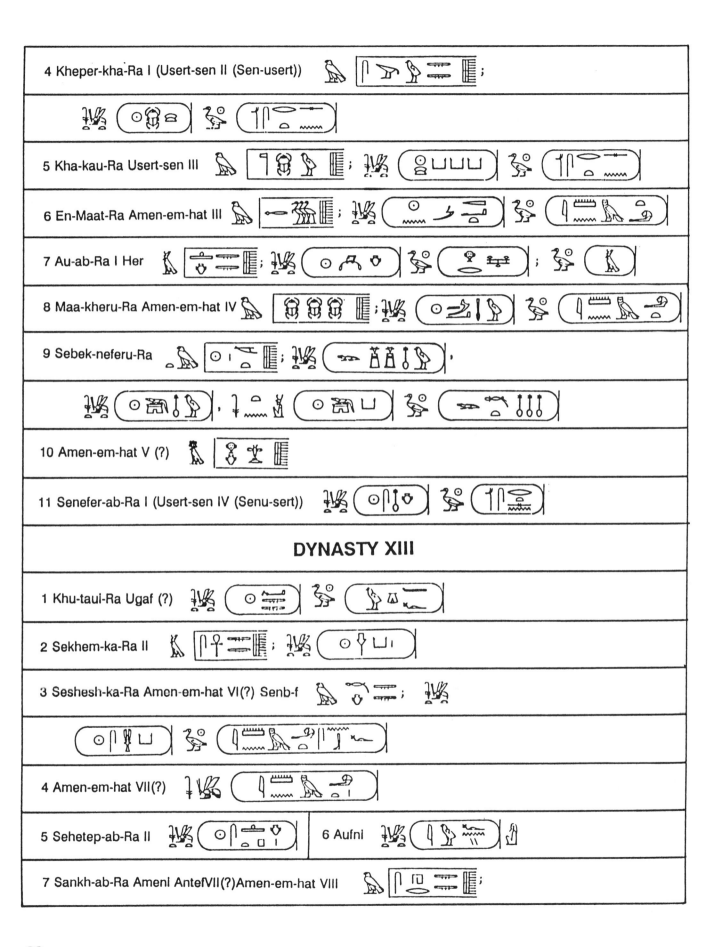

4 Kheper-kha-Ra I (Usert-sen II (Sen-usert))

5 Kha-kau-Ra Usert-sen III

6 En-Maat-Ra Amen-em-hat III

7 Au-ab-Ra I Her

8 Maa-kheru-Ra Amen-em-hat IV

9 Sebek-neferu-Ra

10 Amen-em-hat V (?)

11 Senefer-ab-Ra I (Usert-sen IV (Senu-sert))

DYNASTY XIII

1 Khu-taui-Ra Ugaf (?)

2 Sekhem-ka-Ra II

3 Seshesh-ka-Ra Amen-em-hat VI(?) Senb-f

4 Amen-em-hat VII(?)

5 Sehetep-ab-Ra II

6 Aufni

7 Sankh-ab-Ra Ameni AntefVII(?)Amen-em-hat VIII

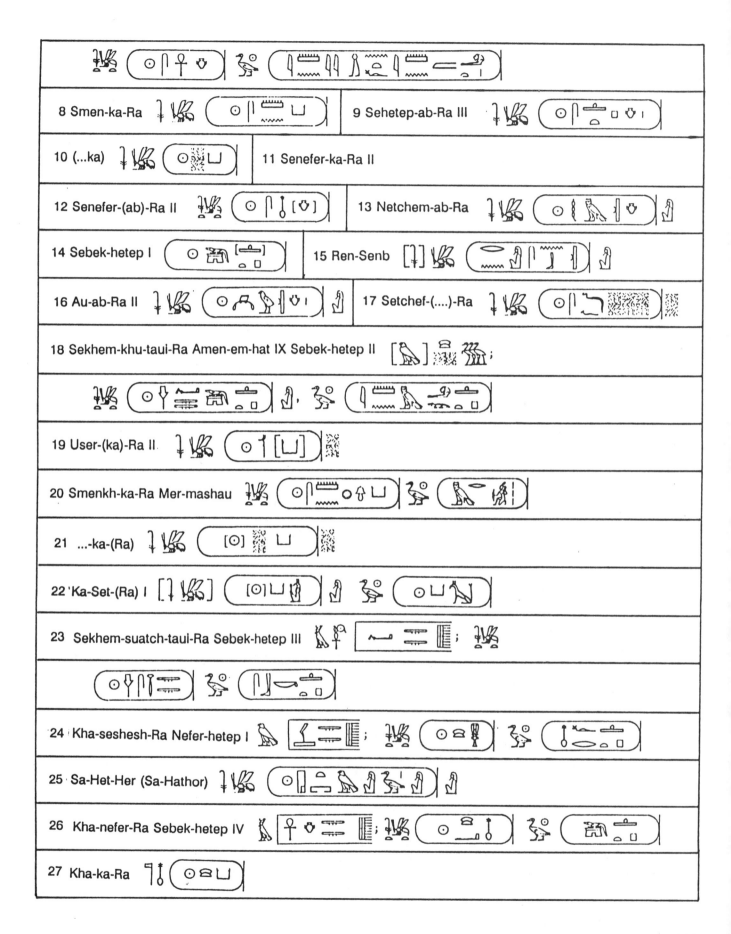

8 Smen-ka-Ra   9 Sehetep-ab-Ra III

10 (...ka)   11 Senefer-ka-Ra II

12 Senefer-(ab)-Ra II   13 Netchem-ab-Ra

14 Sebek-hetep I   15 Ren-Senb

16 Au-ab-Ra II   17 Setchef-(....)-Ra

18 Sekhem-khu-taui-Ra Amen-em-hat IX Sebek-hetep II

19 User-(ka)-Ra II

20 Smenkh-ka-Ra Mer-mashau

21 ...-ka-(Ra)

22 'Ka-Set-(Ra) I

23 Sekhem-suatch-taui-Ra Sebek-hetep III

24 Kha-seshesh-Ra Nefer-hetep I

25 Sa-Het-Her (Sa-Hathor)

26 Kha-nefer-Ra Sebek-hetep IV

27 Kha-ka-Ra

28 Kha-ankh-Ra Sebek-hetep V	
29 Kha-hetep-Ra Sebek-hetep VI	
30 Uah-ab-Ra I Aa-ab	As-ab
31 Mer-nefer-Ra AI I	
32 Mer-hetep-Ra I An (Ana)	
33 Mer-hetep-Ra II Sebek-hetep VII	
34 Sankh-en-Ra Senb (?)	
35 Mer-sekhem-Ra I An...	
36 Suatch-ka-Ra Herua	
37 Mer-netchem-Ra	
38 Mer-ankh-Ra Menthu-hetep VI	
39 Mer-kheper-Ra	
40 Mer-ka(kau)-Ra Sebek-hetep VIII	
41 Tet-nefer-Ra Tatu-mes	
42 Neb-maat-Ra I	
43 Uben-Ra I	
44 ...ka-Ra	45 Neb-maat-Ra II

101

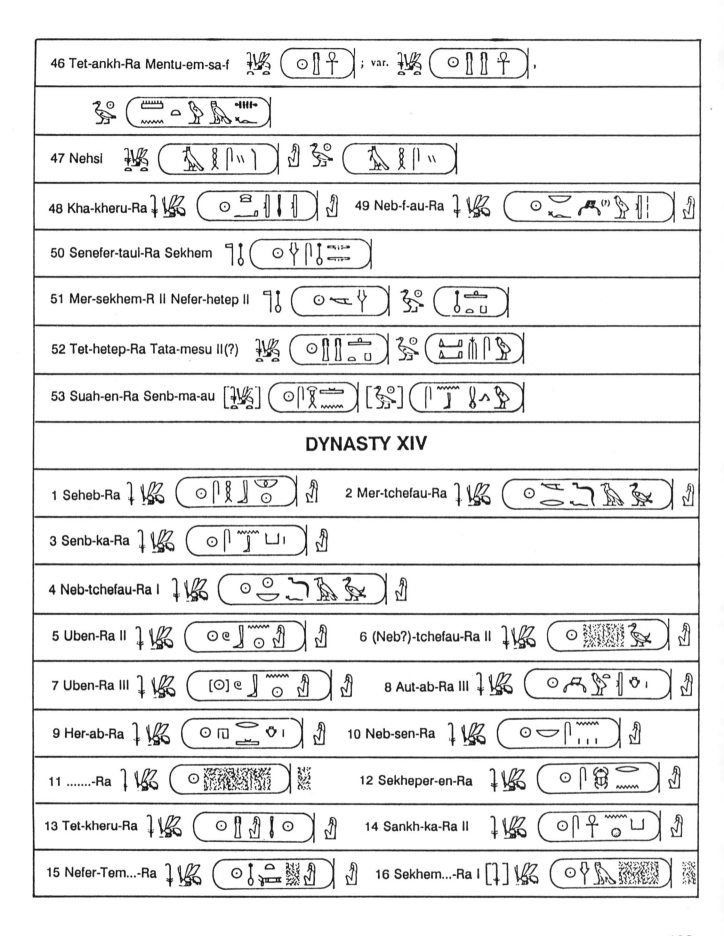

46 Tet-ankh-Ra Mentu-em-sa-f ; var. ,

47 Nehsi

48 Kha-kheru-Ra   49 Neb-f-au-Ra

50 Senefer-taul-Ra Sekhem

51 Mer-sekhem-R II Nefer-hetep II

52 Tet-hetep-Ra Tata-mesu II(?)

53 Suah-en-Ra Senb-ma-au

DYNASTY XIV

1 Seheb-Ra   2 Mer-tchefau-Ra

3 Senb-ka-Ra

4 Neb-tchefau-Ra I

5 Uben-Ra II   6 (Neb?)-tchefau-Ra II

7 Uben-Ra III   8 Aut-ab-Ra III

9 Her-ab-Ra   10 Neb-sen-Ra

11 ....-Ra   12 Sekheper-en-Ra

13 Tet-kheru-Ra   14 Sankh-ka-Ra II

15 Nefer-Tem...-Ra   16 Sekhem...-Ra I

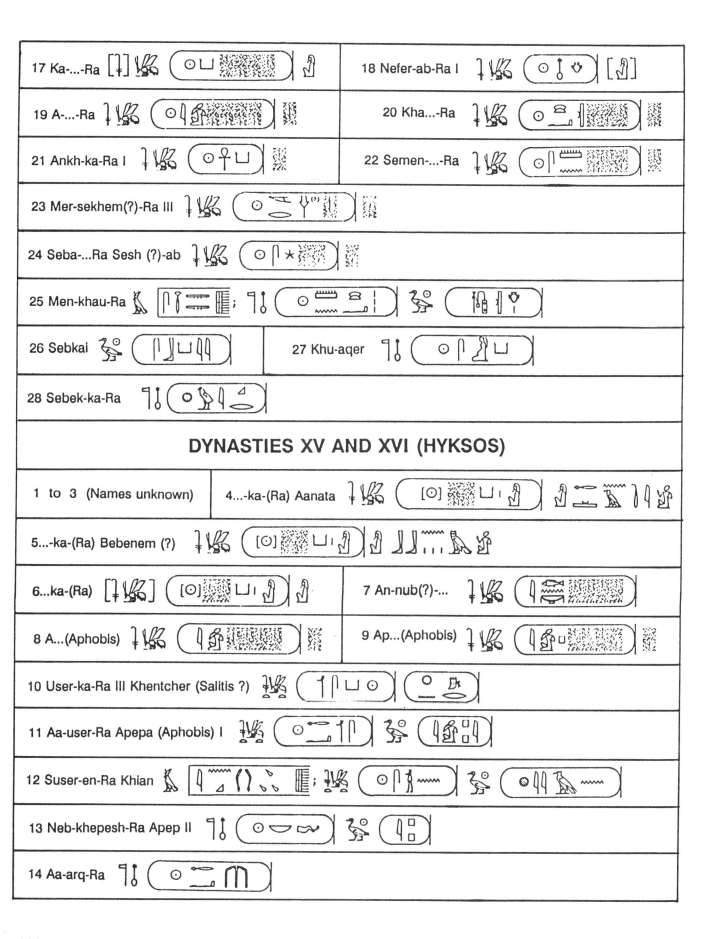

17 Ka-...-Ra		18 Nefer-ab-Ra I	
19 A-...-Ra		20 Kha...-Ra	
21 Ankh-ka-Ra I		22 Semen-...-Ra	
23 Mer-sekhem(?)-Ra III			
24 Seba-...Ra Sesh (?)-ab			
25 Men-khau-Ra			
26 Sebkai		27 Khu-aqer	
28 Sebek-ka-Ra			

DYNASTIES XV AND XVI (HYKSOS)

1 to 3 (Names unknown)	4...-ka-(Ra) Aanata		
5...-ka-(Ra) Bebenem (?)			
6...ka-(Ra)		7 An-nub(?)-...	
8 A...(Aphobis)		9 Ap...(Aphobis)	
10 User-ka-Ra III Khentcher (Salitis ?)			
11 Aa-user-Ra Apepa (Aphobis) I			
12 Suser-en-Ra Khian			
13 Neb-khepesh-Ra Apep II			
14 Aa-arq-Ra			

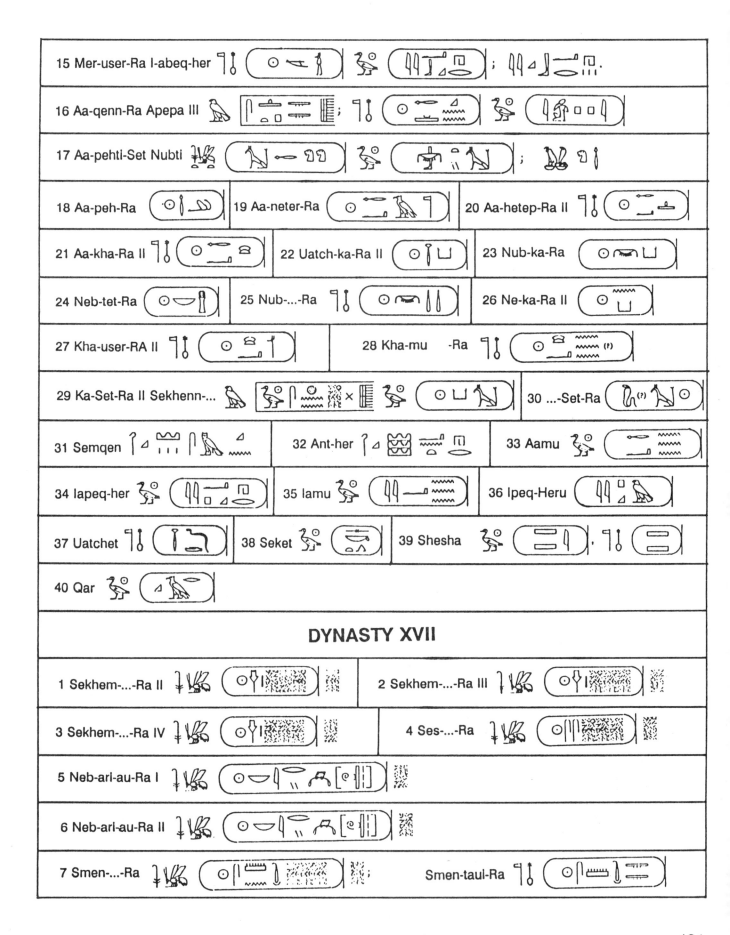

15 Mer-user-Ra I-abeq-her

16 Aa-qenn-Ra Apepa III

17 Aa-pehti-Set Nubti

18 Aa-peh-Ra

19 Aa-neter-Ra

20 Aa-hetep-Ra II

21 Aa-kha-Ra II

22 Uatch-ka-Ra II

23 Nub-ka-Ra

24 Neb-tet-Ra

25 Nub-...-Ra

26 Ne-ka-Ra II

27 Kha-user-RA II

28 Kha-mu   -Ra

29 Ka-Set-Ra II Sekhenn-...

30 ...-Set-Ra

31 Semqen

32 Ant-her

33 Aamu

34 Iapeq-her

35 Iamu

36 Ipeq-Heru

37 Uatchet

38 Seket

39 Shesha

40 Qar

DYNASTY XVII

1 Sekhem-...-Ra II

2 Sekhem-...-Ra III

3 Sekhem-...-Ra IV

4 Ses-...-Ra

5 Neb-arl-au-Ra I

6 Neb-arl-au-Ra II

7 Smen-...-Ra

Smen-taul-Ra

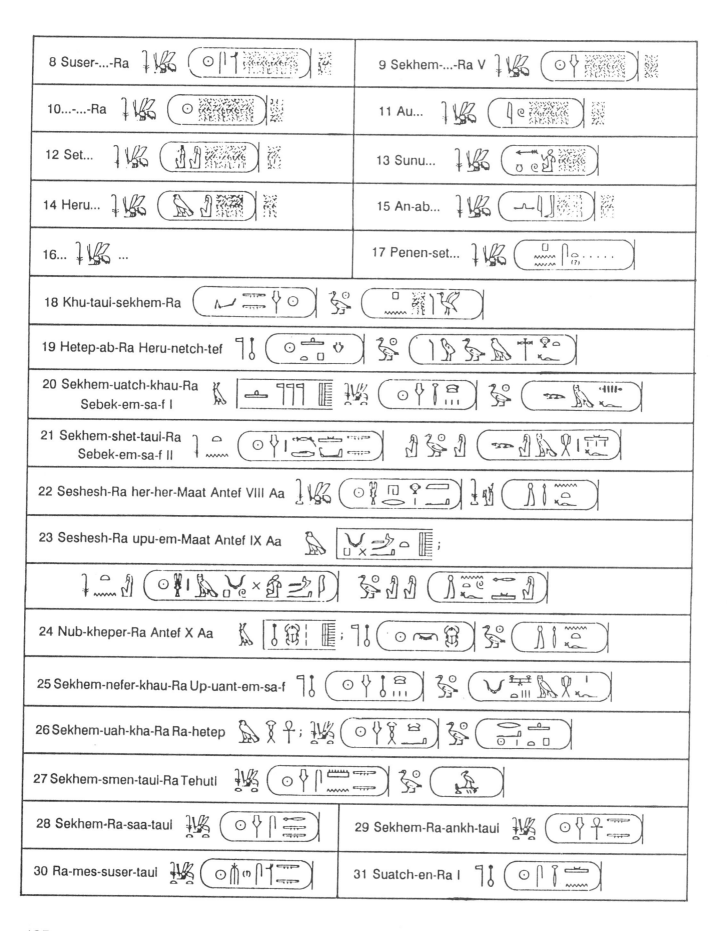

8 Suser-....-Ra	9 Sekhem-....-Ra V
10...-...-Ra	11 Au...
12 Set...	13 Sunu...
14 Heru...	15 An-ab...
16...	17 Penen-set...
18 Khu-taui-sekhem-Ra	
19 Hetep-ab-Ra Heru-netch-tef	
20 Sekhem-uatch-khau-Ra Sebek-em-sa-f I	
21 Sekhem-shet-taui-Ra Sebek-em-sa-f II	
22 Seshesh-Ra her-her-Maat Antef VIII Aa	
23 Seshesh-Ra upu-em-Maat Antef IX Aa	
24 Nub-kheper-Ra Antef X Aa	
25 Sekhem-nefer-khau-Ra Up-uant-em-sa-f	
26 Sekhem-uah-kha-Ra Ra-hetep	
27 Sekhem-smen-taui-Ra Tehuti	
28 Sekhem-Ra-saa-taui	29 Sekhem-Ra-ankh-taui
30 Ra-mes-suser-taui	31 Suatch-en-Ra I

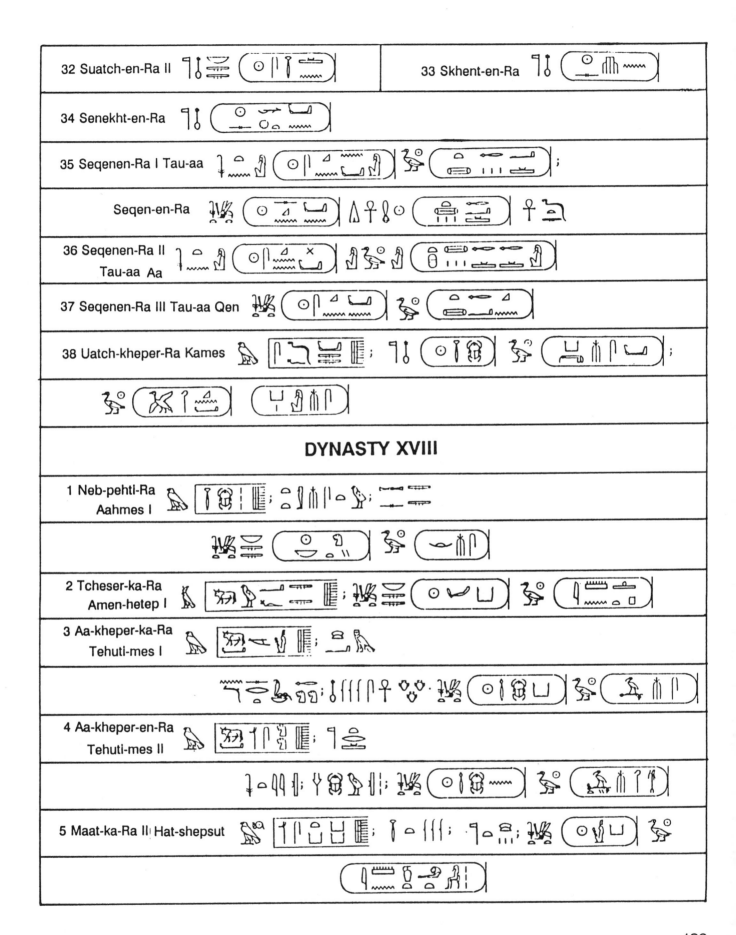

32 Suatch-en-Ra II	33 Skhent-en-Ra

34 Senekht-en-Ra

35 Seqenen-Ra I Tau-aa

Seqen-en-Ra

36 Seqenen-Ra II
Tau-aa Aa

37 Seqenen-Ra III Tau-aa Qen

38 Uatch-kheper-Ra Kames

DYNASTY XVIII

1 Neb-pehti-Ra
Aahmes I

2 Tcheser-ka-Ra
Amen-hetep I

3 Aa-kheper-ka-Ra
Tehuti-mes I

4 Aa-kheper-en-Ra
Tehuti-mes II

5 Maat-ka-Ra II Hat-shepsut

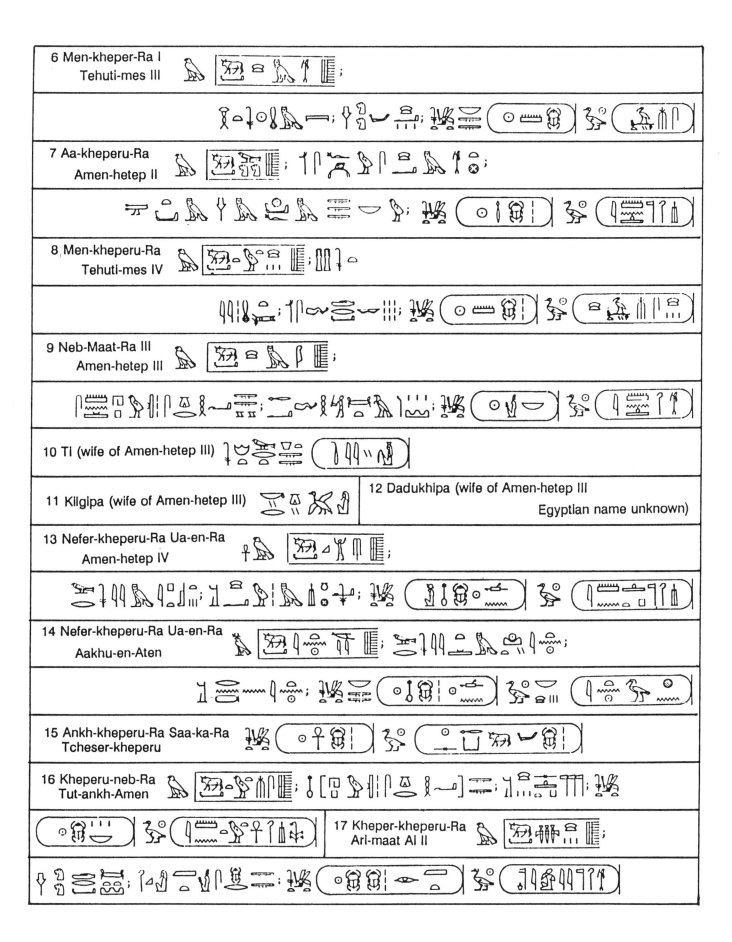

6 Men-kheper-Ra I
Tehuti-mes III

7 Aa-kheperu-Ra
Amen-hetep II

8 Men-kheperu-Ra
Tehuti-mes IV

9 Neb-Maat-Ra III
Amen-hetep III

10 Ti (wife of Amen-hetep III)

11 Kilgipa (wife of Amen-hetep III)

12 Dadukhipa (wife of Amen-hetep III
Egyptian name unknown)

13 Nefer-kheperu-Ra Ua-en-Ra
Amen-hetep IV

14 Nefer-kheperu-Ra Ua-en-Ra
Aakhu-en-Aten

15 Ankh-kheperu-Ra Saa-ka-Ra
Tcheser-kheperu

16 Kheperu-neb-Ra
Tut-ankh-Amen

17 Kheper-kheperu-Ra
Ari-maat Ai II

18 Tcheser-kheperu-Ra Amen-em-heb mer-en-Heru	

DYNASTY XIX

1 Men-pehti-Ra Rameses I	
2 Men-maat-Ra I Seti I meri-Ptah	
3 User-maat-Ra I setep-en-Ra Rameses II	
4 Ba-en-Ra I Mer-en-Ptah I (Menephthah) hetep-her-maat	
5 Men-ma-Ra Amen-meses	
6 User-kheperu-Ra mer Amen Seti II Mer-en-Ptah II	
7 Aakhu-en-Ra setep-en-Ra Sa-Ptah I Mer-en-Ptah III	
8 Arsu	

DYNASTY XX

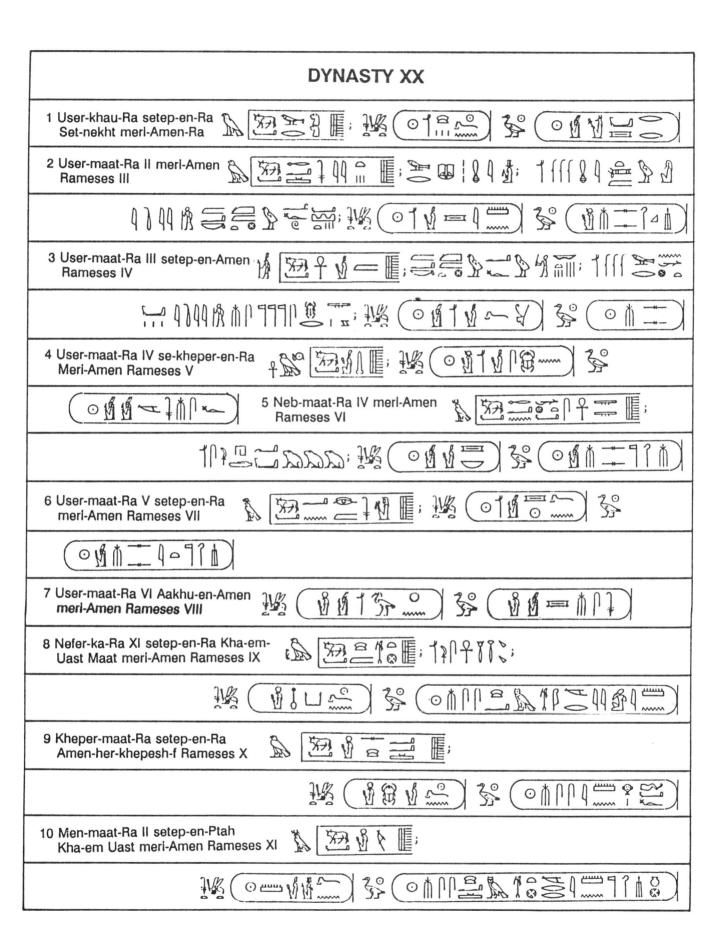

1 User-khau-Ra setep-en-Ra
Set-nekht meri-Amen-Ra

2 User-maat-Ra II meri-Amen
Rameses III

3 User-maat-Ra III setep-en-Amen
Rameses IV

4 User-maat-Ra IV se-kheper-en-Ra
Meri-Amen Rameses V

5 Neb-maat-Ra IV meri-Amen
Rameses VI

6 User-maat-Ra V setep-en-Ra
meri-Amen Rameses VII

7 User-maat-Ra VI Aakhu-en-Amen
meri-Amen Rameses VIII

8 Nefer-ka-Ra XI setep-en-Ra Kha-em-
Uast Maat meri-Amen Rameses IX

9 Kheper-maat-Ra setep-en-Ra
Amen-her-khepesh-f Rameses X

10 Men-maat-Ra II setep-en-Ptah
Kha-em Uast meri-Amen Rameses XI

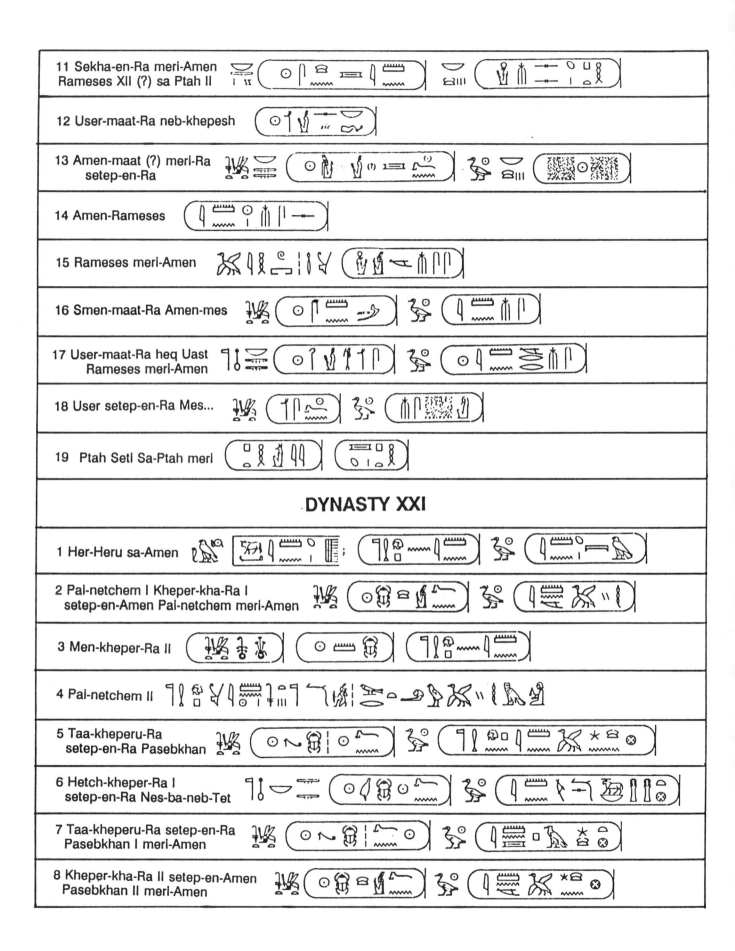

11 Sekha-en-Ra meri-Amen
Rameses XII (?) sa Ptah II

12 User-maat-Ra neb-khepesh

13 Amen-maat (?) meri-Ra
setep-en-Ra

14 Amen-Rameses

15 Rameses meri-Amen

16 Smen-maat-Ra Amen-mes

17 User-maat-Ra heq Uast
Rameses meri-Amen

18 User setep-en-Ra Mes...

19 Ptah Seti Sa-Ptah meri

DYNASTY XXI

1 Her-Heru sa-Amen

2 Pai-netchem I Kheper-kha-Ra I
setep-en-Amen Pai-netchem meri-Amen

3 Men-kheper-Ra II

4 Pai-netchem II

5 Taa-kheperu-Ra
setep-en-Ra Pasebkhan

6 Hetch-kheper-Ra I
setep-en-Ra Nes-ba-neb-Tet

7 Taa-kheperu-Ra setep-en-Ra
Pasebkhan I meri-Amen

8 Kheper-kha-Ra II setep-en-Amen
Pasebkhan II meri-Amen

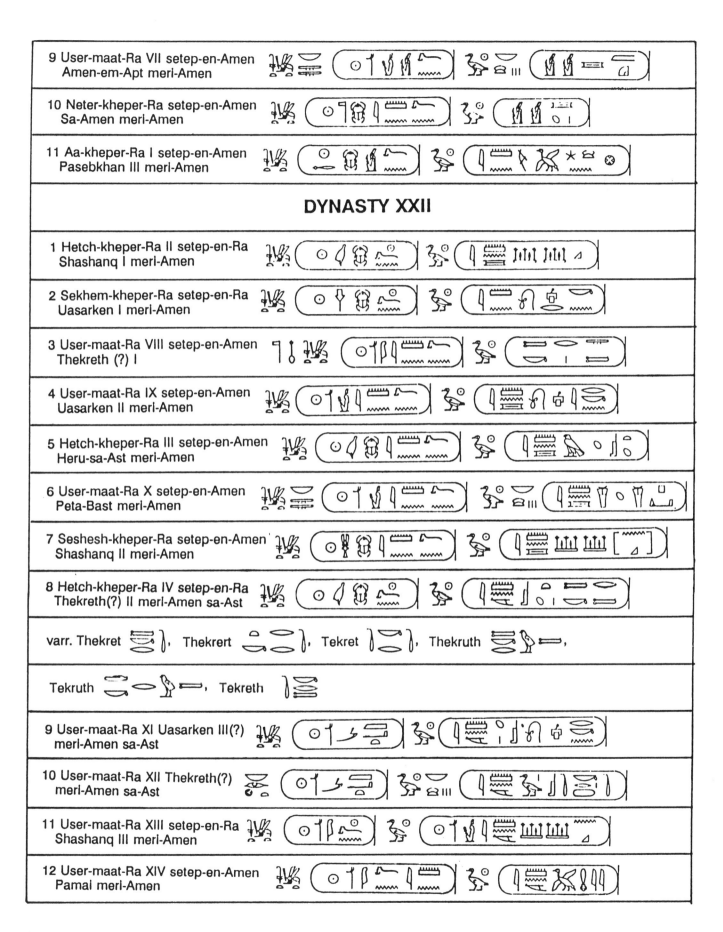

9 User-maat-Ra VII setep-en-Amen
Amen-em-Apt meri-Amen

10 Neter-kheper-Ra setep-en-Amen
Sa-Amen meri-Amen

11 Aa-kheper-Ra I setep-en-Amen
Pasebkhan III meri-Amen

DYNASTY XXII

1 Hetch-kheper-Ra II setep-en-Ra
Shashanq I meri-Amen

2 Sekhem-kheper-Ra setep-en-Ra
Uasarken I meri-Amen

3 User-maat-Ra VIII setep-en-Amen
Thekreth (?) I

4 User-maat-Ra IX setep-en-Amen
Uasarken II meri-Amen

5 Hetch-kheper-Ra III setep-en-Amen
Heru-sa-Ast meri-Amen

6 User-maat-Ra X setep-en-Amen
Peta-Bast meri-Amen

7 Seshesh-kheper-Ra setep-en-Amen
Shashanq II meri-Amen

8 Hetch-kheper-Ra IV setep-en-Ra
Thekreth(?) II meri-Amen sa-Ast

varr. Thekret, Thekrert, Tekret, Thekruth,

Tekruth, Tekreth

9 User-maat-Ra XI Uasarken III(?)
meri-Amen sa-Ast

10 User-maat-Ra XII Thekreth(?)
meri-Amen sa-Ast

11 User-maat-Ra XIII setep-en-Ra
Shashanq III meri-Amen

12 User-maat-Ra XIV setep-en-Amen
Pamai meri-Amen

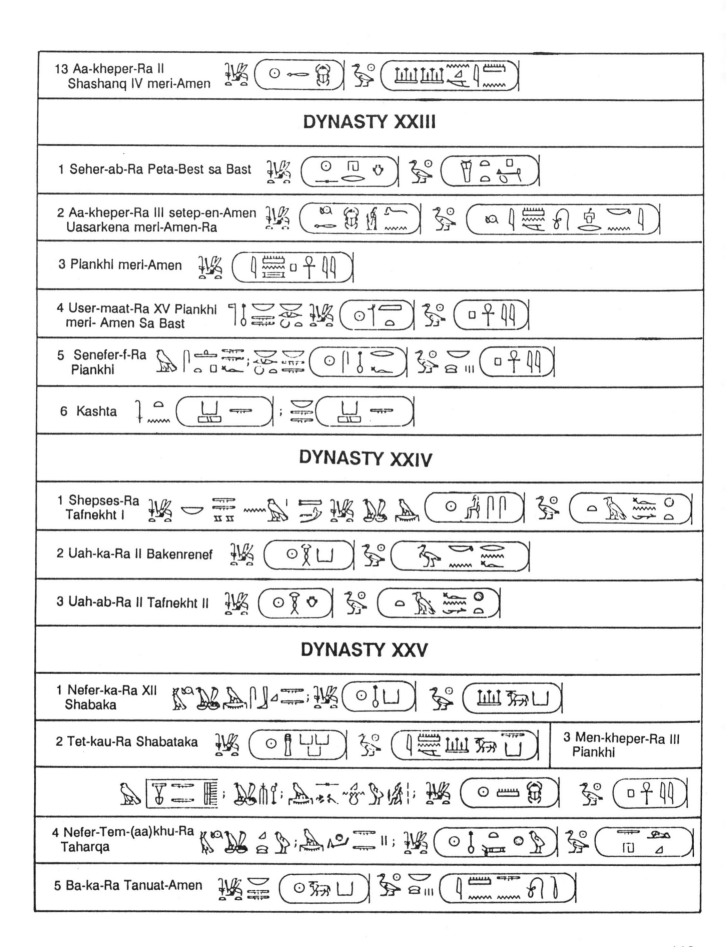

13 Aa-kheper-Ra II
Shashanq IV meri-Amen

DYNASTY XXIII

1 Seher-ab-Ra Peta-Best sa Bast

2 Aa-kheper-Ra III setep-en-Amen
Uasarkena meri-Amen-Ra

3 Piankhi meri-Amen

4 User-maat-Ra XV Piankhi
meri- Amen Sa Bast

5 Senefer-f-Ra
Piankhi

6 Kashta

DYNASTY XXIV

1 Shepses-Ra
Tafnekht I

2 Uah-ka-Ra II Bakenrenef

3 Uah-ab-Ra II Tafnekht II

DYNASTY XXV

1 Nefer-ka-Ra XII
Shabaka

2 Tet-kau-Ra Shabataka

3 Men-kheper-Ra III
Piankhi

4 Nefer-Tem-(aa)khu-Ra
Taharqa

5 Ba-ka-Ra Tanuat-Amen

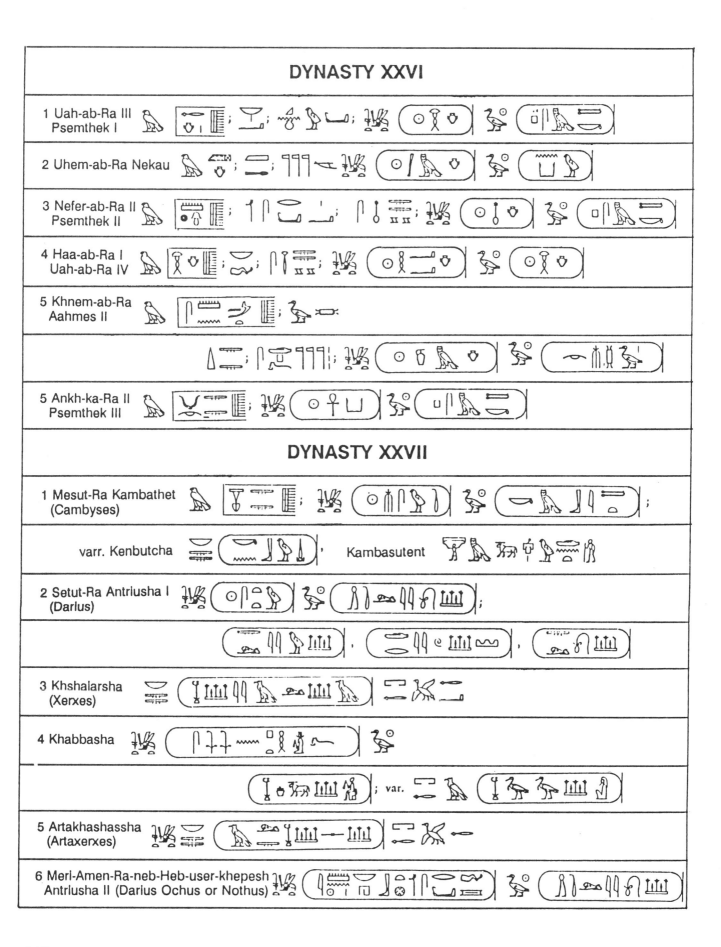

DYNASTY XXVI

1 Uah-ab-Ra III
Psemthek I

2 Uhem-ab-Ra Nekau

3 Nefer-ab-Ra II
Psemthek II

4 Haa-ab-Ra I
Uah-ab-Ra IV

5 Khnem-ab-Ra
Aahmes II

5 Ankh-ka-Ra II
Psemthek III

DYNASTY XXVII

1 Mesut-Ra Kambathet
(Cambyses)

varr. Kenbutcha   Kambasutent

2 Setut-Ra Antriusha I
(Darius)

3 Khshalarsha
(Xerxes)

4 Khabbasha

; var.

5 Artakhashassha
(Artaxerxes)

6 Meri-Amen-Ra-neb-Heb-user-khepesh
Antriusha II (Darius Ochus or Nothus)

DYNASTY XXVIII
(Wanting)

DYNASTY XXIX

1 Ba-en-Ra II Naifaaurut

2 Khnem-maat-Ra
  Hagr

3 Ptah-user setep-en-Ra
  Psa-Mut

DYNASTY XXX

1 Senetchem-ab-Ra setep-en-Amen
  Nekht-Heru-heb meri-Amen

2 Ari-maat-en-Ra Tche-Her
  setep-en-An-her

3 Kheper-ka-Ra II Nekht-neb-f

4 Qa-ka-Ra II An II

5 User-maat-Ra XVI Setep-en-Amen
  Amen-rut meri-Amen

HELLENIC KINGS IN EGYPT

6 Meri-Amen setep-en-Ra Arksantrs
  (Alexander The Great)

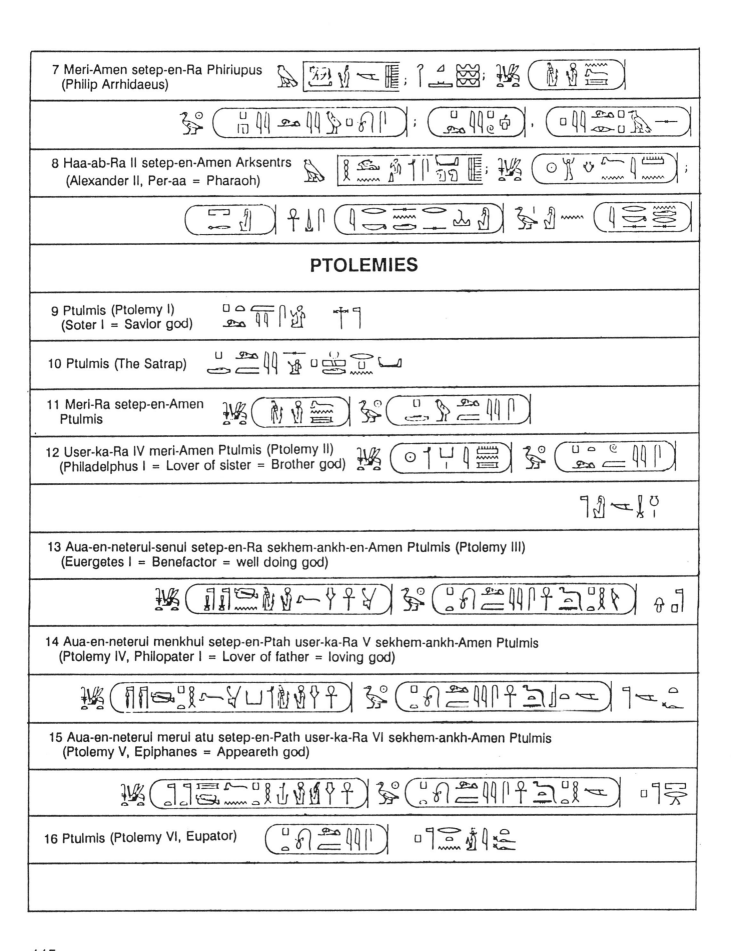

7 Meri-Amen setep-en-Ra Phiriupus
(Philip Arrhidaeus)

8 Haa-ab-Ra II setep-en-Amen Arksentrs
(Alexander II, Per-aa = Pharaoh)

PTOLEMIES

9 Ptulmis (Ptolemy I)
(Soter I = Savior god)

10 Ptulmis (The Satrap)

11 Meri-Ra setep-en-Amen Ptulmis

12 User-ka-Ra IV meri-Amen Ptulmis (Ptolemy II)
(Philadelphus I = Lover of sister = Brother god)

13 Aua-en-neterui-senui setep-en-Ra sekhem-ankh-en-Amen Ptulmis (Ptolemy III)
(Euergetes I = Benefactor = well doing god)

14 Aua-en-neterui menkhui setep-en-Ptah user-ka-Ra V sekhem-ankh-Amen Ptulmis
(Ptolemy IV, Philopater I = Lover of father = loving god)

15 Aua-en-neterui merui atu setep-en-Path user-ka-Ra VI sekhem-ankh-Amen Ptulmis
(Ptolemy V, Epiphanes = Appeareth god)

16 Ptulmis (Ptolemy VI, Eupator)

17 Aua-en-neterui-perui I Kheper-Ptah setep-en-Amen ari-maat-Ra Ptulmis
(Ptolemy VII, Philometer I)

18 Neos Philopator-P-neter hunnu Tef-f-meri
(Ptolemy VIII, Philopator II)

19 Aua-en-neterui perui II setep-en-Ptah ari-maat-Ra sekhem-ankh-Amen Ptulmis
(Ptolemy IX, Euergetes II)

20 Aua-en-neter-menkh I (Aua-en)-neter-t Netchti-menkh-t setep-en-Ptah ari-maat-Ra
sekhem-ankh-Amen Ptulmis (Ptolemy X, Soter II, Philometer II)

21 Aua-en-neter-menkh II (Aua-en)-neter-t-menkh-t-Ra setep-en-Ptah ari-maat-Ra
senen-ankh-en-Amen Ptulmis (Ptolemy XI, Alexander I, Philometer III)

22 Ptolemy XII, Alexander II (Cartouches unknown)

23 Aua-en-p-neter-enti-nehem setep-en-Ptah ari-maat-Ra sekhem-ankh-Amen Ptulmis
(Ptolemy XIII, Philopator III, Philadelphus II)

24 Ptolemy XIV (Cartouches unknown)

25 Ptolemy XV (Cartouches unknown)

26 Ptulmis, Philopator Philometor, Caesar lord of crowns
(Ptolemy XVI, Philopator IV, Philometor IV)

PTOLEMAIC QUEENS AND PRINCESSES

1 Berenice I (Barniga), fourth wife of Ptolemy I

2 Arsinoe (Arsenai), Philadelpha, daugther of Ptolemy I and sister and wife of Ptolemy II

3 Arsinoe II Philadelpha Khnem-ab-en-Maat meri-neteru Arsenai (?)

4 Philtera (Pilutera), youngest daughter of Ptolemy I

5 Berenice II (Barniga), wife of Ptolemy III

6 Berenice III (Barniga), daughter of Ptolemy III and Berenice II

7 Arsinoe III (Arsenai), sister and wife of Ptolemy IV

8 Cleopatra (Qlauptra) I Syra, daughter of Antiochus III and wife of Ptolemy V

9 Cleopatra II Soteira, sister and wife of Ptolemy VII, and sister of Ptolemy IX

10 Cleopatra III Kokke, niece and wife of Ptolemy IX

11 Cleopatra IV Berenice IV wife of Ptolemy XI

12 Cleopatra V, Tryphaena sister and wife of Ptolemy XIII

13 Cleopatra VI, and her Son Caesarion

117

CHAPTER 4

HIEROGLYPHIC (ANCIENT EGYPTIAN FIGURE LANGUAGE)

The Rosetta Stone (See Figure No. 43)

This stone led to the decipherment of Hieroglyphics. In 1799 Napolean's solders were demolishing a wall of Fort Julian, on the west branch of the Nile river, at the village of Rosetta, located just a few miles from the Mediterranean Sea and found a stele (stone tablet) which was a black basalt slab with part of the top and bottom broken off. Even in its broken off state the Rosetta stone is of good size, measuring 3 ft. 9 inches in height, 2 ft. 4 1/2 inches in width, and 11 inches thick. It weighed about 1,500 pounds.

At the top of this slab were parts of 14 lines of Hieroglyphics, the middle section contained parts of 32 lines of Demotic (cursive script which replaced hieratic for general use), and in the bottom section there were parts of 54 lines of Greek capital letters. The importance of the stone's three distinct inscriptions was recognized at once that they could be versions of a single text in three different scripts: Hieroglyphics, Demotic and the Greek language in capital letters. As it finally turned out, this stone contained the Decree of a council of priests of Memphis in 196 B.C. The text concerns the honors bestowed on Ptolemy V by the priests and temples of Egypt in return for the service rendered by him to Egypt, at home and aboard. Priestly privileges, especially those of an economic nature, are listed in great detail.

The broken off missing lines of the Decree were later obtained from other similar stelae: the stele of Damanhur, and from a copy of the Decree on the wall of the temple of Isis, on the island of Philae. By comparing the Hieroglyphics of the Rosetta stone, the Damanhur stone, other inscriptions and the Banks Obelisk, it was

determined that all royal names were placed in elongated ovals, , called "cartouches". It was further determined that the Hieroglyphic figures in the cartouches represented the sounds of the Greek letters and thus they represented the Greek form of royal names as shown below:

Ptolemy

P T O L E M Y

Kleopatra

K L E O P A T R A 10 11

The numbers 10 and 11 have no Greek letter equivalents but were used only for the ending of feminine names.

Hellenic Kingdoms In Egypt (333-30 B.C.)

Alexander The Great was the first of the Hellenic kings mentioned in the Rosetta text, but he lived only a short time and died at the age of 33 years. His vast Greek-Macedonian Kingdom was divided into four parts between his four general: Ptolemy I (Egypt), Cassander (Macedonia), Lysimachus (Thrace), and Seleucus (Syria).

It is Alexander and the first five Ptolemy kings and there Queens that are mentioned in the text of the Rosetta Stone. It is their Greek names that led to the decipherment of their equivalent Hieroglyphic figures. Their Hieroglyphic cartouches can be referred to by checking their listings in Dynasty XXX at the end of Chapter 3.

FIGURE	SOUND	FIGURE USED	FIGURE	SOUND	FIGURE USED
		A PSEUDO HIEROGLYPHIC ALPHABET			
🦅	A	VULTURE		R & L	LION
	A or I	FLOWERING REED		H	REED SHELTER
	A	FOREARM AND HAND		H	WICK OF TWISTED FLAX
	I or Y	TWO FLOWERING REEDS		KH	SIEVE
\\	I or Y	OBLIQUE STROKES		S	DOOR BOLT
	U or W	QUAIL CHICKEN		S	FOLDED CLOTH
	U or W	ROPE		SH	POOL
	B	FOOT		K	BASKET WITH HANDLE
	P	STOOL		K	HILL
	F	HORNED VIPER		G	JAR STAND
	M	OWL		T	LOAF
	M	SIDE		T	CLUB
~~	N	WATER		TH	TETHERING ROPE
	N	RED CROWN OF NORTH EGYPT		T or D	HAND
	R & L	MOUTH		TCH, S	SNAKE

THE ROSETTA STONE

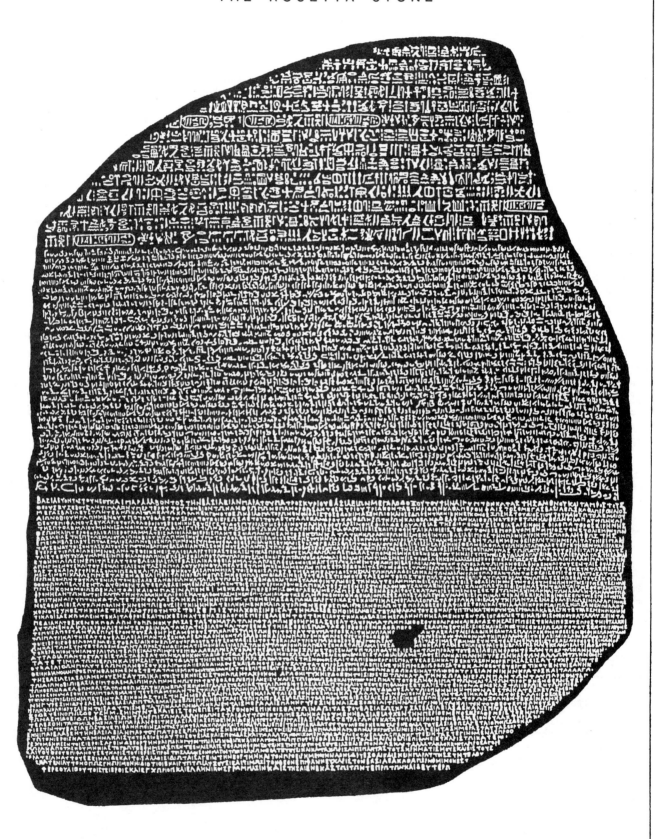

Hieroglyphics

The origin of this ancient Egyptian Figure Language is not known, but its use started before the Dynastic Period about (4400 B.C.). Except for names and a few titles, the oldest inscriptions cannot be read. In the period of the 3rd Dynasty (3966-3766 B.C.) many of the principles of Hieroglyphic writings were standardized and the number of figures used were held at about 2,000. The form of the figures expressed and communicated their ideas by using a combination of all kinds of: animals, birds, reptiles, insects, trees, plants, buildings, ships, men, women, limbs of men, limbs of animals, celestial objects, instruments, etc. For this writing does not express the intended idea by a combination of syllables, one with another, but by the outward appearance of what has been copied. Hieroglyphics was used mostly by the priests and their scribes in the Temples, and it was perpetuated by them. Most people outside the Temples, even the kings, couldn't read and write it. Hieroglyphics was used for the last time about 394 A.D.

Decipherers of Hieroglyphics: Jean Francois Champollion (father of the decipherment), Dr. Thomas Young, J. Zoega, DuThell, A. I. Silvestre de Sacy, J. D. Akerbald, Athanasius Kircher, and many others.

For centuries scholars were not able to decipher the Hieroglyphics until the Rosetta stone was found in 1799 by Napolean's solders. This tablet of hard stone was inscribed with the, "Decree Of Memphis", of 196 B.C. This Decree was drafted in Greek by a council of priests containing the good deeds of king Ptolemy V and honors which they proposed to pay him were listed. They further ordered that a copy of the Greek Decree, together with its translation in Egyptian Demotic Script and Hieroglyphic languages be engraved on tablets of hard stone and set up in every temple of Egypt. Greek was the Royal language of the Ptolemy Kings and for this reason the Degree was first written in Greek.

Now at long last it was possible to translate immediately the Greek Decree and use it as the key to decipher its corresponding Hieroglyphic Figures. Scholars found that royal names were always placed in an elongated oval, "cartouche", as was mentioned before. Thus they were able to relate the Greek letter sounds of Alexander, Cleopatra, and Ptolemy to their corresponding Hieroglyphic Figures. For this reason Hieroglyphics has no true Alphabet and true vowels as we know them in the English language, but is made up of figures which the scholars equated to the Greek language sounds of its letters by using consonants and pseudo vowels. Since combinations of consonants are not pronounceable, the letter "e" is usually placed between the consonants to make them pronounceable. Hieroglyphic writing follows these basic principles:

(1) A Hieroglyphic figure can be used in a pictorial way. The figure of a man with his hand to his mouth might stand for the word "eat". Similarly, the word "sun" would be represented by a large circle with a smaller circle in its center.

(2) A Hieroglyphic figure can be used in a phonetic way. The figures are used only for their sounds regardless of what they actually represent.

(3) A Hieroglyphic figure might represent or imply another word suggested by the figure. If the figure for the word "sun", large circle with a smaller circle in its center, is followed by a single stroke, it could serve as the figure for "day", "month", "time", etc. Also, the figure for the word "sun" serves as the name of the Sun god Ra. The figure for "eat" could also represent the more conceptual word "silent" by suggesting the covering of the mouth.

(4) The figures also serve as representatives of words that shared consonants in the same order. Thus the Egyptian word for "pool" and "lake", both spelled with the consonants, mn(men), could be rendered by the same Hieroglyphic figure.

(5) Hieroglyphic figures can stand for individual and or a combination of consonants.

(6) Normally, Hieroglyphic figures are read opposite to the direction that the figures are facing which may be either left or right. Also, they may be read in vertical columns. All royal names, kings and queens are placed in an elongated oval called a "cartouche".

In Hieroglyphic Inscriptions

The figures are used in two ways: (1) pictorial and (2) phonetic. In the pictorial system a word is expressed by its figure thus: ～～～ = mu = "water". In the phonetic system the word for "water" is written, 🦉 ⌒ = m + u, with no regard being paid to the fact that, 🦉 , represents an owl, and, ⌒ = a rope, because only their sounds are needed.

Phonetic figures are: (1) Alphabetic, 🦉 = m, ∏ = s, and 🦅 = u; or (2) Syllabic, as ⊏ = mer, 🪲 = kheper, and ⊏ = hetep. The figure ⌀ = nefer can be written in many ways: ⌀⊂ , ⊏⌀ , ⊏⌀ , ⌀⊏ , ～～⌀⊏ .

The pictorial figures are also used as determinatives, and are placed after words written phonetically to determine their meaning. For example, "nem" has several meaning: "to sleep", "to walk", "to go back", "again", and without a determinative the meaning of the word "nem" when used alone can easily be mistaken.

Determinatives are of two kinds: (1) pictorial, and (2) generic. Thus if after the word, 🦆🦉 = mau, the figure of a cat, 🐈 , is placed then the meaning is "cat" (this is a pictorial determinative). If after, ⊏🦅 = kerh, the figure of a night sky with a star in it, ⊡ , is placed, then the meaning is "darkness" (this is a generic determinative).

A word has frequently more than one determinative for example: in the word, 🦵🦅🦆🦉～～⊞ = bah = "to over flow"; 🦆 is a determinative of the sound bah; ～～ is a determinative of water; ⊞ is a determinative of a lake or collection of water; and ˅ is a determinative of ground.

Plurals and their variants are expressed in the following ways: By writing their figure three times 🦆🦆🦆 = offerings; 🏔🏔🏔 = fields; and ⊏🦅🦉: = great ones. By writing the determinative three times, 🦅⊏🐈🐈🐈 = goddesses; ∏🔲▦▦▦ = nomes (states); and 🪶🪶🪶 = gods and goddesses. By adding three strokes, ⫶ ,once to the pictorial figure: 🦅⫶ = gods; 🦅🦅🪶⫶ = gods; and 🪶⫶ = gods.

The word "temple" is expressed pictorially, ⬚⬚ , or ⬚⬚ , that is god's house. The word for "queen" is expressed by the figures for king and women, ⬚⬚ . ⬚⬚ ⬚⬚ = Per-aa, literally, "house great", from which we obtain the word "Pharaoh".

As examples of sound of pictorial figures which have become mere syllables, in other words, maybe quoted,

⬚⬚ = "men" in ⬚⬚ = breasts. ⬚⬚ = "mes" in ⬚⬚ = ear; and ⬚⬚ = skin.

⬚⬚ = "mer" in ⬚⬚ = urgent. ⬚⬚ = "shen" in ⬚⬚ = tempest.

DETERMINATIVES USED IN WORDS	
= to eat	= stars
= to speak words	= to drink
= priest	= flower
= Syria	= city of Abydos
= west	= house
= fish	= feeble, exhausted
= violence	= men
= sandstone	= to stand
= two arms	= mouse
= time	= flesh
WORDS WITH TWO DETERMINATIVES	
= cool water	= taste
WORDS WITH THREE DETERMINATIVES	
= bath	= to slay

IN THE INSCRIPTION BELOW THE DETERMINATIVES
ARE MARKED WITH THE LETTER D AND THE SYLLABLES
ARE MARKED WITH THE LETTER S

Not   a daughter   of a poor man   did I harm;

not   a widow   did I oppress;

not   a field laborer   did I repulse   him;

not a shepherd did I quarrel with; not was there the chief

of a gang of 5 men from   I took away   his men

for   labor taxes;   not existed   oppression

in   my   time;   not was there   a hungry man

in   my   time;   when came   years

hungry   I stood up,   I plowed

the fields   all

Rameses II

He was one of the leading Pharaohs of a line of kings that covers a period of forty centuries of Egyptian history. His monuments are extensive, beginning at Memphis and go on increasing up the Nile to Karnak, Luxor, Aswan, and ending with the Temple of Rameses II at Abu Simbel. This temple is one of the largest and finest in all of Egypt. Rameses II built it to commemorate his victory over the Kheta in Syria (see Figure No. 43).

This temple is cut out of solid rock to a depth of 185 feet, and the surface of the rock was cut away for a space of 100 feet square to form the front of the temple, which is ornamented by four colossal statues of Rameses II, 66 feet high, seated on thrones, cut out of the rock. A cornice is decorated with twenty-one figures, , and beneath it, in the middle, is a line of Hieroglyphics, , ta-na-nek-ankh-user-neb ("I give to thee life and strength"). On the right side of this, are four figures of Ra, (sun-god), , and eight cartouches containing the "prenomen" of Rameses II, , Ra-user-maat-en-Ra (Ra strong in truth approved of Ra), with a uraeus on each side. On the left side are four figures of Amen (king of the gods), and eight cartouches as on the right side. Around the base of the four large colossi are many small statues of gods and many Hieroglyphic inscriptions. Over the door to the temple is a statue of Harmakhis (alternative name of Ra), ,and on each side of him is a figure of Rameses II making offerings to him, . Each colossal has the "prenomen" name of Rames II, , inscribed upon each shoulder and breast.

On the south wall, inside the temple, is the following inscription, sculptured in high relief and elaborately colored, honoring Rameses II for his works. The columns are read left to right, top to bottom. The spaces A, and B, at the end of column No. 5 contain the "prenomen" and "nomen" names of Rameses II. A detailed translation, column by column, and figure by figure follows on the next four pages.

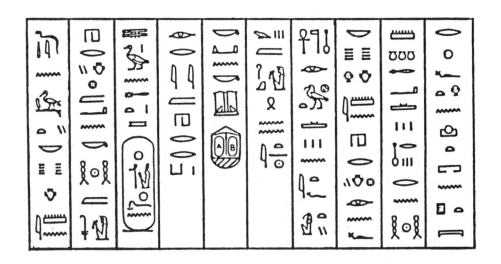

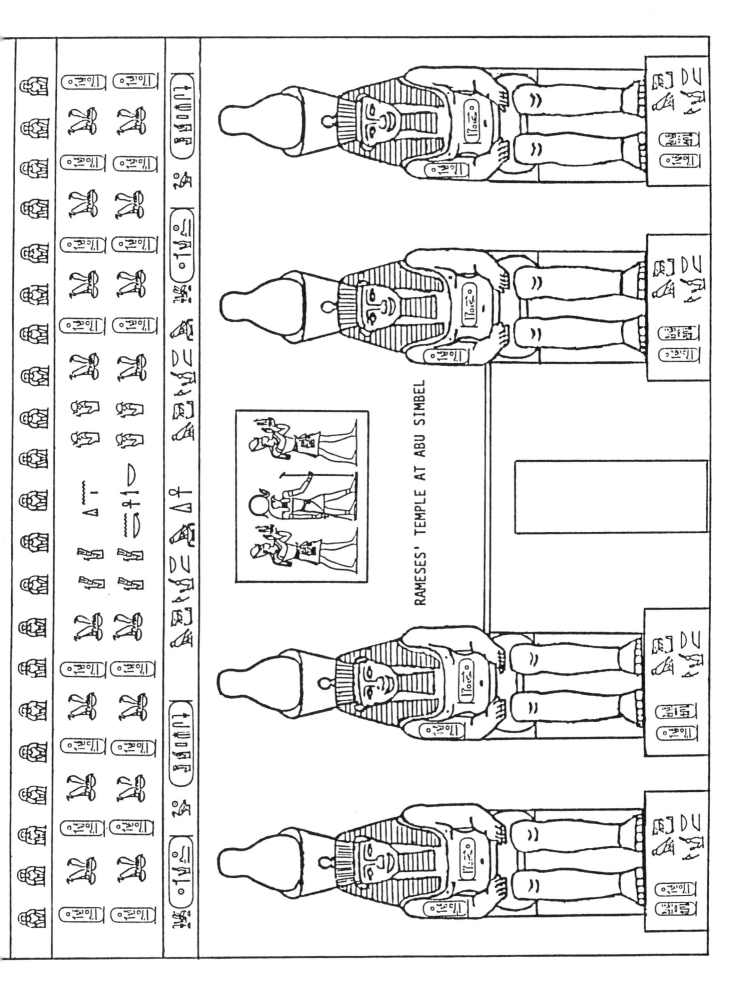

RAMESES' TEMPLE AT ABU SIMBEL

FIGURE NO. 44
RAMESES II (THE GREAT)
MAKING OFFERING TO THE SUN GOD

RAMESES' "NOMEN"
AND "PRENOMEN" NAME

RAMESES' "PRENOMEN"
AND "NOMEN" NAME

Translation Of Rameses' Inscription

A figure by figure and column by column translation was made by the author using the technique of comparing various inscriptions having similar Hieroglyphic figures.

It is impossible to know exactly what the original scribe of the inscription wrote back there in about 1,321 B.C., because there is no way of knowing how he communicated his ideas with these Hieroglyphic figures.

However, the reader of this translation will obtain some idea of what the scribe wrote, about 3,321 years ago honoring Rameses The Great when he built his temple at Abu Simbel. Also, the reader will appreciation and understand these ancient Hieroglyphic figures which were first used about 6,000 years ago.

Column 1 Reading Top To Bottom.	
	"said": figures of a snake, a club, and a flowering reed was used.
	"by": figure for water was used.
	"god Thoth"; figures of a feather, a bird, a forearm, a loaf, and two slant strokes are used.
	"lord of Sesenu": figures of a vase, a vase, 8 horizontal strokes (8 primeval gods)', a heart, a musical instrument, a flowering reed, and water were used. Column 1 translation: "said by the god Thoth, lord of Sesenu"

Column 2 Reading Top To Bottom.	
	"residence: figure of a reed shelter was used.
	"in": figure for a mouth was used.
	"Amen-Heri" (a place): figures of 2 slant strokes, a heart, a town, and the side figure were used.
	"I give": figure of a forearm was used.
	"to you": figures for water and a basket with a handle were used.
	"ever lasting": figures of 2 wicks of twisted flax and the sun's disk were used.
	"sovereignty": figures of the papyrus plant (king of the South of Egypt), and a king holding a whip and a scepter were used.
	"over": figure for a side (earth?) was used. Column 2 translation: "residing in Amen-Heri, I give to you an ever lasting sovereignty over".

	Column 3 Reading Top To Bottom	
	"two lands": figure for land was used twice (North and South Egypt).	
	"son": figures of a bird and one vertical stroke were used.	
	"of": figure for water was used.	
	"body": figures of a club (body), one vertical stroke, and a loaf were used.	
	"beloved": figure for a water pool was used.	
	"cartouche": figure for an elongated oval was used to encloses Rameses' "Prenomen" name.	
	"Ra the Sun god": figure for the Sun's disk was used.	
	"strong": figure for the limb of an animal ("user", in front of statue) was used.	
	"statue of Maat, the goddess of law and truth"; feather is emblematic of law.	
	"Ra the Sun god": figure for the Sun's disk was used.	
	"approved": figure for an instrument ("setep") used to open the mouths of mummies.	
	"of": figure for water was used.	

Column 3 translation: "two lands, son of my body, Rameses (Ra-user-Maat-setep-en-Ra), Ra strong in truth, approved of Ra.

Column 4 Reading Top To Bottom.

	Column 4 Reading Top To Bottom	
	"maker": figures of an eye, a mouth, and two flowering reeds were used.	
	"of": figure for a side (earth) was used.	
	"funerary abode": figures for a reed shelter, and two mouths were used for the mythical funerary abode of Ka, double of Rameses.	
	"Ka, double of Rameses": figures of arms of a man and one vertical stroke.	

Column 4 translation: "maker of the funerary abode for your Ka" (statue of the deceased used as a double.

Column 5 Reading Top To Bottom.

	Column 5 Reading Top To Bottom	
	"all kinds": figure for a basket with handle was used.	
	"to give": figure of a man's forearm was used.	
	"many": figures for water and a basket with handle were used.	
	"festival": festival figure celebrated every thirty years.	
	"festivals of Rameses": A is the "Prenomen" and B is "Nomen" names of Rameses.	

Column 5 translation: "I give to you many festivals of Rameses".

	Column 6 Reading Top To Bottom.
ᗐ III	"much loved": figures of a frog (100,000) and 3 vertical strokes were used.
⊂▭	"of": figure for side (earth) was used.
⸮⚭	"prince": figures of a scepter of dominium, a hill, and a divine being holding a whip.
Ⴡ	"circular course of the sun": figure of a looped string was used.
∿∿	"water": figure for water was used.
ᑫ ▱⊙	"every place where the sun revolves": figures of a flowering reed, a loaf, a horizontal line, and the sun's disk were used.

Column 6 translation: "much beloved prince", of every place where the sun"s disk revolves.

	Column 7 Reading Top To Bottom.
⚲⊤⚯	"the living, god, beautiful": figures of life, hatchet (signifies royalty), and a musical instrument were used.
⬤━	"maker": figure for the right eye was used.
⬭⚲ ⊂▭ III	"of things": figures of a loaf, a bird, season, roll of papyrus, and three vertical strokes were used
∿∿	"for": figure for water was used.
ᑫ▱	"father": figures of a flowering reed, a loaf, and a horned viper were used.
⚭▱⑊	"god Thoth": figures of the magical god Thoth, a loaf, and two slant strokes were used.

Column 7 translation: "the beautiful living god, maker of things for his father Thoth",

	Column 8 Reading Top To Bottom.
▱ ☰ ☰ ⚲ ⚯ ᑫ ▱∿ ⊓ ▱ ⟍♡⊙	"lord of Sesenu, residing in Amen-Heri"; see bottom of Column 1 and top of Column 2 for details of figures used.
⬤━ ∿∿ ⚲	"maker of things for his father": figures of a right eye, water, and a horned viper were used.

Column 8 translation: "lord of Sesenu, residing in Amen-Heri, maker of things for his father".

Column 9 Reading Top To Bottom.	
	"permanent": figure for a musical instrument was used.
	"storage": figure of three jars was used.
	"great": figure for a body was used.
	"I give": figure of a forearm was used.
	"things": figures of a roll of papyrus and 3 vertical strokes were used.
	"beautiful": figures of a musical instrument, a mouth, and 3 vertical strokes were used.
	"in": figure of a mouth was used.
	"of": figure for water was used.
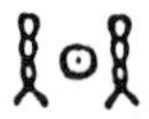	"everlasting": figures of 2 wicks of twisted flax, and the sun's disk were used.
Column 9 translation: "He made and gave permanent storages, great beautiful everlasting things".	
Column 10 Reading Top To Bottom.	
	"in": figure of a mouth was used.
	"Sun": figure of the sun's disk was used.
	"facing": figures of a horned viper, a loaf, and a face were used.
	"of": figure for water was used.
	"eastern": figure of the rising sun was used.
	"monuments": figures of a loaf and a house were used.
	"of": figure for water was used.
	"horizon of heaven": figures of a stone, loaf, and the sky were used.
Column 10 translation: "monuments facing the eastern horizon of heaven".	

THE EGYPTAIN YEAR HAD 360 DAYS

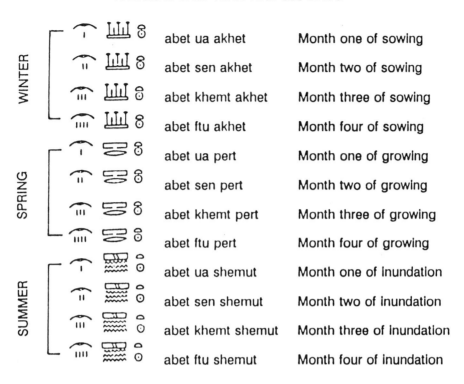

WINTER		abet ua akhet	Month one of sowing
		abet sen akhet	Month two of sowing
		abet khemt akhet	Month three of sowing
		abet ftu akhet	Month four of sowing
SPRING		abet ua pert	Month one of growing
		abet sen pert	Month two of growing
		abet khemt pert	Month three of growing
		abet ftu pert	Month four of growing
SUMMER		abet ua shemut	Month one of inundation
		abet sen shemut	Month two of inundation
		abet khemt shemut	Month three of inundation
		abet ftu shemut	Month four of inundation

EGYPT HAD THREE SEASONS

akhet, began on July 19.

pert, began on November 15.

shemut, began on March 16 and ended on July 13.

ADDING FIVE DAYS TO EACH YEAR

365 DAYS TO EACH YEAR

Some Of The 2,000 Principal Hieroglyphic Figures
Used As Pictorial And Or Determinative Figures

FIGURES OF MEN

	MAN WASHING, CLEAN, PURE, PRIEST		MAN WITH HIS RIGHT HAND TO HIS MOUTH, DETERMINATIVE OF ALL THAT IS DONE WITH THE MOUTH
	MAN WEARING EMBLEM OF YEAR, A LARGE, INDEFINITE NUMBER		TO HIDE
	A GOD WEARING THE SUN'S DISK AND GRASPING A PALM BRANCH IN EACH HAND		TO GIVE OR OFFER A VESSEL OF WATER TO A GOD OR MAN
	TO WRITE		TO MAKE AN OFFERING
	DEAD PERSON WHO HAS OBTAINED POWER IN THE NEXT WORLD		MAN HIDING HIMSELF, TO HIDE, HIDDEN
	DEAD PERSON, HOLY BEING		KING WEARING THE WHITE CROWN AND HOLDING AND
	A DIVINE PERSON		KING WEARING THE RED CROWN AND HOLDING AND
	A DIVINE KING		KING WEARING THE RED AND WHITE CROWNS AND HOLDING
	DIVINE BEING HOLDING THE SCEPTER		KING WEARING THE RED AND WHIT CROWNS AND HOLDING
	DIVINE BEING HOLDING THE SCEPTER		IBIS-HEADED BEING, THOTH
	DIVINE BEING HOLDING THE WHIP		A WATCHMAN, TO GUARD, TO WATCH
	DIVINE BEING HOLDING AND		A DIVINE PERSON, LIVING OR DEAD
	MAN WITH HIS HANDS TIED BEHIND HIM, CAPTIVE		A DIVINE PERSON
	MAN TIED TO A STAKE, CAPTIVE		A PERSON SITTING IN STATE
	MAN TIED BY HIS NECK TO A STAKE		TO FALL DOWN
	BEHEADED MAN TIED BY HIS NECK TO A STAKE		A DEAD PERSON
	MAN KNEELING ON ONE KNEE		TO SWIM
	TO CRY OUT TO, TO INVOKE		A MAN SWIMMING, TO SWIM

134

	TO GIVE A LOAF OF BREAD, TO GIVE		A CHILD WEARING THE RED CROWN
	TO MAKE AN OFFERING		A CHILD WEARING THE SUN'S DISK AND URAEUS
	MAN PERFORMING AN ACT OF WORSHIP		A MAN BREAKING IN HIS HEAD WITH AN AXE OR STICK, ENEMY, DEATH, THE DEAD
	MAN THROWING WATER OVER HIMSELF, A PRIEST		MAN ARMED WITH A BOW AND ARROWS, BOWMAN, SOLDIER
	MAN SPRINKLING WATER, PURITY		MAN ARMED WITH SHIELD AND SWORD, BOW, SOLDIER
	A MAN SKIPPING WITH A ROPE		PYGMY
	MAN BUILDING A WALL, TO BUILD		IMAGE, FIGURE, STATUE, MUMMY
	MAN USING A BORE, TO DRILL		A DEAD BODY IN THE FOLD OF A SERPENT
	A MAN WITH A LOAD ON HIS HEAD, TO BEAR, TO CARRY, WORK		GREAT, GREAT MAN, PRINCE, CHIEF
	MAN SUPPORTING THE WHOLE SKY, TO STRETCH OUT		MAN LEANING ON A STAFF, AGED
	MAN HOLDING A PIG BY THE TAIL		MAN ABOUT TO STRIKE WITH A STICK, STRENGTH
	TO BIND TOGETHER, TO FORCE SOMETHING TOGETHER		MAN STRIPPING A BRANCH
	MAN HOLDING THE ☊ SCEPTER, PRINCE, KING		TO DRIVE AWAY
	PRICE, KING		TWO MEN PERFORMING A CEREMONY (?)
	PRINCE OR KING WEARING WHITE CROWN		MAN HOLDING AN INSTRUMENT
	PRINCE OR KING WEARING RED CROWN		MAN ABOUT TO PERFORM A CEREMONY WITH TWO INSTRUMENTS
	PRINCE OR KING WEARING WHITE AND RED CROWNS		TO PLAY A HARP
	GREAT MAN, PRINCE		MAN STANDING WITH INACTIVE ARMS AND HANDS, SUBMISSION
	A BABY SUCKING ITS FINGERS, CHILD, YOUNG PERSON		TO CALL, TO INVOKE
	A CHILD		MAN IN A PLEADING ATTITUDE

135

	TO PRAY, TO PRAISE, TO ADORE, TO ENTREAT		TO HOLD A CHILD IN THE ARMS
	TO BE HIGH, TO REJOICE		TO NURSE, TO SUCKLE A CHILD
	MAN MOTIONING SOMETHING TO GO BACK, TO RETREAT		TO GIVE BIRTH
	MAN CALLING AFTER SOMEONE, TO BECKON		A PREGNANT WOMEN
	TO DANCE		A GUARDIAN, WATCHMAN
	MAN BOWING, TO PAY HOMAGE		A DIVINE FEMALE, A STATUE
	MAN RUNNING AND STRETCHING FORWARD TO REACH SOMETHING		A DIVINE FEMALE, STATUE
	TO POUR OUT WATER, TO URINATE		A WOMAN SEATED
	TWO MEN GRASPING HANDS, FRIENDSHIP		WOMAN WITH DISHEVELLED HAIR
	A MAN TURNING HIS BACK, TO HIDE, TO CONCEAL		

FIGURES OF GODS AND GODDESSES

	TO PLOW		THE GOD OSIRIS
	A DIVINE PERSON HOLDING A ROPE, A GUARDIAN		THE GOD PTAH
	TO BEAR, TO CARRY		PTATH HOLDING A SCEPTER, AND WEARING A MENAT
	SUBMISSION, INACTIVITY		THE GOD TA-TUNEN
	TO PRAISE, TO PRAY, TO ADORE		THE GOD PTATH-TANEN

FIGURES OF WOMEN

			THE GOD AN-HERU
	TWO WOMEN GRASPING HANDS, FRIENDSHIP		AMEN, OR MENU, OR AMSU
	WOMEN BEATING A TAMBOURINE, TO REJOICE		AMEN WEARING PLUMES AND HOLDING
	TO BEND, TO BOW		AMEN WEARING PLUMES AND HOLDING MAAT
	THE SKY GODDESS NUT		AMEN WEARING PLUMES AND HOLDING A SHORT, CURVED SWORD

	THE GOD TANEN		ISIS HOLDING PAPYRUS SCEPTER
	AMEN HOLDING THE USER SCEPTER		ISIS HOLDING SYMBOL OF LIFE
	THE MOON GOD		ISIS HOLDING PAPYRUS SCEPTER
	THE GOD KHENSU		NEPHTHYS HOLDING SYMBOL OF LIFE
	THE GOD SHU		THE GODDESS NUT
	THE GOD SHU		THE GODDESS SESHETA
	GOD RA AS THE MIGHTY ONE OF MAAT		THE GODDESS MAAT WITH SCEPTER OF STRENGTH
	THE GOD RA WEARING THE WHITE CROWN		THE GODDESS MAAT
	RA HOLDING SCEPTERS OF THE HORIZONS OF EAST AND WEST		THE GODDESS ANQET
	RA HOLDING THE SCEPTER		THE GODDESS BAST
	RA WEARING SUN'S DISK, URAEUS AND HOLDING		THE GODDESS SEKHET
	RA WEARING THE SUN'S DISK AND URAEUS		THE GOD UN
	HORUS (RA) WEARING WHITE AND RED CROWNS		THE GODDESS MEHIT
	RA WEARING DISK AND HOLDING SYMBOL OF "LIFE"		A DEITY
	RA WEARING DISK, URAEUS, PLUMES AND HOLDING SCEPTER		A GOD WHO FRIGHTENS, TERRIFIES, OR DRIVES AWAY
	THE GOD SET		THE GOD BES
	THE GOD ANUBIS		THE GOD KHEPERA
	THE GOD THOTH	PARTS OF THE HUMAN BODY	
	THE GOD KHNEMU		THE HEAD, THE TOP OF ANYTHING
	THE NILE GOD		THE FACE, UPON

	THE HAIR, TO WANT, TO LACK		THE TWO LIPS
	A LOCK OF HAIR		LIP RAISED SHOWING THE TEETH
	THE BEARD		JAWBONE WITH TEETH
	THE RIGHT EYE, TO SEE, TO LOOK AFTER SOMETHING, TO DO		EMIT, MOISTURE
	THE LEFT EYE		A WEAPON OR TOOL
	TO SEE		THE BACKBONE
	AN EYE WITH A LINE OF STIBIUM BELOW THE LOWER EYE-LID		THE SPINE
	AN EYE WEEPING, TO CRY		THE BREAST
	TO HAVE A FINE APPEARANCE		TO EMBRACE
	THE TWO EYES, TO SEE		NOT HAVING, TO BE WITHOUT, NEGATION
	THE RIGHT EYE OF RA, THE SUN		THE BREAST AND ARMS OF A MAN, THE DOUBLE
	THE LEFT EYE OF RA, THE MOON		HANDS GRASPING A SACRED STAFF, SOMETHING HOLY
	THE TWO EYES OF RA		HANDS GRASPING A PADDLE, TO TRANSPORT, TO CARRY AWAY
	AN UTCHAT IN A VASE, OFFERINGS		ARMS HOLDING SHIELD AND CLUB, TO FIGHT
	THE PUPIL OF THE EYE		TO WRITE
	TWO EYES IN A VASE, OFFERINGS		HAND HOLDING A WHIP OR LASH, TO BE STRONG, TO REIGN
	EYEBROW		HAND AND ARM OUTSTRETCHED, TO GIVE
	EAR		TO BEAR, TO CARRY
	NOSE, WHAT IS IN FRONT		TO GIVE
	OPENING, MOUTH, DOOR		TO GIVE

	TO OFFER			TO FLEE, TO RUN AWAY
	TO OFFER FRUIT			TO INVADE, TO ATTACK
	AN ACT OF HOMAGE			TO HOLD, TO POSSES
	TO BE STRONG, TO SHOW STRENGTH			HILL, KNEE, (LETTERS Q AND K)
	TO DIRECT			A LEG AND FOOT
	HAND			ARM + HAND + LEG
	TO RECEIVE			HAND + LEG
	TO HOLD IN THE HAND			HORN + LEG
	TO CLASP, TO HOLD TIGHT IN THE FIST			PIECE OF FLESH, LIMB
	FINGER, THE NUMBER 10,000		**ANIMALS**	
	TO BE IN THE CENTER, TO GIVE EVIDENCE			HORSE
	THUMB			OX
	A GRAVING TOOL			COW
	PENIS, WHAT IS MASCULINE, HUSBAND, BULL			CALF
	TO BEGET			RAM
	RESEMBLE, PICTURE			NUBIAN RAM OF AMEN
	MALE ORGANS			ORYX
	WOMAN, FEMALE ORGAN			ORYX, THE TRANSFORMED BODY, THE SPIRITUAL BODY
	TO GO, TO WALK, TO STAND			A WATER BAG
	TO GO BACKWARD, TO RETREAT			DONKEY

	DOG		THE GOD SET
	APE		RAT
	THE APE OF THOTH		OX
	APE WEARING RED CROWN		NOSE, WHAT IS IN FRONT
	APE BEARING UTCHAT, OR EYE OF THE SUN		HEAD AND NECK OF AN OX
	LION		STRENGTH
	L, R, LION LYING DOWN WITH HEAD UP		HEAD AND NECK OF A RAM
	THE LIONS OF YESTERDAY AND TODAY		TO BE WISE
	CAT		HEAD AND NECK OF A LION, STRENGTH
	JACKAL, WISE PERSON		TWO-FOLD STRENGTH
	THE GOD ANUBIS, THE GOD AP-UAT		HEAD AND PAW OF A LION, FORE PART OF ANYTHING, BEGINNING
	A MYTHICAL ANIMAL		HOUR, SEASON
	WILD BOAR		THE TOP OF ANYTHING, THE FOREPART
	A HARE		RANK, DIGNITY
	ELEPHANT		OPENING OF THE YEAR, THE NEW YEAR
	HIPPOPOTAMUS		HORN, WHAT IS IN FRONT
	RHINOCEROS		TOOTH
	PIG		TO DO THE DUTY OF SOMEONE, VICAR, EAR, TO HEAR
	GIRAFFE		TO ATTAIN TO, TO END
	THE GOD SET, WHAT IS BAD, DEATH, ETC.		THIGH

LEG OF AN ANIMAL, TO REPEAT		HORUS-SEPT
PAW OF AN ANIMAL		SACRED FORM, OR IMAGE
SKIN OF AN ANIMAL		HORUS OF THE TWO PLUMES
SKIN OF AN ANIMAL, ANIMAL OF ANY KIND		VULTURE
AN ARROW TRANSFIXING A SKIN, TO HUNT		THE VULTURE CROWN AND THE URAEUS CROWN
BONE AND FLESH, HEIR, OFFSPRING		OWL

BIRDS

		TO GIVE
EAGLE		BEFORE
EAGLE + SICKLE		IBIS
EAGLE + ⊂		TO FIND
A BIRD OF THE EAGLE CLASS		TO SNARE, TO HUNT
HAWK, THE GOD HORUS, GOD		THE GOD THOTH
HAWK WITH A WHIP, OR FLAIL		THE HEART-SOUL
THE TWO HORUS GODS		SOULS
HORUS WITH DISK AND URAEUS		TO TOIL, TO LABOR
HORUS WEARING THE WHITE AND RED CROWNS		THE SPIRIT-SOUL
THE "GOLDEN HORUS"		A BIRD IDENTIFIED WITH THE PHOENIX
GOD, DIVINE BEING, KING		TO FLOOD, TO INUNDATE
THE WEST		TO MAKE FAT
"HORUS THE UNITER OF THE TWO LANDS"		RED

BREAD, CAKE, FOOD		EYE OF A HAWK
GOOSE, SON		WING, TO FLY
TO MAKE TO SHAKE WITH FEAR, TO TREMBLE		FEATHER, WHAT IS RIGHT AND TRUE
DUCK, TO GO IN		TO BEAR, CARRY
TO DESTROY		FOOT OF A BIRD
TO FLY		TO CUT, TO ENGRAVE
TO HOVER, TO ALIGHT		SON, WITH ⬯ T = DAUGHTER
TO MAKE, TO LIFT UP, TO DISTINGUISH		

AMPHIBIOUS ANIMALS

SWALLOW, GREAT		TURTLE, EVIL, BAD
SPARROW, LITTLE		LIZARD, ABUNDANCE
A BIRD OF THE EAGLE KIND		CROCODILE, TO GATHER TOGETHER
INTELLIGENT PERSON, MANKIND		PRINCE
CHICKEN		CROCODILE
BIRDS' NEST		THE GOD SEBEK
DEAD BIRD, FEAR, TERROR		CROCODILE SKIN, BLACK
SOUL		THE GODDESS HEQT

PARTS OF BIRDS

		YOUNG FROG, 100,000
GOOSE, FEATHERED FOWL		SERPENT, GODDESS
HEAD OF VULTURE		THE GODDESS MEHENT
HEAD OF THE BENNU BIRD		SHRINE OF A SERPENT GODDESS

𓆙	WORM	**TREES AND PLANTS**	
𓆙	THE ADVERSARY OF RA, APOPHIS		TREE, WHAT IS PLEASANT
𓆑	SERPENT, SNAKE, BODY		PALM TREE
𓆑	F, A VIPER, ASP		ACACIA
𓆟	TO COME FORTH		BRANCH OF A TREE, WOOD
𓆟	TO ENTER IN		SHOOT, YOUNG TWIG, YEAR
𓆡	TO BREAK OPEN		ETERNAL YEAR
FISH			TIME
𓆛	FISH		A THORN
𓆚	CENTIPEDE		SHOOT, NAME OF A GODDESS AND CITY
𓆜	DEAD FISH, OR THING		KING OF THE SOUTH
𓆝	TO TRANSPORT		SOUTH, NAME OF A CLASS OF PRIESTESS
𓆞	THIGH		SOUTH
INSECTS			SOUTH
𓆤	BEE		FEATHER
𓆥	"KING OF THE SOUTH AND NORTH"		TO GO
𓆣	TO ROLL, TO BECOME, TO COME INTO BEING		PLANTS GROWING IN A FIELD
𓆦	FLY		AN OFFERING
𓆧	GRASSHOPPER		LOTUS AND PAPYRUS FLOWERS GROWING, FIELD
𓆨	SCORPION		CLUSTER OF FLOWERS, OR PLANTS

CLUSTER OF LOTUS FLOWERS		
THE NORTH, THE DELTA COUNTRY, THE LAND OF THE LOTUS		
THE SOUTH, THE PAPYRUS COUNTRY		
YOUNG PLANT, WHAT IS GREEN		
FLOWER		
FLOWER BUD		
LOTUS FLOWER		
FLOWER		
TO GIVE COMMANDS		
WHITE, SHINING, LIGHT		
AN INSTRUMENT, TO TURN BACK		
TO GIVE BIRTH		
THE UNION OF THE SOUTH AND NORTH		
BARLEY		
GRAIN		
GRANARY, STOREHOUSE		
GRAPES GROWING, WINE		
POMEGRANATE		
SWEET, PLEASANT		
SWEET, PLEASANT		

SKY, EARTH, WATER

	WHAT IS ABOVE, HEAVEN
	SKY WITH A STAR OR LAMP, NIGHT
	WATER FALLING FROM THE SKY, DEW, RAIN
	LIGHTNING
	ONE HALF OF HEAVEN
	THE SUN GOD, DAY
	RADIANCE
	THE SUN GOD RA
	THE SUN SENDING FORTH RAYS, SPLENDOR
	THE SUN'S DISK WITH URACI
	WINGED DISK
	THE RISING SUN
	CAKE, OFFERING, NINE GODS
	A RIB, TO ARRIVE AT
	MOON, MONTH
	STAR, STAR OF DAWN, HOUR, TO PRAY
	THE UNDERWORLD
	LAND
	MOUNTAINOUS LAND

Symbol	Meaning	Symbol	Meaning
	FOREIGN, BARBARIAN		**BUILDINGS**
	MOUNTAIN, WICKEDNESS		TOWN, CITY
	HORIZON		HOUSE, TO GO OUT
	NOME (STATE)		SEPULCHRAL MEALS OR OFFERINGS
	THE LAND ON ONE SIDE OF THE NILE = ALL OF EGYPT		"WHITE HOUSE", TREASURY
	LAND		QUARTER OF A CITY
	A ROAD, A WAY		HOUSE, TEMPLE
	SIDE		TEMPLES, SANCTUARIES
	STONE		GOD'S HOUSE
	SAND, GRAIN, FRUIT, NUTS		GREAT HOUSE
	N, SURFACE OF WATER, WATER		LADY OF THE HOUSE, I.E., NEPHTHYS
	WATER		HOUSE OF HORUS (HATHOR)
	DITCH, WATERCOURSE, TO LOVE		GREAT HOUSE, PALACE
	LAKE		HALL, COURTYARD
	TO GO		WALL, FORT
	THE GOD AMEN		TO OVERTHROW
	ISLAND		FORTIFIED TOWN
	THE TWO HORIZONS (EAST AND WEST)		DOOR, GATE
	SWAMP, MARSH		CORNER, AN OFFICIAL
	METAL, IRON ORE OR COPPER ORE		TO HIDE

	PYRAMID		TO STAND
	OBELISK		HELM, RUDDER
	MEMORIAL TABLET		PADDLE, VOICE
	PILLAR		THE NAME OF A SACRED BOAT
	A DESIGN OR PATTERN		BOATS OF THE SUN
	A HALL, COUNCIL CHAMBER	**TABLES, SEATS, ETC.**	
	FESTIVAL CELEBRATED EVERY THIRTY YEARS		SEAT, THRONE, THE GODDESS ISIS
	FESTIVAL		SEAT, THRONE
	DOUBLE STAIRCASE, TO GO UP		TO LIE DOWN IN SLEEP OR DEATH
	STAIRCASE TO GO UP		CLOTHES, LINEN
	LEAF OF A DOOR, TO OPEN		TABLE OF OFFERINGS
	A BOLT, TO CLOSE		WHAT IS UNDER, BENEATH
	TO BRING, TO BRING QUICKLY		FUNERAL CHEST, SARCOPHAGUS
	TO TIE IN A KNOT		ZONE, DISTRICT
	THE GOD AMSU, OR MIN		TO PROVIDE WITH
SHIPS AND PARTS OF SHIPS			PILLAR, LIGHT TOWER
	BOAT, TO SAIL DOWN STREAM		SQUEEZING JUICE FROM GRAPES, THE GOD SHESMU OF SESHMU
	LOADED BOAT, TO TRANSPORT		TO USE VIOLENCE
	TO SAIL UPSTREAM		LINEN, CLOTHING, GARMENTS
	WIND, BREEZE, AIR, BREATH		PILLOW

146

	MIRROR		HELMET
	FAN, SHADOW		THE WHITE CROWN OF THE SOUTH
	SCALES, TO WEIGHT		THE SOUTH LAND
	TO BALANCE, TO TEST BY WEIGHING		THE RED CROW OF THE NORTH
	TO RAISE UP, TO WAKE UP		THE NORTH LAND
	A REED WHISTLE, WHAT IS RIGHT OR STRAIGHT		THE WHITE AND RED CROWNS UNITED
	STANDARD		ROPE, CORD, THE NUMBER ONE HUNDRED

TEMPLE FURNITURE

			TWO FEATHERS
	ALTAR		PLUMES, DISK AND HORNS
	FIRE STANDARD		CROWN, TIARA
	AXE, KING, OR SOME INSTRUMENT USED IN THE PERFORMANCE OF MAGICAL CEREMONIES		BREAST PLATE
	THE UNDERWORLD		COLLAR
	THE TREE TRUNK THAT HELD THE DEAD BODY OF OSIRIS, STABILITY		GARMENT OF NETWORK
	TO UNITE		TUNIC
	BROTHER		LINEN, GARMENTS, APPAREL
	THE LEFT SIDE		TONGUE, DIRECTOR
	TO BE IN		SANDAL
	NAME OF A GODDESS (SESETA)		CIRCLE, RING

CLOTHING, ETC.

			TO COLLECT, TO JOIN TOGETHER
	HEAD GEAR		BUCKLE

147

♀	LIFE		WHAT IS HOSTILE
	A SEAL AND CORD		AXE
	AN INSTRUMENT WORN AND CARRIED BY DEITIES AND MEN		THE FIRST, THE BEGINNING
	TO BE EQUIPPED		SCIMITAR
	TO DIRECT, TO GOVERN		KNIFE
	TO BE STRONG, TO GAIN THE MASTERY		DAGGER
	THE RIGHT SIDE		KNIFE
	FLY FLAPPER		BLOCK OF SLAUGHTER
	THE EMBLEM CONTAINING THE HEAD OF OSIRIS WORSHIPPED AT ABYDOS		BOW
	SCEPTER, TO RULE		THE FRONT OF ANY THING
	SCEPTER, DOMINION		TO STRETCH OUT, TO EXTEND
	THEBES		ARROW, TO SHOOT
	SCEPTER, STRENGTH, TO BE STRONG		THE SIDE OR BACK
	NAME OF A SCEPTER		GREAT
	FAIL OR WHIP, SCEPTER		BODY
	THE FIRSTBORN SON OF OSIRIS		CHARIOT
	FRINGE	**TOOLS, ETC.**	
ARMS AND ARMOR			EMANATION
	FOREIGN PERSON, TO MAKE, FINGER		TO SELECT, TO CHOOSE
	WHAT IS OPPOSITE, MIDDLE		ADZE (CARPENTER'S CUTTING TOOL)

TO FIGHT, TO SMITE			SILVER
SICKLE			REFINED COPPER
SICKLE CUTTING A REED			FOWLER'S NET
TO PLOW, HALL, GROWING THINGS		ROPES, STRINGS, NETWORK	
TO MAKE PERFECT, THE GOD TEMU			ROPE, CORD, THE NUMBER ONE HUNDRED
MIRACULOUS, WONDERFUL			TO PULL, TO HAUL ALONG
METAL			TO BE LONG, EXTENDED
FIRE STICK			PIOUS, SACRED
GOOD, TO PERFORM			TO FETTER, LINEN BANDAGE
WORKMAN			TO UNFASTEN, BOOK, WRITING
TO OPEN OUT A WAY			TO BRING TO THE END
DISEASE, DEATH			TO FILL
TO BREAK			TO GAIN POSSESSION OF
ONE			PART OF A FOWLER'S NET
THE GODDESS NEITH			CIRCUIT
TO FOLLOW AFTER, FOLLOWER			OUTLINE FOR FOUNDATION OF A BUILDING
BONE			MAGICAL KNOT
ESTATE, FARM			PLANT, GROWING THINGS
TO HIDE AWAY			AMULET, PROTECTION
GOLD			H, ROPE, WICK OF TWISTED FLAX

	H + R		TO BRING
	H + A		HEART
	TO PLACE, BE PERMANENT		TO BE CLEAN, CEREMONIALLY PURE
	OFFERINGS		AS, LIKE
	TO GO AROUND ABOUT		MISTRESS, LADY, BROAD
	TO TAKE POSSESSION OF		CAKE, BREAD
	TO BANDAGE, SUBSTANCE WHICH HAS A STRONG SMELL		FIRE
	FLOWING LIQUID		BOWL CONTAINING GRAINS OF INCENSE ON FIRE

VESSELS

			BOWL CONTAINING FRUIT
	NAME OF A CITY AND OF A GODDESS		K, LIBATION VASE
	TO SING, TO PRAISE, TO BE FAVORED		LORD, ALL, BOWL
	COLD WATER, COOLNESS		FLAT BOWL WITH RING HANDLE
	KING, MAJESTY, SERVANT		FESTIVAL
	DIVINE SERVANT, PRIEST		GRAIN, BARLEY AND THE LIKE
	WHAT IS IN FRONT		**OFFERINGS**
	TO UNITE, TO BE JOINED TO		BREAD, CAKE
	MILK		BREAD, CAKE
	URGENT		COMPANY OF NINE GODS
	WINE		TIME, SEASON
	LIQUID		A SIEVE

	TO GIVE			WHAT IS SAID
	BRONZE			"ANOTHER READING", I.E., VARIANT READING
MUSICAL INSTRUMENTS, WRITING MATERIALS, ETC.				BOUNDARY, BORDER
	WRITING REED, INK POT AND PALETTE, TO WRITE, TO PAINT			NAME
	A PAPYRUS ROLL, BOOK			TO DEPART
	TO PLAY MUSIC, HARP			CAPTIVE
	SISTRUM (PERCUSSION INSTRUMENT)			PART OF A PALACE OR TEMPLE
	INSTRUMENT LIKE A LUTE, GOOD, BEAUTIFUL			GRAIN, WHEAT, BARLEY
	THE GOD NEFER TEMU			P, DOOR
	SYRINX (VOCAL ORGAN OF BIRDS), TO KNOW			SIDE, HALF
	TO ABIDE			

VARIOUS CHARACTERS

	THE NUMBER ONE
	FIGURES FOR PLURALS (MORE THAN ONE)
	SIGN OF DUAL
	TO SPLIT
	THE NUMBER TEN, ∩∩ = TWENTY, THIRTY = ∩∩∩
	FEAR, AWE
	TO SPLIT, TO SEPARATE
	T, CAKE

151

IN THE PAPYRUS OF RAMESES III THE FOLLOWING AMOUNTS WERE LISTED
NUMBER OF LARGE LOAVES OF BREAD AND NUMBER OF BIRDS
GIVEN TO TEMPLES DURING THE YEAR FOR VARIOUS FESTIVALS

NUMBER OF LARGE LOAVES OF BREAD					
BREAD	LARGE	(100,000 x 9)	(10,000 X 9)	(1,000 X 2)	(100 X 7)	(10 X 5)
900,000 + 90,000 + 2,000 + 700 + 50 = 992,750 Loaves of Bread					

TOTAL NUMBER OF BIRDS COUNTED						
	𝔁	𝔢	∩∩		=	6,820
	𝔁	𝔢	∩		=	1,410
	𝔁	𝔢	∩∩∩	IIII	=	1,534
		𝔢	∩∩∩∩∩		=	150
	𝔁		∩∩∩∩∩∩		=	4,060
‖	𝔁		∩∩		=	25,020
‖‖‖	𝔁	𝔢	∩		=	57,810
‖	𝔁	𝔢			=	21,700
	𝔁	𝔢	∩∩∩∩		=	1,240
	𝔁	𝔢	∩		=	6,510
TOTAL NUMBER OF BIRDS COUNTED						
(10,000 X 9)	+ (1,000 X 32)	+ (100 X 40)	+ (10 X 25)	+ 4	=	126,254 Birds

152

	NUMBERS				
NUMBER FORM	PHONETIC FORM	VALUE	NUMBER FORM	PHONETIC FORM	VALUE
I		1	∩∩∩		30
II		2	∩∩ ∩∩		40
III		3	∩∩ ∩∩∩		50
IIII		4	∩∩∩ ∩∩∩		60
II III ★		5	∩∩∩ ∩∩∩∩		70
III III		6	∩∩∩∩ ∩∩∩∩		80
III IIII		7	∩∩∩∩ ∩∩∩∩∩		90
IIII IIII		8	℮		100
IIII IIIII		9			1,000
∩		10			10,000
∩∩		20			100,000
					1,000,000
			Ω		10,000,000

153

O R D I N A L S

Value	Masculine	Feminine
First	𓂝 ▢ \\\\	𓂝 ▢ ᴗ
Second	‖ ᴗ	‖ ᴗ ▢ ᴗ
Third	‖‖ ᴗ	‖‖ ᴗ ᴗ
Fourth	‖‖‖ ᴗ	‖‖‖ ᴗ ᴗ
Fifth	‖‖‖‖ ᴗ	‖‖‖‖ ᴗ ᴗ
Sixth	‖‖‖ / ‖‖‖ ᴗ	‖‖‖ ᴗ / ‖‖‖ ᴗ
Seventh	‖‖‖ / ‖‖‖‖ ᴗ	‖‖‖ ᴗ / ‖‖‖‖ ᴗ
Eight	‖‖‖‖ / ‖‖‖‖ ᴗ	‖‖‖‖ ᴗ / ‖‖‖‖ ᴗ
Ninth	‖‖‖‖ / ‖‖‖‖‖ ᴗ	‖‖‖‖ ᴗ / ‖‖‖‖‖ ᴗ
Tenth	∩ ᴗ	∩ ᴗ ᴗ

T I M E

𓊪𓄿𓏤	Second	𓎛	60 years
𓃭𓏤	Minute	𓎛𓎛	120 years
𓃀𓏤	Hour	𓂙	100,000 years
▢ / ⬯	Day	𓆷	1,000,000 years
𓂋	Month	𓆳	Eternity
𓊪	Year	Ω / 𓊪	10,000,000 years
𓊪𓊪	30 years		

FIGURE No. 45
BROKEN WALL INSCRIPTION AT KARNAK

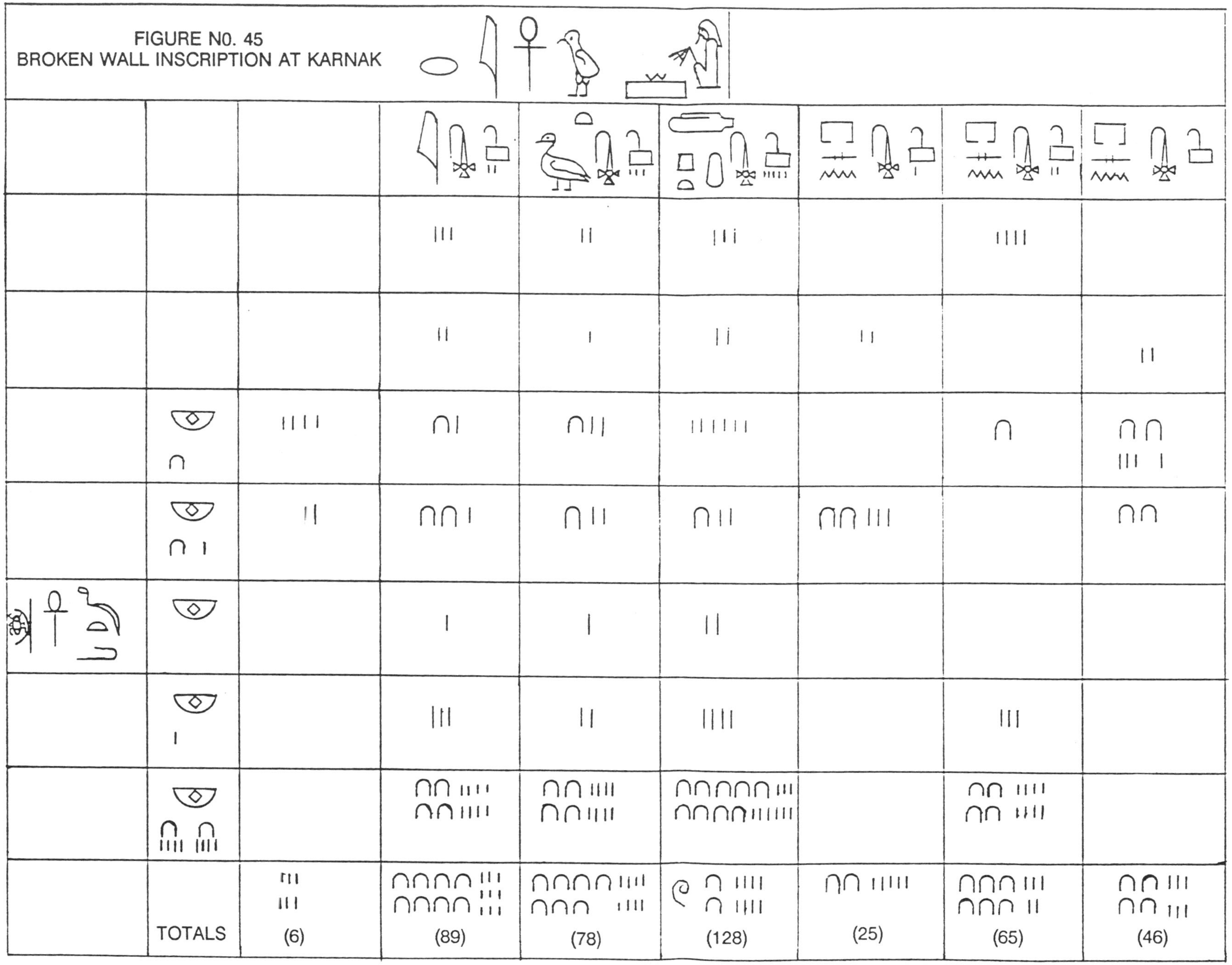

								(46)
								(65)
								(25)
								(128)
								(78)
								(89)
								(6)
								TOTALS

A Broken Wall Inscription At Karnak

Translation of the Broken Wall Inscription At Karnak (See Figure No. 45) will be by Rows (horizontal direction) and Columns (vertical direction) as follows:

Row 1: Reading across, left to right, contains a mouth, a flowering reed, the cross figure for Life, a chicken, a roll of papyrus, and the figure of a king hold a whip. These are read as, "A King's List".

Row 2: Reading across, left to right, lists persons, and temples to whom (flame, fire, and or heat), and

measures of grain, are given; 2 vertical strokes equals 2 measures of grain.

Row 2, Columns 1-3: these can't be read because they are broken off.

Row 2, Column 4: inscription is partially broken off, but the flowering reed indicates that a king receives,

and 2 measures (II) of grain .

Row 2, Column 5: lists a bird + loaf equal daughter, she gets and 3 measures (III) of grain .

Row 2, Column 6: lists a hand, a jar, and loaf equals storage, gets and 5 measures (IIIII) of grain

.

Row 2, Columns 7, 8, and 9: Temples are shown by the house, and door bolt figures, by the

river (Nile) ; receive and measures of grain .

Row 7. Column 1: list a king's name in a broken off, elongated oval (cartouche) with just the beetle

figure of his name showing; followed by the life figure , a loaf , a serpent , and a folded

cloth .

These four figures are read as, "Life Eternal".

It is possible that one of the king's names below was in the broken cartouche:

Men-kheper-Ra I Tehutimes III;   Aa-kheper-Ra II Shashang IV meri-Amen;   Men-kheper- Ra III Piankhi
(6th. king of Dynasty XVIII)   (13th. king of Dynasty XXII)   (3rd. king of Dynasty XXV)

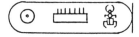      

Column 2: reading, top to bottom, identifies the monthly festivals by use of the festival figure ⌣◇⌣ .

Row 5, Column 2: lists the 10th festival of the month, ⌣◇⌣ ∩ .

Row 6, Column 2: lists the 11th festival of the month, ⌣◇⌣ ∩ I .

Row 7, Column 2: partially broken off, shows only the festival figure, ⌣◇⌣ .

Row 8, Column 2: lists the 1st festival of the month, ⌣◇⌣ I .

Row 9, Column 2: lists the 28th festival of the month, ⌣◇⌣ ∩∩ IIII IIII .

Rows 3-9, Columns 3-9: lists the quantities of ⋔ and ⊔ given.

Row 10: reading across, left to right, lists the total quantities of ⋔ and ⊔ given.

When the figure, ⋔ , is used with the festival figure, ⌣◇⌣ , then the meaning is the burning of incense, which is a resin from the   Pistacia Terebinthus Tree, a relative of the tree that yield pistachio nuts.

From earliest times the ritual significance of incense centered around its fragrance and smoke it produced. The fragrance was thought to please the gods and to drive off evil spirits. Its smoke was thought to carry prayers to divine ears to conduct the souls of the departed to heaven.

157

Source Of The Resin Used For Incense In The Temples

George F. Bass, Abell Professor of Nautical Archaeology at Texas A & M had the following to say about two most exciting discoveries which lead to the source of the resin used for incense in the ancient temples of Egypt:

The first discovery was made at a second hand book sale in College Station Texas. The find? A slim brown book published in French in Cairo in 1949. The subject? The use of terebinthine resin in ancient Egypt. It solved one of the major puzzles presented by the second discovery, the ship I have excavated for the past five years, a ship that crashed against a rocky Turkish cape in the 14th century B.C.

The ship carried mostly materials, including six tons of copper ingots, and tin ingots to mix with the copper to form bronze for weapons and tools. Also on board were ingots--the earliest ever found--of cobalt blue, raw ivory in the form of hippopotamus and elephant tusks, and unworked logs of African blackwood (ebony). There were ostrich eggshells, tortoise shells, jars of olives, and whole pomegranates.

But the second largest item in the cargo was a ton of resin in 150 Canaanite amphoras, or two-handled jars. At first identified as myrrh, it was instead, we now know, resin from the Pistacia terebinthus tree--a relative of the tree that yields pistachio nuts.

Since no large quantities of terebinthine resin had ever before been found by archaeologists, I was perplexed by this enormous amount. Where was it from? What was its destination? Its purpose? There were no written clues in the ancient text I consulted.

The little book I found written by Egyptologist Victor Loret to prove his theory that a certain ancient word, written

(sonter and or sunta) in hieroglyphics, , meant terebinthine resin. This interpretation allowed him to translate Egyptian texts describing tons of the stuff being imported from the Syro-Palestinian coast, the home of the Canaanites, for use as incense in the Egyptian religious ritual during the 14th century B.C. No wonder archaeologists had never found much of it! All that reached Egypt had been burned for the gods thousands of years ago.

An Egyptian painting mentioned by Loret shows a Canaanite jar like those on our wreak, but inscribed with the word (sonter and or sunta) to indicates its contents.

Our cargo of terebinthine resin, then suggests that our ship sailed from the Syro-Palestinian coast and sank on the way to Egypt (by way of the Aegean). Weighing all such bits of evidence will one day bring to life a voyage from the time of Tutankhamen.

WRITE YOUR FIRST NAME IN ANCIENT EGYPTIAN HIEROGLYPHICS BY USING THE SPECIAL ALPHABET BELOW AS FOLLOWS: (1) MAKE ONE PHOTOSTAT OF THE LARGE OVAL (CARTOUCHE) ON THE NEXT PAGE. (2) MAKE 2 PHOTOSTATS OF THE ALPHABET BELOW. (3) CUT OUT THE FIGURES THAT SPELL YOUR FIRST NAME. (4) GLUE THESE FIGURES IN THE LARGE CARTOUCHE MADE IN (1) JUST LIKE THE EXAMPLE FOR THE NAME WILLIAM IN THE CARTOUCHE TO THE LEFT. (5) MAKE A PHOTOSTAT OF THE CARTOUCHE WITH YOUR NAME IN IT. (6) COLOR IN THE FIGURES. (7) MOUNT THE COLORED CARTOUCHE IN A FRAME.

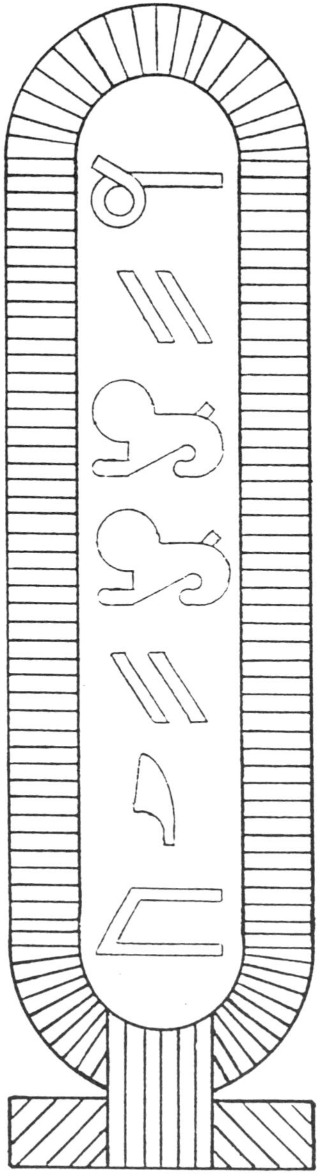

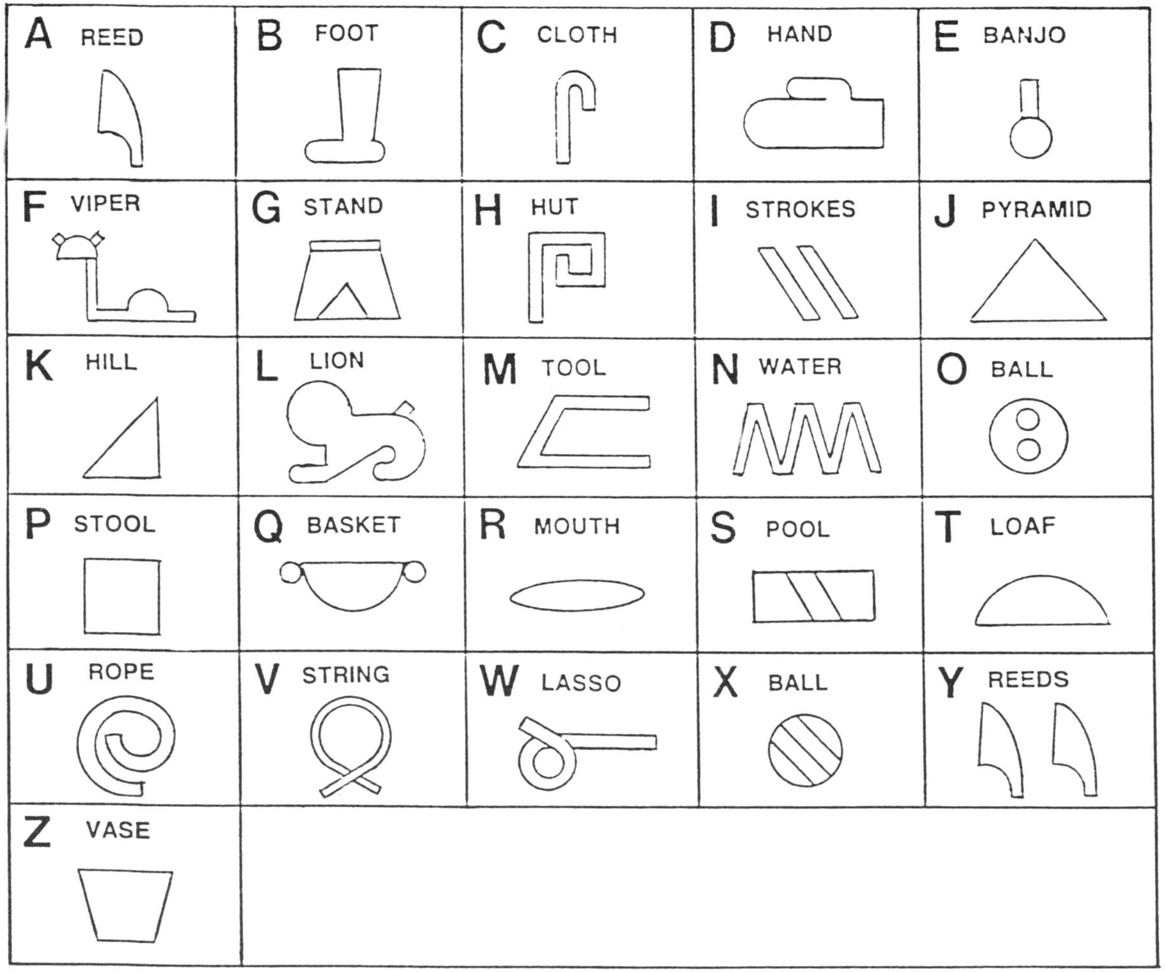

A REED	B FOOT	C CLOTH	D HAND	E BANJO
F VIPER	G STAND	H HUT	I STROKES	J PYRAMID
K HILL	L LION	M TOOL	N WATER	O BALL
P STOOL	Q BASKET	R MOUTH	S POOL	T LOAF
U ROPE	V STRING	W LASSO	X BALL	Y REEDS
Z VASE				

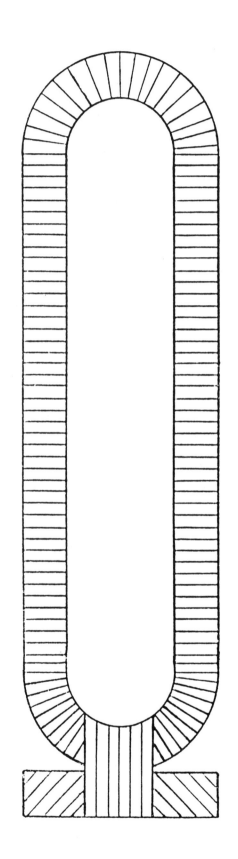

BIBLIOGRAPHY

Author	Text

Budge, E. A. Wallis   "An Egyptisn Reading Book".
London: Kegan Paul, Trench, Trubner & Co. Ltd., 1896.

Budge, E. A. Wallis   "Cleopatra's Needles".
London: The Religious Tract Society, 1926.

Budge, E. A. Wallis   "Egyptian Language: Easy Lessions In Egyptian Hieroglyphics".
London: Kegan Paul, Trench, Trubner & Co. Ltd., 1910.

Budge, E. A. Wallis   "The Nile".
London: Thos. Cook & Sons, 1912.

Cole, J. H.   "Determination Of The Exact Size And Orientation Of The Great Pyramid Of Giza".
Cairo: Government Press, 1925.

Capps, E.
Page, T. E.
Rouse, W. H. D.   "Herodotus - Books I And II".
London: William Heinemann, 1920.

Murray, John   "An Egyptian Hieroglyphic Dictionary - Volumns I And II".
London: Harrison & Sons, 1920.

Taylor, John   "The Great Pyramid: Why Was It Built? And Who Built It?
London: Longmans, Green, 1864.

Tompkins, Peter   "Secrets Of The Great Pyramid".
New York: Harper & Row Publishers, 1978.

APPENDIX

Translation Of Queen's Hatshepsut's Obelisk At Karnak (See Page 10)

The Horus, Usritkau, Lord of the Vulture and Serpent Crowns (i.e. chosen by the goddess Nekhebit and Uatchit), Flourishing in years, The Horus of gold, Divine one of crowns, King of the South and the North, Lord of the Two Lands, Maat-ka-Ra. She made them as her monument for her father Amen, Lord of Thebes, setting up for him two great obelisks before the august pylon called, "Amen, mighty one of terror." It is worked (i.e. covered over) with a very great quantity of shining, refined copper, which lights up Egypt like Athen (i.e. the solar Disk). Never was the like made since the world began. May it make for him the son of Ra, Hatshepsut, the counterpart of Amen, the giving of life, like Ra, forever.

Translation Of King Thothmes' III Obelisk At Karnak (See Page 11)

Horus (name) Ka-nekht-kha-em-Uas. Nebti (name) Uaht sutenit-ma-Ra-em-pet. Golden Horus (name) Tcheser-khau-kherp-pehti. Nesubati (name Men-kheper-Ra-setep-en-Ra. Son of Ra (name) Tehuti-mes-nefer-kheper. He made (this obelisk) as his monument for his father Amen-Ra, lord of the thrones of the Two Lands. He set up one obelisk in the court of the temple facing the Apts (Karnak). It was the first time one obelisk had been set up in Thebes. He did it that life might be given to him.

Translation Of King Thothmes' III Obelisk At Heliopolis (See Page 14)

Same Horus (name) as above. Nesubati, King of the South and North, Men-kheper-Ra. He made as his monument for father, (Harakhthes), Horus Ra of the two horizons. He set up two obelisks great, the pyramidions of electrum, at his third time of the Set Festival, through the greatness of his love of Father Tem. He made them, the son of RA, Thothmes, Nefer-kheper, of Ra-Harakhthes, beloved, living forever.

INDEX